FiNALE
online.de

Wissen, was drankommt

FiNALE online.de ist die digitale Ergänzung zu deinem FiNALE- Abiturband. Hier findest du eine Vielzahl an Angeboten, die dich zusätzlich bei deiner Prüfungsvorbereitung in Englisch unterstützen!

W0172339

✓ **Original-Prüfungsaufgaben mit Lösungen**

Schalte dir mit dem Code auf Seite 4 die aktuellen Original-Prüfungsaufgaben frei.

✓ **Audiodateien Englisch**

Passend zu deinem FiNALE-Arbeitsbuch kannst du dir die Audiodateien zu den Hörverstehensübungen anhören.

✓ **Tipps zur Prüfungsvorbereitung**

Mit unseren Tipps zur Prüfungsvorbereitung entsteht Lernstress erst gar nicht.

✓ **Abi-Checklisten**

Mit den Abi-Checklisten ist die Vorbereitung auf die Englisch-Abiturprüfung noch einfacher. Einfach als PDF oder in beschreibbarem WORD-Format herunterladen und den eigenen idealen Zeitplan erstellen. Hake in der Checkliste ab, was du kannst und noch nicht kannst, um deinen Wissensstand zu überprüfen.

Die **Abi-Checklisten** helfen dir, den Überblick über den Prüfungsstoff zu behalten.

www.finaleonline.de

FiNALE online.de

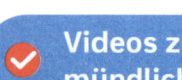

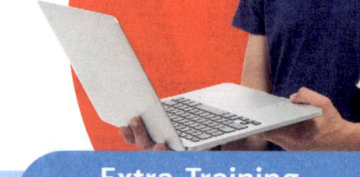

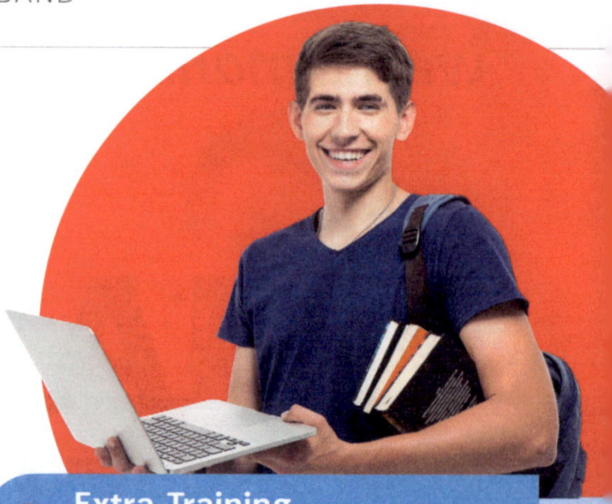

Videos zur mündlichen Prüfung

Keine Angst vor der mündlichen Prüfung! Die Videos geben dir Einblick in den Ablauf der Prüfung und Tipps für die richtige Vorbereitung.

Extra-Training Rechtschreibung

Punktabzug durch Schreibfehler? Das muss nicht sein! Mit dem Extra-Training auf finaleonline.de kriegst du die Rechtschreibung in den Griff.

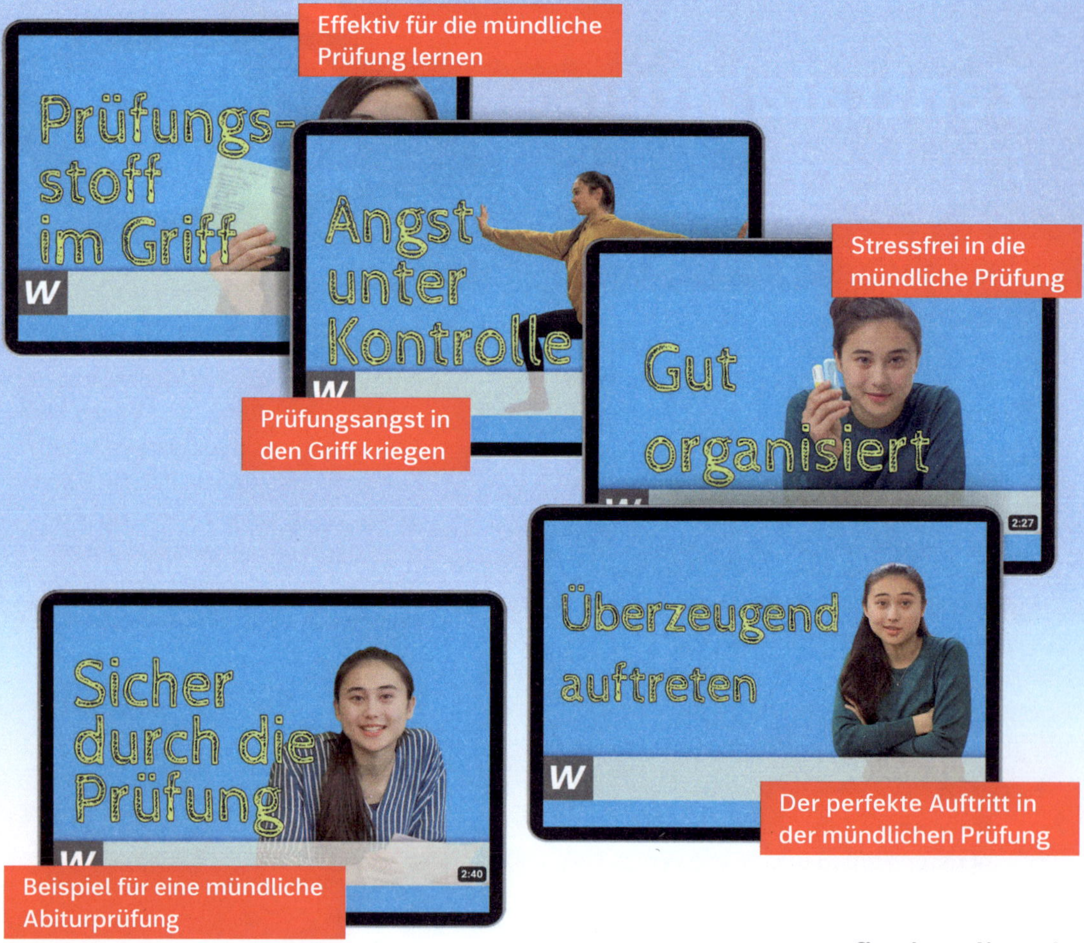

www.finaleonline.de

westermann

FiNALE
Prüfungstraining

2025
Nordrhein-Westfalen

Zentralabitur
Englisch

Thomas Lehnen

Miriam Schulz

sowie: Anne Böker

Liebe Schülerin, lieber Schüler,

sobald die Original-Prüfungsaufgaben zur Veröffentlichung frei-
gegeben sind, können sie unter **www.finaleonline.de** zusammen
mit ausführlichen Lösungen kostenlos heruntergeladen werden.
Gib dazu einfach diesen Code ein:

EN3Z6A9

Einfach mal reinschauen: www.finaleonline.de

© 2024 Westermann Lernwelten GmbH, Georg-Westermann-Allee 66, 38104 Braunschweig
www.westermann.de

Bildnachweis:
|iStockphoto.com, Calgary: chekat Titel, 1.2; DeanDrobot 2.1; guoya 176.1. |stock.adobe.com, Dublin:
leonidkos Titel, 1.1.

Druck A[1]/Jahr 2024
Alle Drucke der Serie A sind im Unterricht parallel verwendbar.

Redaktion: Federlese GbR – Christina & Boris Kühne, Grevenbroich
Kontakt: finale@westermanngruppe.de
Layout: LIO Design GmbH, Braunschweig
Umschlaggestaltung: Janssen Kahlert Design & Kommunikation GmbH, Hannover
Umschlagfoto: stock.adobe.com, Dublin, leonidkos; iStockphoto.com, Calgary, chekat
Druck und Bindung: Westermann Druck GmbH, Georg-Westermann-Allee 66, 38104 Braunschweig

ISBN 978-3-07-**172517**-1

Inhaltsverzeichnis

Informationen und Tipps zur Prüfung

Basiswissen

Methoden der Textarbeit

Literarische Texte

Sach- und Gebrauchstexte

Sprachmittlung

Zieltextformate

Letter/Email

Speech Script

Beispiele für Prüfungsaufgaben zu den Fokusthemen

Original-Prüfungsaufgaben 2023 und 2024

Die sprachliche Leistung im Abitur

Arbeiten mit FiNALE

FiNALE Prüfungstraining Englisch möchte Ihnen eine praxisnahe Hilfe zur Vorbereitung auf die Abiturprüfung sein. Im Praxis-Teil finden sich zu allen geforderten Themenbereichen authentische Aufgaben, die dem aktuell geltenden neuen Format entsprechen. Daneben finden Sie die Original-Prüfungsaufgaben 2023.

Ihr Abiturjahrgang erfährt eine Reihe Neuerungen, die uns zu einer Neustrukturierung unseres Buches veranlasst haben. Vielleicht kennen Sie die FiNALE-Bände aus der Schule oder von Ihren älteren Geschwistern. Anders als in den vergangenen 14 Jahren werden Sie nun keine vollständigen Klausuren mehr vorfinden. Das Abitur 2025 sieht die Überprüfung von vier Teilkompetenzen vor. Lesen, Schreiben und Sprachmittlung werden ergänzt durch eine Aufgabe zum Hörverstehen. Dies führt zu einem ganz neuen Abiturprüfungsformat und zu einem neuen Bewertungsschlüssel. Überdies wurde der thematische Zusammenhang der einzelnen Prüfungsteile aufgegeben. Deshalb haben wir uns entschlossen, die verschiedenen Kompetenzen in unterschiedlichen Kapiteln zu behandeln. Sie finden also jeweils ein Kapitel mit authentischen Aufgaben zum Hörverstehen, zur Mediation sowie zum kombinierten Leseverstehen und Schreiben.

Daneben bietet Ihnen der aktuelle Titel wie gewohnt die Original-Prüfungsaufgaben von 2023. Trotz der von der Landesregierung vorgenommenen Änderungen sind diese Aufgaben eine sinnvolle Lernhilfe für Sie, denn das Format und der Schwierigkeitsgrad der Schreibaufgabe und der Sprachmittlungsaufgabe sind weitgehend gleich geblieben. Was das Hörverstehen angeht, erachten wir es nicht für sinnvoll, eine Vielzahl von Beispielaufgaben zu erstellen, die diese Kompetenz lediglich begrenzt und für einen spezifischen Kontext trainieren. Wir konzentrieren uns daher auf eine Beispielaufgabe und bieten Ihnen zusätzlich Tipps zum Umgang mit den Hörtexten und den Items der Aufgabenstellung sowie Hinweise, wie Sie auch kurzfristig noch Ihr Hörverstehen trainieren können.

Unter unseren Beispielaufgaben sind sowohl Beispiele für Grundkurse als auch für Leistungskurse. Im Abitur unterscheidet sich die Aufgabe für Leistungskurse von denen für Grundkurse einerseits durch den Textumfang, andererseits durch den Schwierigkeitsgrad der Texte, der sich in der Regel aus der Komplexität der Syntax und des Wortschatzes ergibt. Beide Kriterien spielen für Übungstexte keine große Rolle. Auch als Grundkursschülerin oder -schüler sind Sie durch den Englischunterricht mit längeren und komplexeren Texten vertraut. Als Leistungskursschülerin oder -schüler können Sie eine Textanalyse auch an kürzeren, einfacheren Texten üben. Die inhaltlichen Vorgaben sind für beide Kursarten weitgehend gleich.

Je eine Schreibaufgabe zu einem literarischen Text und einem Sach- und Gebrauchstext sowie eine Sprachmittlungsaufgabe wird kleinschrittig erarbeitet und schließt mit einer Musterlösung. Dies soll für Sie eine exemplarische Hilfe sein auf dem Weg von den Ausgangstexten über das Textverständnis, die Methodik der Textanalyse, die Evaluation und die Sprachmittlung hin zur Gliederung und sprachlichen Darstellung der Zieltexte. Den weiteren Aufgabenbeispielen folgen Bewertungskriterien ganz in der Form, wie Ihre Lehrerinnen und Lehrer sie zur Korrektur der Abiturarbeiten an die Hand bekommen. Sie dienen Ihnen zur Selbstkontrolle in Ihrem fortschreitenden Prüfungstraining. Zu Ihrer Orientierung haben wir auch entsprechende Punkte vergeben. „Gummipunkte", also Punkte für ein „weiteres aufgabenbezogenes Kriterium", wie es sie im Abitur gibt, erschienen uns für die Beispielaufgaben jedoch wenig sinnvoll.

Geschrieben wurde dieses Buch im Jahr 2024, damit es frühzeitig zur Vorbereitung auf das Abitur 2025 beitragen kann. Die zu diesem Zeitpunkt aktuellen Abituraufgaben 2023 werden jeweils mit einer Musterlösung angeboten. Originallösungen unterliegen weiterhin der Geheimhaltung und können nicht veröffentlicht werden. Dennoch versuchen wir, unsere Musterlösung auf der Grundlage unserer Korrekturarbeit der Abiturarbeiten 2023 zu erstellen. Sie greifen die tatsächlich gegebenen Probleme und Fehlerschwerpunkte der Abiturientinnen und Abiturienten auf.

Der eindringliche Wunsch unserer Abiturienten nach einer kompakten inhaltlichen Übersicht über die verbindlich vorgegebenen Themen des Zentralabiturs hat uns bewogen, diese relevanten Inhalte im Kapitel „Basiswissen" zusammenzustellen. Natürlich kann dieses weder den Englischunterricht der Qualifikationsphase noch dessen Vor- und Nachbereitung ersetzen. Es hilft Ihnen jedoch, das im Unterricht erworbene Wissen zu strukturieren und in seinen Grundzügen abzurufen. Um den Umgang mit dem thematischen Vokabular zu vertiefen, ist dieser Teil in englischer Sprache geschrieben und wird durch Glossare zum thematischen Vokabular ergänzt.
Die sprachliche Leistung spielt in der Fremdsprache trotz aller inhaltlich-thematischer Kompetenz immer noch die herausragende Rolle. Während man in der Abiturklausur für den Inhalt maximal 64 Punkte erreichen kann, erhält man für eine perfekte sprachliche Leistung 96 Punkte. Ein sicherer Umgang mit den Strukturen und Wörtern der englischen Sprache ist also unabdingbar. Deshalb haben wir in FiNALE ein Kapitel zur sprachlichen Leistung aufgenommen, in dem es vor allem um kommunikative Textgestaltung und Ausdrucksvermögen geht, die im Zentralabitur – wie die sprachliche Richtigkeit – mit jeweils 32 Punkten bewertet werden.

Wir wünschen Ihnen viel Erfolg!

Informationen und Tipps zur Prüfung

Inhalte des Faches Englisch in der gymnasialen Oberstufe

Gelegentlich beklagen sich Schülerinnen und Schüler und auch Eltern über die Anforderungen und Inhalte des Englischunterrichts, insbesondere der Klausuren und der schriftlichen Abiturprüfung. Textanalyse und kreative Textproduktion erscheinen ihnen nicht als Fertigkeiten, die man im Leben braucht. Auf Unverständnis trifft gelegentlich auch die Bewertung – hat man doch gerade mit einem Australier gechattet, der sich anerkennend zu den Englischkenntnissen äußerte, oder im Urlaub einen Engländer getroffen, mit dem man sich prima bei einer Cola unterhalten konnte. Die Fähigkeit, sich mit anderen unterhalten zu können, ist also offensichtlich nicht der alleinige Aspekt, der in der Oberstufe und im Abitur bewertet wird.

Primäres Ziel des Englischunterrichts ist die **kommunikative Kompetenz**, also Schüler/-innen in die Lage zu versetzen, im englischsprachigen Ausland oder auch mit dem Englischen als *lingua franca* angemessen zu kommunizieren. Sieht man sich den Kernlehrplan für die Sekundarstufe I an, so wird man schnell erkennen, dass selbst die geforderten Kompetenzen für das Ende der Sekundarstufe I weit über die Kommunikation in Alltagssituationen hinausgehen. Zur Vorbereitung der Schüler/-innen auf ein Studium an der Hochschule, auf einen beruflichen Weg in Großunternehmen oder international tätigen mittelständischen Unternehmen orientiert sich der Kernlehrplan Englisch am Leitziel der interkulturellen Handlungsfähigkeit. Deshalb behandelt der Englischunterricht soziokulturell und global bedeutsame Themen, die in Texten und Medien dargestellt werden.

Funktional kommunikative Kompetenzen sind Leseverstehen, Schreiben, Hör-/Hörsehverstehen, Sprechen und Sprachmittlung. Außerdem zählt man die Verfügbarkeit sprachlicher Mittel dazu, d. h. Wortschatz, Grammatik, Rechtschreibung und Aussprache.
Interkulturelle kommunikative Kompetenz ist das Zusammenspiel von Wissen, Einstellung und Bewusstheit. Vor dem Hintergrund ihrer eigenen Kultur sollen Schülerinnen und Schüler in der Lage sein, sowohl Empathie als auch kritische Distanz gegenüber kulturellen Besonderheiten zu entwickeln.
Für den Erwerb von **Text- und Medienkompetenz** vermittelt der Englischunterricht eine Fülle von Teilkompetenzen. Der Begriff Text umfasst hier – wie immer – Sachtexte sowie literarische Texte, Filme, Bilder, Diagramme, Statistiken, Grafiken etc. Das Kapitel „Methoden der Textarbeit" wird sich eingehend damit befassen.

Für den **Umgang mit Texten** in der Q1 und der Q2 gibt der Kernlehrplan Folgendes vor:
Sach- und Gebrauchstexte
Texte der privaten und öffentlichen Kommunikation:
  Brief, Kommentar, Leitartikel, politische Rede, Leserbrief, Werbeanzeige
Texte in wissenschaftsorientierter Dimension:
  Lexikonauszug, ein längerer Sachbuchauszug
Texte in berufsorientierter Dimension: Stellenanzeige, PR-Material, Exposé, Protokoll

literarische Texte
lyrische Texte: zeitgenössisches Gedicht, Gedicht in historischer Dimension
narrative Texte: zeitgenössischer Roman, Kurzgeschichte
dramatische Texte:
   Auszüge aus einem oder aus verschiedenen Shakespeare-Dramen, ein zeitgenössisches Drama, Auszüge aus einem Drehbuch

diskontinuierlicher Texte
Text-Bild-Kombinationen: Bild, Cartoon
Grafiken: Tabelle, Karte, Diagramm

medial vermittelte Texte
auditive Formate: *radio feature* / Podcast, Auszüge aus einem Hörbuch
audiovisuelle Formate: Spielfilm, *documentary/feature,* Nachrichten
digitale Texte: Blog/Videoblog, Beiträge in Internetforen

Sprachlernkompetenz beinhaltet das selbstständige Gestalten des Lernens durch das Entwickeln von Strategien, aber auch durch den sicheren Umgang mit Hilfsmitteln, z. B. mit dem Wörterbuch.

Sprachbewusstheit beinhaltet Einsichten zum Beispiel in Varianten des Sprachgebrauchs, in verschiedene Register und Stilebenen, in Beziehungen zwischen Sprache und Kultur, aber auch die Bewusstheit von sprachlicher Manipulation.

Obligatorische Themen und Inhalte für das Zentralabitur

Das Ministerium gibt auf der Grundlage der Kernlehrpläne Vorgaben für eine Schwerpunktsetzung im Hinblick auf das Zentralabitur. Konkret gelten für das Abitur 2025 die folgenden Fokussierungen zu der im Kernlehrplan festgelegten Obligatorik. (Die vollständige Übersicht ist zu finden auf der Website des Ministeriums: https://www.standardsicherung.schulministerium.nrw.de/cms/zentralabitur-gost/faecher/getfile.php?file=5559 (Zugriff: 01.04.2024))

Inhaltliche Schwerpunkte

Amerikanischer Traum – Visionen und Lebenswirklichkeiten in den USA
– American myths and realities: freedom and equality
Das Vereinigte Königreich im 21. Jahrhundert – Selbstverständnis zwischen Tradition und Moderne
– Tradition and change in politics and society:
   – the UK in the European context
   – multicultural society (Leistungskurs)

Postkolonialismus – Lebenswirklichkeiten in einem weiteren anglophonen Kulturraum
- Voices from the African Continent: Focus on Nigeria

Chancen und Risiken der Globalisierung
- The international world of work
- Voices from the African continent: focus on Nigeria (Grundkurs)
- Ecological challenges and sustainable lifestyles (Grundkurs)
- Globalisation and global challenges: economic, ecological and political issues (Leistungskurs)
- International relations (Leistungskurs):
  - conflict and cooperation
  - migration

(Literatur und) Medien in ihrer Bedeutung für den Einzelnen und die Gesellschaft
- The impact of the media: information, entertainment, manipulation (Grundkurs)
- Voices from the African continent: focus on Nigeria (Leistungskurs)
- Visions of the future:
  - utopia and dystopia
  - ethical issues of scientific and technological progress (Leistungskurs)

Fortschritt und Ethik in der modernen Gesellschaft (Leistungskurs)
- Visions of the future:
  - utopia and dystopia
  - ethical issues of scientific and technological progress (Leistungskurs)
- Globalisation and global challenges: economic, ecological and political issues (Leistungskurs)

Lebensentwürfe, Studium, Ausbildung, Beruf international – Englisch als *lingua franca*
- Questions of identity and gender:
  - ambitions and obstacles
  - conformity vs. individualism

Zieltextformate

In Teilaufgabe 3 der Lese-/Schreibaufgabe haben die Schülerinnen und Schüler die Wahl zwischen einer Stellungnahme und einer kreativen Aufgabe. Für letztere wird Vertrautheit mit folgenden Textformaten vorausgesetzt:
- *letter/email, letter to the editor*
- *speech script: talk, public/formal speech, debate statement*
- *newspaper/internet article, blog entry*
- nur im Leistungskurs: *(written) interview*
- Ausgestaltung, Fortführung oder Ergänzung eines literarischen Ausgangstextes: narrative Texte; zusätzlich im Leistungskurs: dramatische Texte, *film script*

Für die Sprachmittlung wird Vertrautheit mit folgenden Zieltexten vorausgesetzt:
- *letter/email*
- *newspaper/internet article, blog entry*

Grundsätze der Abiturprüfung

Aufgabenarten

Sie kennen verschiedene Klausurvarianten bereits aus der Qualifikationsphase. Leseverstehen und Schreiben wurden stets entweder mit Hörverstehen oder mit Sprachmittlung kombiniert. Im Abitur erhalten sie eine Kombination von Aufgaben zur Prüfung aller vier Kompetenzen.

Die Prüfung beginnt mit dem Hörverstehen. Nach 30 Minuten werden die Aufgaben eingesammelt. Danach werden die Aufgaben zur Sprachmittlung verteilt. Grundlage ist dabei immer ein deutschsprachiger Sachtext. Diese Aufgaben werden nach 60 Minuten eingesammelt und die Lese-/Schreibaufgabe wird verteilt. Sollten Sie früher mit der Mediationsaufgabe fertig sein, so können Sie diese abgeben und erhalten die Unterlagen für die Lese-/Schreibaufgabe schon dann.

Für den Klausurteil zum Leseverstehen/Schreiben erhalten Sie zwei Aufgabenvorschläge zur Wahl: einen literarischen Text und einen Sachtext. Beide Aufgabenvorschläge beinhalten die Ihnen bekannten drei Teilaufgaben *(comprehension – analysis – evaluation)*. Die dritte Teilaufgabe gibt Ihnen die Wahl zwischen einer kreativen Aufgabe und einer Stellungnahme.

Der englische Text hat im Leistungskurs einen Umfang von maximal 1000 Wörtern, im Grundkurs maximal 800 Wörtern. Der deutsche Text umfasst in beiden Kursarten zwischen 450 und 650 Wörter. Als Ausgangstexte eignen sich nur authentische Texte, d. h. sie dürfen nicht adaptiert oder stark gekürzt sein.

Anforderungsbereiche

Die Teilaufgaben der Prüfungsklausuren entsprechen den folgenden Anforderungsbereichen, die Sie bereits aus der Qualifikationsphase kennen.

> **Anforderungsbereich I:** *comprehension/orientation/context*
> - Wiedergabe der zentralen Aussagen eines Textes (meist Inhaltsangabe)
> - Einordnung des Textes in einen Kontext unter Verwendung von Hintergrundwissen
> - Einleitung eines komplexen Textes

> **Anforderungsbereich II:** *analysis*
> - Anwendung von Fachmethoden: textanalytische Verfahren, Einsatz von Lesetechniken
> - gezielte Anwendung von Kenntnissen und Wissen – z. B. soziokulturelles oder metasprachliches Wissen (= Wissen über Sprache)
> - exakte Arbeit am sprachlichen Detail, Belegen und Zitieren, problemlösende Argumentation

Anforderungsbereich III: *evaluation*

für die analytisch-interpretierende Aufgabenstellung:

- Bewertung der Problemlösung, Einordnen der Ergebnisse in einen größeren Zusammenhang
- persönliche Stellungnahme, eigene Meinung (erst hier und nicht etwa in AFB I oder II)

Anforderungsbereich III: *evaluation/re-creation of text*

für die anwendungs-/produktionsorientierte Aufgabenstellung:

- Umsetzung, Bewertung, Reflexion der Problematik des Ausgangstextes bzw. der Analyse im Aufgabenbereich II in Form einer kreativen Aufgabe: Perspektivwechsel (Sicht einer anderen Figur)
- Füllen von Leerstellen (Weitererzählen, neues Ende)
- Textsortenwechsel (Brief an Protagonisten, Leserbrief, Brief an *agony aunt*, Tagebucheintrag, Dialog etc.)

Die einzelnen Anforderungsbereiche sollen nicht in drei voneinander unabhängigen Texten behandelt werden. Der Zieltext ist ein geschlossener, kohärenter Text, der sich als Essay in seinen drei Teilen etwa in eine Hinführung zum Thema, einen Hauptteil und eine Schlussbetrachtung gliedert. Eine kreative Teilaufgabe wird sich naheliegenderweise nicht in den geschlossenen Zieltext eingliedern, da sie in der Regel ein völlig anderes Textformat hat.

TIPP

Wichtig! Sie sind aus Ihren Oberstufenklausuren gewohnt, Stellungnahmen und kreative Texte mit engem Bezug zum Ausgangstext zu erstellen. Im Abitur wird es auch Aufgaben mit nur thematischem Bezug oder gar themenübergreifendem Bezug geben. Beispiele dazu finden Sie in den Abituraufgaben der Jahre 2023 und 2024 und auch in unseren Beispielaufgaben zum American Dream und zum Brexit.

Treffen Sie im Abitur Ihre Aufgabenauswahl also auch mit besonderem Blick auf den Anforderungsbereich III!

Operatoren

Für die Formulierung der Aufgaben gibt es klare Vorgaben. Verben für die Arbeitsanweisungen (= Operatoren) müssen in ihrer exakten Bedeutung verstanden werden. Eine ungefähre Ahnung, was gefordert ist, reicht keinesfalls aus.

Die folgende Operatorenübersicht ist der Website des Ministeriums entnommen. Die mittlere Spalte definiert die genaue Wortbedeutung des Verbs, die dritte Spalte gibt jeweils ein Beispiel für eine Aufgabenstellung.

Beachten Sie, dass die Operatoren im Anforderungsbereich I vor allem deutlich machen, welcher Umfang der inhaltlichen Wiedergabe von Ihnen verlangt wird. „Outline", „summarise" oder „write a summary" verlangen eine knappe Wiedergabe des Textes oder auch nur einer relevanten Textpassage. „Describe" und „point out" hingegen erwarten eine ausführliche Beschreibung bzw. Erläuterung des im Text dargestellten Sachverhalts. Letzteres kommt vor allem infrage, wenn der Ausgangstext sehr komplex ist, wie z. B. eine Erörterung, oder sehr dicht, wie beispielsweise ein Gedicht. Ihr Textverständnis weisen Sie dann nicht durch eine knappe Zusammenfassung, sondern durch eine Beschreibung oder Erläuterung in Ihren eigenen Worten nach.

TIPP

Achten Sie darauf, dass Sie, auch wenn Sie zu einer Skizzierung *(outline)* oder Zusammenfassung *(summary)* des Inhalts aufgefordert werden, stets die wesentlichen Inhaltspunkte benennen. Eine abstraktere, allgemeiner gehaltene Zusammenfassung kann durchaus eleganter sein, wird aber durch den Punktekatalog der Bewertungskriterien möglicherweise nicht erfasst.

Grundsätzlich können sich alle Operatoren auf alle drei Anforderungsbereiche beziehen, doch definiert die Wortbedeutung meist den Anforderungsbereich (z. B. *analyse oder evaluate)*. Die hier angegebenen Anforderungsbereiche entsprechen daher der üblichen Zuordnung des jeweiligen Operators.

Hörverstehen

Operator	Illustrierendes Aufgabenbeispiel
complete, fill in	Complete the sentences below using 1 to 5 words. Fill in the missing information using about 1 to 5 words.
list, name	List the most important aspects mentioned in the discussion.
match	Match each person with one of the pictures. There is one more picture than you need.
state	State the ideas supported by speaker A.
tick	Tick the correct answer.

Sprachmittlung
Die Aufgabenstellung für die Sprachmittlung enthält einen situativen Kontext mit Hinweisen zu Adressat/-in und Zieltextformat.

Operator	Erläuterung	Illustrierendes Aufgabenbeispiel
explain	make sth. clear taking into account culture-related differences if necessary	Based on the text on environmental policy, explain the principle of waste separation in Germany in an email to your British friend.

outline	give a concise account of the main points or ideas of a text, clarifying culture-related aspects if necessary	Outline Mr. Liu's career in Germany in an article for your international school project's website on *Successful Immigrants*.
present	give a concise account of the main points or ideas of a text, clarifying culture-related aspects if necessary	For an international school project in the EU, present the relevant information on the image of migrants in German media in a formal email to your partner school in Spain.
summarise, sum up	give a concise account of the main points or ideas of a text, clarifying culture-related aspects if necessary	Sum up Manuel's views on working and living as a gap year student in India for your blog. Where necessary, add information which might help to avoid possible misunderstandings.
write (+ text type)	produce a text with specific features	Using the information in the German text write an article in English for your project website in which you inform your Polish partners how to get a sports scholarship at a German university.

Schreiben, Leseverstehen integriert

Operator	Erläuterung	Illustrierendes Aufgabenbeispiel	AFB
analyse	describe and explain in detail	Analyse the opposing views on class held by the two protagonists. Examine the author's use of language.	II
assess	express a well-founded opinion on the nature or quality of sb./sth.	Assess the importance of standards in education.	III
evaluate	express a well-founded opinion on the nature or quality of sb./sth.	Evaluate the author's view of the present impact of the American Dream ...	III
examine	describe and explain in detail	Examine the opposing views on social class held by the two protagonists.	II
give/write a characterisation of	provide a thorough analysis of a character	Characterise / Write a characterisation of the principal figures in the play.	II

comment (on)	state one's opinion clearly and support one's view with evidence or reasons	Comment on the writer's view of gender roles.	III
compare	show similarities and differences	Compare the attitude of the two characters towards war.	II
describe	give a detailed account of what sb./sth. is like	Describe the way the playwright creates an atmosphere of suspense.	I II
discuss	give arguments or reasons for and against, especially to come to a well-founded conclusion	Discuss the message of the cartoon, referring to work done on the British monarchy.	III
explain	make sth. clear by giving reasons for and details/aspects of sth.	Explain the protagonist's obsession with money.	II
illustrate	use examples to explain or make clear	Illustrate the way in which, according to the author, school life in Britain differs from that in Germany.	II
interpret	explain the meaning, purpose or message of sth.	Interpret the sonnet, focusing on the way structure and imagery are used to express the speaker's insight into the nature of time.	II
outline	give the main features, structure or general principles of sth.	Outline the author's views on love, marriage and divorce.	I
point out	find and explain certain aspects	Point out the author's main ideas on …	I
state	present the main aspects of sth. briefly and clearly	State the author's key reasons for taking a gap year.	I
summarise, sum up	give a concise account of the main points or ideas of a text, issue or topic	Summarise / Sum up the information about green energy given in the text.	I
write (+ text type)	produce a text with specific features	Write the ending of the story / a letter to the editor / a dialogue, etc. Write an interior monologue that reflects the character's view of the situation and her/his feelings.	III

Quelle: https://www.standardsicherung.schulministerium.nrw.de/cms/zentralabitur-gost/faecher/getfile.php?file=5794 (Zugriff: 01.04.2024)

Dauer der Prüfung

Leistungskurs: 315 Minuten (30 Minuten Hörverstehen; 285 Minuten für Sprachmittlung und Schreiben/Leseverstehen (integriert) einschließlich Auswahlzeit; davon max. 60 Minuten für Sprachmittlung)

Grundkurs: 285 Minuten (30 Minuten Hörverstehen; 255 Minuten für Sprachmittlung und Schreiben/Leseverstehen (integriert) einschließlich Auswahlzeit; davon max. 60 Minuten für Sprachmittlung)

Bewertung

Die Lehrer/-innen nutzen ein Bewertungsraster mit Bewertungskriterien, sowohl für die sprachliche als auch für die inhaltliche Leistung, sowie ein Schlüssel zur Übertragung der Punkte aus dem Hörverstehen. Es können in der Abiturklausur insgesamt 200 Punkte erreicht werden. Dabei entfallen 40 Punkte auf das Hörverstehen, 50 Punkte auf die Sprachmittlung und 110 Punkte auf die Lese-/Schreibaufgabe.

Innerhalb der Sprachmittlung werden für den Inhalt höchstens 20 und für die Sprache 30 Punkte vergeben; in der Schreibaufgabe sind maximal 44 Punkte für den Inhalt und 66 Punkte für die Sprache erreichbar. Die jeweiligen Punktzahlen für die drei Teilaufgaben können variieren.

Grundsätze für die Bewertung (Notenfindung)

Für die Zuordnung der Notenstufen zu den Punktzahlen wird folgende Tabelle verwendet:

Note	Punkte	Erreichte Punktzahl
sehr gut plus	15	190 – 200
sehr gut	14	180 – 189
sehr gut minus	13	170 – 179
gut plus	12	160 – 169
gut	11	150 – 159
gut minus	10	140 – 149
befriedigend plus	9	130 – 139
befriedigend	8	120 – 129
befriedigend minus	7	110 – 119
ausreichen plus	6	100 – 109
ausreichend	5	90 – 99
ausreichend minus	4	80 – 89
mangelhaft plus	3	66 – 79
mangelhaft	2	54 – 65
mangelhaft minus	1	40 – 53
ungenügend	0	0 – 39

Hörverstehen

Hörverstehen ist Ihnen aus dem Unterricht und den Klassenarbeiten der Sekundarstufe I sowie den Klausuren der gymnasialen Oberstufe längst bekannt. Im Abitur wurde Hörverstehen bisher nicht überprüft – Sie sind der erste Jahrgang.

In den ersten 30 Minuten Ihrer Abiturprüfung werden Ihnen hierzu drei Hörtexte von insgesamt zehn Minuten Dauer präsentiert. Sie dürfen die Texte zweimal hören. Es wird Ihnen auch Zeit gegeben, vorher die Einzelaufgaben in Ruhe zu lesen.

Zu erwarten sind authentische Hörtexte, also nicht extra für die Prüfung fabrizierte und eingesprochene Texte. Es wird Mitschnitte aus Nachrichtensendungen geben, aus Interviews, Reportagen, Reden, Gesprächen, Diskussionen oder Hintergrundberichten und auch Ausschnitte aus Hörbüchern. Videos sind nicht vorgesehen. Thematisch werden die Texte an Ihre Unterrichtsinhalte angebunden sein, sie können aber ausdrücklich auch ganz allgemeinen lebensweltlichen Bezug haben.

Zur Bearbeitung der Aufgabe sollten Sie sich der verschiedenen Hörstile bewusst sein, die in den Aufgaben auch gezielt berücksichtigt werden:

Globales Verstehen: Die Kernaussage wird erfasst.

Detailliertes Verstehen: Hauptinformationen und bestimmte Details werden erfasst.

Selektives Verstehen: Bestimmte Einzelinformationen an der Textoberfläche werden erfasst (z.B. Uhrzeiten, Daten, Preise etc.)

Inferierendes Verstehen (LK): Stimmungen und Einstellungen der sprechenden Person werden erfasst. („zwischen den Zeilen")

Zur Überprüfung des Hörverstehens werden bestimmte Aufgabenformate eingesetzt:

Multiple-Choice-Aufgaben: Sie kreuzen aus vier vorgegebenen Antwortmöglichkeiten die richtige an. Es gibt immer nur eine richtige Antwort. Dabei folgen die Einzelaufgaben in ihrer Reihenfolge dem Verlauf des Textes und sind gleichmäßig über den gesamten Text verteilt. Dabei sind sie voneinander unabhängig, d. h. eine Lösung setzt nicht eine andere voraus.

Matching (Zuordnungsaufgaben): Insbesondere im Bereich des Globalverstehens kommen Zuordnungsaufgaben zum Einsatz. Z. B. kann einer sprechenden Person eine zusammenfassende Kernaussage zugeordnet werden.

Es wird auch **Ergänzungsaufgaben** sowie Aufgaben geben, in denen Sie **Kurzantworten** geben müssen.

Die verschiedenen Formate sollten Ihnen aus Ihren Klausuren bekannt sein. Darüber hinaus stellt die Website des Ministeriums unter dem folgenden Link Beispielaufgaben zur Verfügung, nicht nur für das Abitur, sondern auch für Klausuren der Qualifikationsphase: https://www.standardsicherung.schulministerium.nrw.de/cms/front_content.php?idart=442 („Beispielaufgaben Englisch Aufgabenformat ‚Hörverstehen'")

Unser Aufgabenbeispiel ist dazu gedacht, Sie mit dem Format der Hörverstehensprüfung vertraut zu machen. Hörverstehen selbst können Sie mit drei 3-Minuten-Texten leider nicht trainieren. Sollten sie Probleme beim Verstehen gesprochener englischsprachiger Texte haben, so können Sie dies auch kurzfristig noch effektiv trainieren:

TIPP zum Punktesammeln

Schauen Sie Ihre Lieblingsserien und Filme in englischer Sprache! Wenn Sie ohnehin Zeit auf Video- und Streamingplattformen verbringen, suchen Sie sich doch gezielt englischsprachige Beiträge aus!

Informieren Sie sich zum Weltgeschehen in den Medien der englischsprachigen Welt, zum Beispiel bei der BBC, CNN oder dem News-Channel TLDR!

BBC Sound bietet Podcasts zu unterschiedlichen Themen. Suchen Sie sich Ihr Lieblingsthema aus!

Englische Audio- und Videobeiträge finden sich bekanntlich auch in den Sozialmedien. Darüber hinaus wissen Sie selbst am besten, wo es im Internet etwas zu hören gibt. Tun Sie es auf Englisch, auch in Ihrer Freizeit!

Und lassen Sie sich nicht entmutigen, wenn Sie etwas nicht verstehen! Das wird schon.

Die mündliche Abiturprüfung im Fach Englisch

Während einige von Ihnen Englisch als schriftliches Abiturfach gewählt haben, werden andere sich für Englisch als 4. Abiturfach entschieden haben und damit eine mündliche Abiturprüfung ablegen.

Auch für den Fall, dass Sie Englisch als schriftliches Abiturfach gewählt haben, könnte es trotzdem sein, dass Sie an einer mündlichen Nachprüfung teilnehmen müssen, nämlich wenn Sie Ihre Prüfungen nicht bestanden haben. In bestimmten Fällen besteht auch die Möglichkeit, die Abiturnote durch die Teilnahme an einer freiwilligen mündlichen Nachprüfung zu verbessern.

Ganz egal, welcher Fall für Sie von Bedeutung ist: Die Vorbereitung und der Ablauf der mündlichen Prüfung im Fach Englisch ist immer gleich.

Die mündliche Prüfung im Fach Englisch dauert insgesamt **mindestens 20,** aber **höchstens 30 Minuten** und ist in zwei Prüfungsteile aufgeteilt, deren Dauer ungefähr gleich lang ist.

Vor Beginn der Prüfung haben Sie **30 Minuten Zeit,** das Ihnen von Ihrem Fachlehrer oder Ihrer Fachlehrerin für den ersten Prüfungsteil vorgelegte **Material vorzubereiten.** Als Hilfsmittel stehen Ihnen hier ein **ein- und zweisprachiges Wörterbuch** und **gegebenenfalls ein herkunftssprachliches Wörterbuch** zur Verfügung. Die Notizen, die Sie hier anfertigen, dürfen Sie mit in die Prüfung nehmen und als Grundlage für Ihren Vortrag nutzen.

Anders als im schriftlichen Abitur können Sie hier **nicht** zwischen verschiedenen Materialien auswählen.

Das Material, das Ihnen von Ihrem Fachlehrer oder Ihrer Fachlehrerin vorgelegt wird, stellt einen **Bezug zu den Themenfeldern der Qualifikationsphase** her. Zur häuslichen Vorbereitung verweisen wir hier auf die Kapitel zum Basiswissen auf den Seiten 21 bis 77.

Im **ersten Prüfungsteil** sollen Sie – auf Basis des Ihnen zur Vorbereitung vorgelegten Materials – einen **zusammenhängenden und weitgehend freien Vortrag** halten, selbstständig eine **nachvollziehbare Argumentation** entwickeln und **eine Einordnung in den entsprechenden Themenkomplex** vornehmen.

Grundsätzlich ist der erste Prüfungsteil nichts anderes als eine „mündliche Version" einer Klausur. Daher empfehlen wir Ihnen, die in diesem Buch enthaltenen Klausuren zur Vorbereitung auf die mündliche Prüfung durchzuarbeiten.

Im Grunde bestehen zwei Möglichkeiten, wie das von Ihnen vorzubereitende **Material** aussehen kann.

Es können Ihnen ein oder mehrere Texte beziehungsweise ein längeres Zitat mit einem Wortumfang von **ca. 200 bis 300 Wörtern** vorgelegt werden. Bei den Texten kann es sich um **literarische Texte** oder um **Sach- und Gebrauchstexte** handeln.

Ihr Fachlehrer oder Ihre Fachlehrerin kann Ihnen aber auch eine oder mehrere visuelle **Darstellungen** (Diagramm, Grafik, Cartoon, Statistik, Bild) vorlegen, die er/sie gegebenenfalls um einen Text ergänzt.

Im **zweiten Prüfungsteil** wird Ihnen kein weiteres Material vorgelegt. Gegenstand dieses Prüfungsteils sind ein weiterer bzw. mehrere weitere **Themenkomplexe zu den Themenfeldern der Qualifikationsphase**.

Hier sollen Sie zeigen, dass Sie **größere Zusammenhänge erkennen und herstellen** können.

Da neben Ihrer inhaltlichen Leistung auch Ihre sprachliche Leistung bewertet wird, sei an dieser Stelle nochmals auf die Listen mit nützlichen Wörtern und Wendungen im Buch (ab S. 210) verwiesen.

Beachten Sie auch die Strategien zur Wortschatzarbeit und zur Vermeidung „gängiger" Fehler.

Achten Sie in beiden Prüfungsteilen darauf, dass Ihre Ausführungen für die Prüfungskommission verständlich und nachvollziehbar sind.

Bemühen Sie sich darum, im ersten Prüfungsteil Ihre Gedanken und Anmerkungen möglichst strukturiert und frei vorzutragen.

Nutzen Sie die Vorbereitungszeit dazu, Ihre Notizen zu strukturieren. Selbstverständlich dürfen und sollen Sie auf diese zurückgreifen, aber lesen Sie keinesfalls alles von Ihrem Notizzettel ab.

Basiswissen

American Myths and Realities: Freedom and Equality

Concepts of the American Dream

The USA

The USA was – and still is – a country of unlimited opportunities, where people can work their way "from rags to riches". It has attracted millions of both legal and illegal immigrants over the centuries, who hoped to find a better life without the kind of persecution or obstacles they faced in their home countries.

> **Keyword**
>
> **The American Dream:** There is no single definition of what the American Dream actually is, as it varies for each and every American.
> The term was first used by James Truslow Adams, an American historian, in his book *The Epic of America,* in 1931: "[The] American Dream [is] the dream of a land in which life should be better and richer and fuller for every man, with opportunity for each according to his ability or achievement."

In the following pages we are going to take a look at some of the key concepts generally associated with the American Dream, many of which are often touched upon in political speeches.
Please note that these key concepts often overlap and are closely related.

Freedom

The first thing many immigrants saw when they came to New York City by ship during the 19th and the first half of the 20th century was the Statue of Liberty, which is located on Liberty Island.

The Statue of Liberty

- given to the USA as a gift from France in 1886, to celebrate the first 100 years of American independence from Britain
- a robed woman, holding a lit torch in her right and a tablet in her left hand, showing the date of the Declaration of Independence (4 July 1776)
- underneath her right foot the remains of broken shackles can be seen
- one of the most famous American icons, symbolising enlightenment, independence, liberty and freedom
- the theme of Emma Lazarus's famous poem "The New Colossus" (1883), which can be seen on a bronze plaque inside the statue
- located in Upper New York Bay, just like Ellis Island

Ellis Island
- the place where most immigrants first set foot on American soil
- an island of hopes but also an island of tears for a number of immigrants, as some of them were detained there for legal or medical reasons or even sent back
- the gateway to a new – better – life for the majority of immigrants
- a federal immigration station from 1892 to 1954

The Puritans

The Puritans' beliefs and values had a lasting impact on New England society:
- towards the end of the 16th century, some English Protestants felt that Protestantism in England was not much different from Catholicism
- decided to leave England, seeking their luck elsewhere
- first settled in Holland (1608), but moved back to England
- wished to remain English subjects but free to worship God the way they wanted to
- intention: to purify the Church of England, not to leave it
- September 1620: a group of 102 people left England, sailed on a ship called the *Mayflower*, arrived in America 65 days later, in a bay they called Plymouth Bay

The New Canaan

In the Bible, Canaan was the land God promised to the Israelites. God ordered Moses to lead the people from captivity in Egypt to Canaan – "a land of milk and honey". America sees itself in this tradition. The idea of America as the "New Canaan", is closely linked to the idea of "manifest destiny".

Manifest Destiny / The frontier
Manifest Destiny

The term "Manifest Destiny" was coined by the American journalist John L. O'Sullivan in 1839:
- stands for the belief that America is the one nation ordered by God to expand across the North American continent
- "The Great Nation of Futurity" by John L. O'Sullivan: "[America is] the nation of progress, of individual freedom, of universal enfranchisement"; the American people have been chosen "to establish on earth the moral dignity and salvation of man – the immutable truth and beneficence of God"[1].
- America as the country that is superior to all other countries
- stresses virtue of the American people, as they are the ones to establish moral rules and values across the globe

American patriotism is deeply rooted in the concept of "Manifest Destiny", while the idea of "Manifest Destiny" is in turn closely linked to the perception of the frontier and its continuing permutations.

---

[1] "The Great Nation of Futurity," *The United States Democratic Review,* Volume 6, Issue 23, pp. 426–430.

The frontier

- the expansion of the American nation from coast to coast, pushing the borderline between civilisation and wilderness further and further back
- Pacific coast was reached in the 2nd half of the 19th century
- after this mission new challenges – new frontiers – were needed, e. g. space exploration (like the moon landing in 1969), scientific and technological progress

Life, liberty and the pursuit of happiness
Declaration of Independence

- written in 1776 by Thomas Jefferson
- all American citizens are created equal: "We hold these truths to be self-evident, that all men are created equal, that they are endowed by their Creator with certain unalienable Rights, that among these are Life, Liberty and the pursuit of Happiness."
- possibility for every American (however, women were excluded from this definition at first) to lead their life the way they want to, making their own personal dreams come true
- stresses the rights of the individual, while at the same time taking the rights of others into consideration
- 1776: the thirteen colonies declared their independence from England and were therefore at war with England
- Declaration of Independence questioned the rights of the British king, George III, in that it stated that everyone was created equal (a revolutionary idea at the time)
- The new American government was to be radically different from that of the British monarchy, as pointed out in the American Constitution.

American Constitution

- written in 1787
- new ideas of a democratic state stated in the preamble of the Constitution: "We the People of the United States, in Order to form a more perfect Union, establish Justice, ensure domestic Tranquility, provide for the common defense, promote the general Welfare, and secure the Blessings of Liberty to ourselves and our Posterity, do ordain and establish this Constitution for the United States of America."

Bill of Rights

- first ten amendments to the American Constitution
- written because some delegates feared that the new American government would threaten everyone's ability to achieve personal freedom and the pursuit of happiness
- First Congress of the United States originally proposed twelve amendments in 1789, ten of which were added to the constitution as a preamble
- amendments known as the Bill of Rights
- guarantee America's citizens certain inalienable rights, e. g. freedom of religion, freedom of speech and the press as well as the right to own and carry weapons

The American Dream today

> **Keywords**
>
> **Multicultural society:** a society where various ethnic groups and their cultural heritage are accepted in their own right
>
> **Salad bowl:** the various ethnicities living in the United States adding their own traditions, cultural values, etc. to the American people; the various heritages do not merge into one but stay distinct ("unity in diversity")
>
> **Melting pot:** ethnic groups do not retain their cultural heritage but amalgamate into one new nation; term first appeared in an essay by Jean de Crèvecœur entitled "Letters from an American Farmer" (1782)
>
> The term "salad bowl" is now considered to be more politically correct.

- The American Dream itself has come to be seen more critically.
- A considerable number of critics regard the American Dream as an illusion, as not everyone has access to the possibilities usually associated with it.
- Examples of American nightmares are the Vietnam War, 11 September 2001 and the financial crisis starting in 2008.

During his election campaign, current US president Joe Biden declared that he would reform the US immigration system and reverse the restrictions implemented by former US president Donald Trump. The number of prospective new immigrants would be increased and those immigrants living in the United States illegally should be pardoned and thereby been given the chance to become legal US citizens. In addition, restrictions would be lifted so that more refugees could be admitted to the USA. The number of green cards issued would be raised to match the increasing demand.

Instead of pursuing Trump's vision of building a wall on the border to Mexico to stop illegal immigration from South American countries, Biden plans to make border screening more effective.

On his first day in office, President Biden sent a bill to Congress to put his plans for a fair, human and reformed immigration system into action.

Unaccompanied minors are allowed to enter the USA while it is decided whether they are allowed to stay or will be sent back to their home country. This has led to false rumours that the US borders are open to migrants and an increased rise in the numbers of unaccompanied migrant children. Sadly, the number of these underage immigrants is still fairly high. Biden has urged families not to send their children unaccompanied on this dangerous journey to the USA.

Legislation proposed by the Biden administration in 2023, however, creates new obstacles for immigrants applying for asylum. With the Republican party driving a particularly hard line on this issue, immigration and border security is likely to be one of the key topics during the run-up to the presidential elections in 2024.

The Present Economic Situation in the US

The question whether the American Dream is still alive today is one which cannot be answered with either "yes" or "no", as the concept of the American Dream is not static. It depends on several aspects, e. g. a person's individual definition of and belief in the concept of the American Dream and the point of view one takes.

With regard to the present economic situation in the US, it is often said that the American Dream has been shattered for many people. The financial crisis that began in 2008 made the aim of achieving financial security a distant prospect for many.

In the following you will find a brief overview of why the quest for financial security has become difficult over the last few years.

For many people, owning a house is the goal of a lifetime. This is also true for US citizens, and for many years getting a loan necessary to build or buy a house was not difficult, even for people without a steady or with a low income. This resulted in people taking bigger loans than they could actually afford. They hoped that in the worst case of not being able to pay back the loan, they could still sell their houses, thereby making a profit. In most cases paying back the loan was not a problem as long as the mortgage rates were low. Hoewever, when the base rate *(Leitzins)* increased, many house owners had difficulties paying back their loans. A huge number of houses suddenly had to be sold, which lowered prices, as there was also a decline in demand. In some cases that actually meant that the price for which a house could be sold was lower than the house owner's loan. So instead of making a profit, selling a house often meant incurring a loss.

In the meantime, the banks had started to speculate with their customers' loans. Loans of good, average and bad credit rating were combined into so-called "Mortgage Backed Securities" (MBS). By combining loans of different credit rankings, banks hoped to limit the risk if someone failed to pay back a loan. These MBS were then sold to other banks worldwide, which meant profit for the seller. This practice went well for several years, but when more and more house owners could not pay back their loans, their banks started to lose large sums of money.

On 15 September 2008, one of America's biggest banks, Lehman Brothers, crashed. This marked the beginning of a series of bank crashes. Unemployment increased, and as many Americans had less money to spend, this led to a drop in consumption as well. The burst of the housing bubble did not remain an American problem for long. It soon affected the economy of other countries, among them Germany, the Benelux countries and Iceland. Government bailouts for banks and economic stimulus plans were decided and put into action. Nevertheless, many countries were hit by recession.

The US economy has fully recovered after the economic crisis of 2008 and unemployment was very low at 3.7 % in January 2024[2] During the COVID-19 crisis, the unemplyoment rate rose as high as 14.7 %, but has stabilised since and appears to be declining steadily again.

[2] http://data.bls.gov/timeseries/LNS14000000 (accessed on 1 April 2024)

For both major parties in the US, economic growth and an increase in the number of jobs are top issues, although their approaches are quite different.

On 3 November 2020, Joseph "Joe" Robinette Biden Jr., the Democratic Party candidate, won the US presidential election against Donald Trump. During both of Barack Obama's terms in office as US president, Joe Biden served as Vice-President of the USA. Prior to his finally successful run for the presidency, Biden had announced his candidacy in 1988 and 2009, but on both occasions he withdrew from the race for presidency.

Born on 20 November 1942, Biden grew up in Pennsylvania and Delaware. He worked as a lawyer until he was sworn in as a senator for the state of Delaware at the age of 29. He kept this position until his election as Vice-President to Barack Obama in 2009. Kamala Harris was elected with Biden as the first female Vice-President of the USA. She is also the first African American and first Asian American to hold this office.

Among Biden's election pledges were fighting COVID-19, dealing with the climate crisis, making healthcare affordable for everyone and renewing the country's immigration system. Rejoining the Paris Climate Agreement, which the USA had left under Donald Trump, was a first step to acknowledging the urgent global challenge of the climate crisis.

Given the relatively narrow margin of Biden's victory in the presidential election, Donald Trump, together with his supporters and many members of the Republican Party, did not readily accept the outcome. Trump continued to use the social micro-blogging platform Twitter to spread his theory of fraudulent elections and a "stolen" victory. Several of his tweets questioned the legitimacy of the election. Many were also regarded as a glorification of violence. As a consequence, Twitter permanently suspended Donald Trump's account. In the build-up to the 2024 presidential elections, Trump's election lie is still spread by a large portion of the Republican party.

The tension in the USA that erupted in the wake of Trump's constant accusations of electoral fraud led to a large number Trump supporters violently storming the Capitol in Washington, D.C. on 6 January 2021 – a mere two weeks before Biden's inauguration. Trump had summoned his supporters to march to Washington to protest against the "stolen" election and Joe Biden's congressional certification. The angry mob that stormed the Capitol wreaked havoc. Photographs and videos taken during the raid showed that some of the protesters were heavily armed and aggressive.

Media coverage of this incident went around the globe and caused horror, shock, disgust and disbelief in governments and citizens worldwide. American and international politicians alike criticised Trump for not condemning but rather inciting, the violence. In the aftermath of the riots, there were attempts to press legal charges against Trump for the role he played in this incident. On 7 January 2021, Donald Trump – again on Twitter – promised a smooth transition of power.

Trump himself did not attend Joe Biden's inauguration ceremony, thereby breaking with a 152-year-long tradition. Instead, outgoing Vice-President Mike Pence paid his respects to Joe Biden and new Vice-President Kamala Harris.

During his election campaign President Joe Biden frequently declared the dangers of climate change to be one of the most pressing current global challenges. He kept his promise to rejoin the Paris Climate Agreement by releasing the following statement on

20 January 2021, only a few hours after being sworn in as President: "I, Joseph R. Biden Jr., President of the United States of America, having seen and considered the Paris Agreement, done at Paris on 12 December 2015, do hereby accept the said Agreement and every article and clause thereof on behalf of the United States of America"[3]. Accordingly, Biden's "Build Back Better Plan" includes initiatives to reduce the effects of climate change.

Glossary – Freedom and Justice

assimilation	Assimilation; Angleichung an Bestehendes
base rate	Leitzins
civil disobedience	bürgerlicher Ungehorsam
Civil Rights Movement	die Bürgerrechtsbewegung
credit rating	Beurteilung der Kreditwürdigkeit, Bonitätsbeurteilung
cultural heritage	Kulturerbe; kulturelles Erbe
Declaration of Independence	Unabhängigkeitserklärung
discrimination; deprivation	Diskriminierung; Mangel/Entzug
drop in consumption	Konsumrückgang
"E pluribus unum"	lat.: „aus vielen Eines"; ursprünglich bezogen auf die verschiedenen Staaten der USA; heute vielmehr bezogen auf die vielen ethnischen Gruppen, aus denen sich die Bevölkerung der USA zusammensetzt
economic stimulus plan	Konjunkturprogramm
entrepreneur	Unternehmer
equality; equal opportunities	Gleichheit; gleiche Chancen
fame	Ruhm
freedom; ~ of speech; ~ of the press; religious ~	Freiheit; Redefreiheit; Pressefreiheit; Religionsfreiheit
frontier	Grenze (zwischen Zivilisation und Wildnis)
gold rush	Goldrausch
government bailouts	Rettungsaktion durch die Regierung
identity	Identität
Immigration Act	Einwanderungsgesetz

[3] White House Briefing Room, https://www.whitehouse.gov/briefing-room/statements-releases/2021/01/20/paris-climate-agreement/ (accessed on 1 April 2024). Biden's act of rejoining the Paris Climate Agreement was internationally received with praise and relief.

"In God we trust"	„Wir vertrauen auf Gott"; offizieller Wahlspruch der USA
inauguration; inaugural speech	Amtseinführung; Amtsantrittsrede
liberation	Befreiung
loan	Darlehen
melting pot vs. salad bowl	„Schmelztiegel" vs. „Salatschüssel" (unterschiedliche Konzepte, die die Vielfalt unterschiedlicher Kulturen in den USA charakterisieren)
mortgage	Hypothek
multiculturalism	Multikulturalität
naturalisation	Einbürgerung
pioneer; pioneer spirit	Pionier/-in; Pioniergeist
Promised Land; the land of milk and honey; God's own country; the New Canaan	das gelobte Land
recession	Rezession
refugee; refugee camp	Flüchtling; Flüchtlingslager
segregation; desegregation	Rassentrennung; Aufhebung der Rassentrennung
success	Erfolg
supply and demand	Angebot und Nachfrage
housing bubble	Immobilienblase
the pursuit of happiness	das Streben nach Glück
to achieve financial security	finanzielle Sicherheit erlangen
to attain self-fulfillment	sich selbst verwirklichen
to be persecuted; religious/political persecution	verfolgt werden; religiöse/politische Verfolgung
from rags to riches; from dishwasher to millionaire	vom Tellerwäscher zum Millionär
to immigrate; immigrant; immigration; an influx of immigrants	einwandern; Einwandernde/-r; Einwanderung; Zustrom von Einwandernden
to incur a loss	(einen) Verlust machen
to pledge allegiance to the flag	den Fahneneid leisten
to prosper	Erfolg haben; in Wohlstand leben
to settle; settler; settlement	besiedeln; Siedler/-in; Siedlung
unalienable/inalienable rights	unveräußerliche Rechte

Tradition and Change in Politics and Society: The UK in the European Context

The Political System of the UK

Keyword

British constitution: not set out in a single document

The British constitution is based on conventions that are universally accepted but which have never been formally defined. It also rests upon numerous acts and resolutions of Parliament, as each individual act of Parliament contributes to the constitution. Thus, it is adaptable to changing political conditions.

Separation of Powers

The following three branches represent the powers and areas of responsibility:

Legislature: Parliament

Executive:
- government departments responsible for national administration
- local authorities
- public corporations responsible for particular nationalised industries (controlled by Government; most of these have now been privatised)

Judiciary: the Courts

There are **two kinds of law:**
- common law: historic body of conventions ('it has always been like that')
- statute law: parliamentary and EU legislation

Parliament

Functions of Parliament
- pass laws
- scrutinise government policy and administration
- debate the major issues of the day

Elements of Parliament

Monarch – House of Lords – House of Commons
- agreement of all three elements required to pass legislation
- Parliament directly responsible to the electorate; no written constitution
- Act of Parliament cannot be disputed by the law courts

The House of Lords (House of Peers, Upper House, Second Chamber)

The House of Lords consists of hereditary peers, who inherit their peerage, and life peers, whose peerages are granted to them personally for their lifetime.

The political power of the peers has been gradually reduced over the years, and they have recognised the supremacy of the elected chamber, the House of Commons.

The House of Commons (Lower House)

650 members are directly elected by voters in their constituencies.
The House of Commons is the actual legislative body of the United Kingdom.

The Monarch

The monarch has no overt power but is formally part of the government system.
As the head of state, the Monarch
- appoints the Prime Minister by inviting the leader of the majority in the House of Commons to form a government,
- summons and dissolves Parliament,
- gives Royal Assent to legislation (as a matter of course),
- formally appoints ministers, judges, officers, diplomats, bishops,
- can pardon people,
- confers peerages (see above) and knighthoods,
- represents the country at home and abroad.

Political parties

The Conservative Party (Tories)

right-wing party, associated with
- nationalism
- law and order
- private enterprise
- minimal interference of the state in the economy

The Labour Party

traditional party of the "working class", formerly associated with
- state control and planning
- nationalisation of key industries
- welfare
- affiliation to the trade unions

However, with Tony Blair the party now known as New Labour changed direction away from socialist ideals towards an acceptance of the free market economy, opening itself to voters from the middle classes.

Devolution

Devolution is the granting of powers to the parliaments of Scotland, Wales and Northern Ireland. At the end of the 1990s, the National Assembly of Wales and the Scottish Parliament were inaugurated, with competence to rule on issues like agriculture, fisheries and forestry, education, health and tourism, whereas Westminster (the UK government) retained power in fields such as foreign affairs, defence, taxation, fiscal policy and labour market policy. Because of the Troubles, devolution in Northern Ireland was only implemented in 2007. In the 2014 referendum on full independence held in Scotland, there was a narrow majority for the country to remain in the UK.

After the Brexit decision the Scottish Parliament decided to ask the British Government to be allowed to hold a second referendum on independence in order to give Scotland the chance to stay in the EU.

Society
Class
The British are very class-conscious. Class distinctions are recognisable in speech, habits, style, tastes and values. The Office of National Statistics produced a detailed socio-economic classification in 2020[1]. Although many top-ranking people may earn a lot of money, the classification is not based on income alone but on the differences mentioned above. In the last three decades class differences have become less obvious. The country has become more of a meritocracy, i. e. a society where achievement counts most. But traditional everyday terms are still used to refer to social classes: *upper class, upper-middle class, lower-middle class, working class.*

Ethnicity
Britain has become a multinational society in the last half century (see chapter "Multi-cultural society", p. 34).

Britain and Europe

A European context has been relevant to the UK since the 1950s.
Before: Britain as imperial power with military alliances
In 1957, France, West Germany, Belgium, Italy, Luxembourg and the Netherlands signed the Treaty of Rome, which was the foundation of the European Economic Community (EEC), the predecessor the European Union. Economic cooperation between European nations, especially in the coal and steel industry, was believed to prevent war.
When the United Kingdom applied for membership in the EEC in 1963, France's President Charles de Gaulle vetoed its application because he thought Britain was leaning towards America rather than Europe.

Britain and the EU

Traditionally, Britain has preferred to stay out of Europe. The terms "Europe" and "the Continent" have always referred to the European mainland.
Britain had been a member of the EU since 1973 (then the EC). Britain never joined the monetary union (i. e. they did not have the euro) and never signed the Schengen Agreement, which permits travelling between 25 European countries.
On 23 June 2016, a referendum about Britain's membership in the EU was held (cf. p. 32). There is a continuing debate on Brexit in Britain between those in favour of the EU and the "Eurosceptics", who are usually to be found among the supporters of the nationalist

[1] https://www.ons.gov.uk/methodology/classificationsandstandards/standardoccupationalclassificationsoc/soc2020/
soc2020volume3thenationalstatisticssocioeconomicclassificationnssecrebasedonthesoc2020#classes-and-collapses
(accessed on 1 April 2024)

right and the Conservative party but also among Labour Party members. Anti-European propaganda is to be found particularly in tabloid papers like the *Sun* or the *Daily Mail*.

Main arguments of the Eurosceptics

According to Eurosceptics, the EU is
- expensive to run,
- dominated by wealthy countries at the expense of the less affluent members,
- too powerful and undemocratic
- trying to impose regulation in policy areas that should be the responsibility of national governments (e.g. health, education, law, tax, etc.),
- corrupt and money-wasting,
- a security risk with its open borders,
- host to millions of immigrants, some of them hostile and violent.

Arguments in favour of the European Union

- has created the world's largest international trade market
- choice to live and work anywhere in the EU
- formerly poor countries have prospered in the EU; poor regions receive special grants
- cooperation on crime (Europol)
- many laws to ensure better environmental, consumer and health standards
- free medical aid for tourists
- easier and cheaper travel
- improved human rights legislation

Brexit

> **Keyword**
> **Brexit:** shorthand way of saying the UK is leaving the EU – **Br**itain and **exit**

Cause: referendum on 23 June 2016 → „Leave" campaign won by 52 % to 48 %.
The referendum turnout was 71.8 %, with more than 30 million people voting.

UK Breakdown

England voted for Brexit by 53.4 % to 46.6 %
Wales voted for Brexit by 52.5 % to 47.5 %.
Scotland and Northern Ireland both backed staying in the EU.
Scotland backed Remain by 62 % to 38 %.
Northern Ireland voted Remain by 55.8 % to 44.2 %.

After the referendum

Prime Minister David Cameron, who was against Brexit, resigned.
Britain was supposed to leave the EU on 29 March 2019, but the departure date had to be postponed. There were lengthy negotiations after the referendum. Basically, they concerned the 'deal', the conditions under which the UK would leave the EU. The outcome of these negotiations was the "Withdrawal Agreement", which covered several key points,

the most controversial of which dealt with the border between the Republic of Ireland and Northern Ireland. This border, which is invisible today, would become an external border of the EU. Hardening this border was an unpopular idea for many. Although the Withdrawal Agreement was approved by the EU and UK negotiators, it was never approved by the British Parliament. Prime Minister Theresa May's deal was rejected three times by Parliament. Therefore, she resigned.

In July 2019, Boris Johnson became Prime Minister and promised to take Britain out of the EU by 31 October, with or without a deal, but this deadline was again extended to 31 January 2020.

Johnson persuaded enough opposition MPs to agree to an early general election. His Conservative Party won an 80-seat majority, which in turn voted for his Withdrawal Agreement ("Get Brexit done."). The most important changes to the deal agreed by Theresa May with the EU concerned the Irish border after Brexit.

The new agreement replaced the controversial Irish backstop plan in Theresa May's deal. It established a customs border between Northern Ireland (which is part of the UK) and the Republic of Ireland (which is part of the EU), but in practice there are no border checks. The actual checks are between Great Britain and the island of Ireland, with goods being checked at "points of entry" into Northern Ireland.

On 31 January 2020, Britain left the EU. There was a transition period until 31 December 2020. During this transition period, everything stayed as it was. In the meantime, there were to be negotiations on the future relationship between the UK and the EU regarding all details. The Corona crisis hit Britain in spring 2020, which further hindered progress of the negotiations with the EU.

Finally, Britain and the EU reached a deal just in time on 24 December: The deal contained new rules for how the UK and EU will live, work and trade together. Important issues were workers' rights, social and environmental regulations, travel, fishing and financial services. The UK now follows its own trade policy and hopes to negotiate deals with other countries, particularly the US, Australia and New Zealand. There is no longer freedom of movement between the UK and the EU. For longer stays, people now need visas.

Many of the EU's rules stay in effect in Northern Ireland in order to avoid a hard border with the Republic of Ireland. Checks are carried out on goods leaving Great Britain for Northern Ireland. At the time FiNALE 2025 is being written, a new plan has been proposed under PM Rishi Sunak that formulates checks only for goods destined for the Republic of Ireland from Great Britain. Pro-British Unionists in Northern Ireland, however, fear alienation from the UK.

For up-to-date information you should check websites such as those of the BBC, the Guardian or TLDR News, especially shortly before your English exam, in order to deal with a possible task on Britain leaving the EU and its consequences.

Consequences of Brexit

Free movement between the UK and EU has ended. Europeans living in the UK must have permits from the UK government allowing them to remain.

New border rules have led to a significant disruption of trade and delays on the border.

Travellers between the EU and the UK must have passports ready to show.

The UK must pay a "divorce bill" of approximately 34 billion pounds by 2064. This is to fulfil any remaining financial commitments made while a member of the EU.

The economy has slowed, and many businesses have moved their headquarters to the EU. Employers are having a hard time finding employees. One reason is that EU workers left the UK and immigration rules are stricter. This hits low-skilled and medium-skilled occupations most. Shortage of lorry drivers has led to supply shortages.

The UK must negotiate new trade agreements with countries outside of the EU, which had more than 45 trade agreements with over 70 countries.

Consequences for EU

Brexit has weakened forces in the EU that favour integration and multiculturalism. Members of right-wing, anti-immigration, anti-EU parties in France and Germany are becoming stronger. However, the majority of EU citizens still strongly support the union.

Scotland

Scotland's former first minister, Nicola Sturgeon, said it was "democratically unacceptable" that Scotland had to leave the EU when it voted overwhelmingly to remain. There might be a second independence referendum for the country (cf. Devolution, p. 30).

Northern Ireland

The Republic of Ireland is part of the EU. Northern Ireland voted to remain. Some politicians see this as a reason for a vote on reunification. We will have to wait and see how this issue develops (see above).

Tradition and Change in Politics and Society: Multicultural Society

> **Keyword**
> **Imperial Act (1914):** Inhabitants of the colonies were given British citizenship.

- Between the 1960s and 1980s, many Indians, Pakistanis and Bangladeshis immigrated to Britain. They now form the largest immigrant communities.
- Many of them settled in the Midlands or in towns in Lancashire, Yorkshire and Strathclyde, where they worked in the textile industry.

Britain today

- Britain consists of three countries (England, Scotland, Wales). Together with Northern Ireland it forms the United Kingdom. 12.4 % of the population in the UK were born abroad (2013).[1]
- **Ethnic diversity** enriches Britain, not only when it comes to music, fashion and food.

---

[1] http://visual.ons.gov.uk/uk-perspectives-a-recent-history-of-international-migration (accessed on 1 April 2024)

- Others fear that "Britishness" will eventually be lost; they interpret multiculturalism as meaning that various cultures coexist peacefully but without having a common basis of shared values.
- **Second generation immigrants,** i. e. children born to parents who immigrated to Britain prior to (or shortly after) their children's birth, face a variety of problems:
  - They often experience a clash of cultures. Outside their parents' home they adopt a western lifestyle, similar to that of their friends and classmates. At home, however, they live according to values, beliefs and traditions typical of their parents' home countries, which many of these children and teenagers have never visited. Quite often they do not speak their parents' language any more either. For some, the transition between these two different lifestyles is not easy.
  - They have difficulties when it comes to living up to the expectations of their parents, friends, teachers, etc.
  - They often face discrimination.

Glossary – Tradition and Change

act/law; bill the law	Gesetz; Gesetzesentwurf das Gesetz
agreement	Abkommen
asylum seekers	Asylsuchende
to blend in	sich einfügen/integrieren
citizen; citizenship	Bürger/-in; Staatsangehörigkeit
clash between/of two cultures	das Aufeinanderprallen zweier Kulturen
conservative Conservative Party a conservative	konservativ die Conservative Party ein/-e Konservative/-r
constitution	Verfassung
delegate	Delegierte/-r
democracy	Demokratie
to discriminate against someone	jemanden benachteiligen/diskriminieren
to elect; to be elected; election electorate election period election campaign	wählen; gewählt werden; Wahl Wählerschaft Wahlperiode Wahlkampf
ethnic minorities ethnicity	ethnische Minderheiten Ethnizität/Volkszugehörigkeit
executive	die Exekutive
federal	Bundes-...
government; to govern	Regierung; regieren

to hold racist attitudes	eine rassistische Einstellung haben
House	Kammer des Parlaments
imperialism; imperialistic	Imperialismus; imperialistisch
indefinite leave to remain	unbeschränkte Aufenthaltserlaubnis
judiciary	die Judikative
labour	Arbeit
Labour Party	die Labour Party
legislature; legislative	die Legislative; gesetzgebend
loss of identity	Identitätsverlust
minister; ministry prime minister (the Prime Minister)	Minister; Ministerium Premierminister
Member of Parliament (MP)	Abgeordnete/-r
mutual understanding and respect	gegenseitiges Verständnis und Respekt
office; to hold office Home Office; Foreign Office	Amt/Ministerium; ein Amt innehaben Innenministerium; Außenministerium
open-minded; narrow-minded	aufgeschlossen; engstirnig
outsider	Außenseiter/-in
parliament	Parlament
party	Partei
policy economic policy; foreign policy	politisches Ziel / Maßnahmen Wirtschaftspolitik Außenpolitik
pluralistic society	eine pluralistische Gesellschaft
politics; political politician	Politik; politisch Politiker/-in
poll polling station	Abstimmung/Umfrage/Wahl Wahllokal
racial equality	Gleichwertigkeit verschiedener Rassen
to receive / to be granted citizenship	die Staatsbürgerschaft erhalten
referendum	Volksbefragung, Volksentscheid
representative	(Volks-)Vertreter/-in
secretary foreign secretary	Minister/-in Außenminister/-in
the people	das Volk
to support	unterstützen
vote; to vote voter	Stimme; abstimmen/wählen Wähler/-in
wing right/left wing	Flügel rechter/linker Flügel (einer Partei)

Voices from the African Continent: Focus on Nigeria

From Empire to Commonwealth

> **Keywords**
>
> **Postcolonialism:** This term, first used in the middle of the 20th century, refers to the time after the British had left the colonies, i. e. after their formal rule over the colonies had come to an end.
>
> Political independence did not necessarily lead to economic independence. The withdrawal of the British regularly revealed imperialism's harmful legacy, often resulting in problems for the former colonies. Postcolonial nations therefore often struggle to set up a functioning government which guarantees the people the freedom they dream of.
>
> **The Commonwealth:** a group of 56 states; many former British colonies joined at the end of the decolonisation process; aims at racial equality and national sovereignty; the British monarch is the head of the Commonwealth

- At the **beginning of the 17th century**, Britain started to expand its empire across the globe.
- In most cases, the British colonisers ruled with brutal force, seizing land at will, ending rebellion in bloodshed, causing widespread famine as well as implementing slavery and exterminating whole ethnic groups.

- **After the Second World War**, the British Empire changed rapidly.
- Most British colonies had become independent by 1970, but a large number of them stayed closely connected with their former coloniser by joining the Commonwealth.

- While the British ruled the colonies, they regarded their culture, values, traditions and language as superior to those of the colonised.
- Now, after independence, the colonised faced the difficult task of recreating their own identity, bridging the gap between their country's native traditions and values and British ones.
- As people from member countries of the Commonwealth were allowed to immigrate to Britain, lots of people did so in the second half of the 20th century. First they were welcomed, as workers were needed after the Second World War, but in the 1970s, when more and more workers faced unemployment because of the economic crisis, immigration came to be seen more critically.

- Much **postcolonial writing** – both from former the colonies and in Britain – deals with the issue of being caught between two cultures or of trying to find one's identity.

Postcolonialism in an Anglophone Culture: Nigeria

Keywords

The Transatlantic Slave Trade: As part of the trade triangle between Europe, Africa and America, enslaved Africans were transported by Western European slave traders to the Americas, where they had to work on tobacco, coffee, sugar, cotton and cocoa plantations. The transatlantic slave trade started in the late 15th / early 16th century, with the Portuguese being the first nation to engage in it. They were soon followed by other European nations, in particular the British, Spanish, Dutch and French. The trade lasted until the 19th century, when most European countries prohibited slave trade and ended slavery.

Protectorate: (from Latin "protegere" = "protect") a country protected and ruled by another country, often one with superior military power (in Nigeria's case, the British)

Republic: a country in which the power is held by representatives elected by the people

Military rule: a government by an authoritarian body, controlled by the military instead of being elected by the people

Nigerian history
A short overview of British rule in Nigeria and the country's way to independence

- late 15th century: Nigeria starts to be affected by the transatlantic slave trade led by the Portuguese, from whom the Christian religion is initially adopted.
- 18th century: British replace Portuguese as the driving force of the slave trade.
- 1851: Lagos is invaded by British forces and formally annexed in 1865.
- 1901: Nigeria becomes a British protectorate.
- 1914: British protectorates of Northern and Southern Nigeria are joined.
- 1 October 1960: Nigeria succeeds in gaining independence from Britain.
- 1963: Nigeria becomes a republic but remains a member of the Commonwealth.
- 1966: The Nigerian Republic surrenders to military rule.
- 1967: A separatist movement leads to the "Republic of Biafra", and the three-year Nigerian Civil War breaks out, in which over 1 million people lose their lives.
- 1979: Nigeria becomes a single republic again, but the military seize power again in 1983.
- 1993: Plans to establish a third republic are dissolved by the Nigerian dictator, General Sani Abacha. After his death in 1998, a fourth republic is established in 1999, after almost three decades of military rule. President Obasanjo rules until 2007, from 2004 under emergency legislation.
- In 2007, Umaru Yar'Adua is elected president but dies after a long illness in 2010. Goodluck Ebele Jonathan, who had already been acting president, succeeds him.
- In 2015, Jonathan loses in the elections against Muhammadu Buhari, who is also the current president.
- Obasanjo, Jonathan and Buhari were all military generals at one time in their career.

Nigeria today[1]

- **General information:** The country's official name is "Federal Republic of Nigeria"; it is located on the western coast of Africa. The capital is Abuja, the largest and most important city is Lagos. Due to its booming economy and large population it is often referred to as the "Giant of Africa". The country's geography is diverse, with climates ranging from arid to humid/equatorial.
- **Culture:** With its many languages spoken by various ethnic groups, Nigeria has a very rich and diverse national culture. Nigeria is also known for its English language literature. Among the most famous Nigerian writers are Chinua Achebe *(Things Fall Apart)* and the winner of the Nobel Prize for Literature, Wole Soyinka. Since the 1990s, the Nigerian film industry, also dubbed "Nollywood", has become important for the whole of Africa.
- **Society:** Nigeria is considered to be the seventh most populous country in the world and the most populous one in Africa, with the world's third highest youth population after India and China. Primary education, free and compulsory, begins at age six and lasts for six years. Secondary education is free and compulsory for three years. There are 258 universities in Nigeria. The population is half urban, half rural. Over 500 languages are spoken by the more than 250 ethnic groups living in Nigeria. English serves as the official language. In addition to English, Hausa, Yoruba, Igbo, Fula and English Creole are widely spoken. Many of the languages exist in written form. About half of the population are Muslim (mainly in the north); about 48 % are Christians of various denominations.
- The Nigerian **legal and judicial system** contains three codes of law: customary law, Nigerian statute law (following English law) and Sharia (Islamic law).
- **Economy and the environment**: Nigeria is regarded as an emerging global power, due to its oil and natural gas industry, especially in the south of the country. The GDP in 2021 was $ 440 billion, i.e. $ 2,066 per capita.

Challenges

- Nigeria's rapidly growing population causes several problems, e.g. poverty and the inability to provide enough food for everyone without relying on food imports.
- 41 % of the population are under 15, another 28 % are under 30 (2018). The youth literacy rate of the age group 15–24 is 75 %. However, unemployment poses a major challenge.
- inequality between men and women
- battling various forms of crime, e.g. organised crime (especially drug trafficking), child labour and female genital mutilation
- Religious tension between the two major faiths is rising, especially in the "middle belt" of the country. Religious fundamentalism can be noticed in both Muslim and Christian communities, a major cause being the uneven distribution of natural resources and hence wealth.

[1] Statistical information based on: https://www.bpb.de/internationales/weltweit/innerstaatliche-konflikte/176466/nigeria; https://www.britannica.com/place/Nigeria; https://data.unicef.org/country/nga/; http://data.un.org/en/iso/ng.html (all accessed on 1 April 2024)

- Inside the growing Nigerian cities, waste management is a problem and the fact that waste is often simply dumped outside the cities results in the pollution of both waterways and groundwater. Oil spills also threaten the environment.
- Terrorism is another major problem: the Islamic terrorist group Boko Haram is responsible for numerous attacks and the abduction of school children.
- In recent years, the Biafran hostilities between the two major ethnic groups in the south of the country, the Igbo and Yoruba has resurfaced. The conflict first came to a head in the Biafran Civil War (1967–1970) when the Igbo population of south-east Nigeria attempted to form a republic (Biafra) of their own. It remains unsolved, without any prospect of a positive outcome.

Glossary – Voices from the African Continent: Focus on Nigeria

civil war	Bürgerkrieg
corruption	Korruption
to adapt to sth.	sich an etwas anpassen
to be oppressed by someone	von jemandem unterdrückt werden
citizenship	Nationalität, Staatsangehörigkeit
clash between/of two cultures	das Aufeinanderprallen zweier Kulturen
colonialism; coloniser; colonised	Kolonialismus; die/der Besiedelnde; kolonisiert
to discriminate against someone	jemanden benachteiligen/diskriminieren
empire	das Imperium
ethnic minorities	ethnische Minderheiten
ethnicity	Ethnizität, Volkszugehörigkeit
to be excluded (from)	(von) etw. ausgeschlossen sein
to hold racist attitudes	eine rassistische Haltung/Einstellung haben
hostile	feindlich, feindselig, ablehnend
imperialism; imperialistic	Imperialismus; imperialistisch
indigenous	Einheimische/-r eines Landes
loss of identity	Identitätsverlust
hegemony	Vorherrschaft
famine	Hungersnot
infant mortality	Kindersterblichkeit
to bribe someone	jmd. bestechen
to regain independence	Unabhängigkeit wiedererlangen
independence-minded	nach Unabhängigkeit strebend
to decolonise	in die Unabhängigkeit entlassen
to thrive and prosper	wachsen und gedeihen

Globalisation and Global Challenges

> **Keyword**
>
> **Globalisation:** a worldwide movement, involving the integration of financial, economic and communications systems; often seen as an unstoppable process, affecting people all around the globe, no matter whether they live in industrialised or developing countries, in big cities or rural villages; transfer of goods, capital and services, as well as communications, made easier; not everyone profits from the development; smaller economies may suffer
>
> The world is said to be getting smaller, i. e. it has become a "global village". The term was coined by Marshall McLuhan, a Canadian philosopher and media specialist.

It is not easy to say when globalisation actually started:
– Did it start with the discovery of America?
– Does it go even further back in time?
– Is it a phenomenon of the modern era?

Everyone can experience the results of globalisation, e. g. when
– travelling,
– keeping in touch with friends or business partners in distant countries with the help of new means of communication or
– buying goods which come from far away.

Globalisation is not always regarded as a positive process:
– Some people fear that individual cultures will finally blend into a single global culture, thereby losing all their characteristic features.
– Globalisation has failed the thousands of people in developing countries still suffering from malnutrition or dying of curable diseases.
– Others work under cruel working conditions, producing goods which will be shipped to and sold in industrialised countries at a low price.
– One of the latest financial crises, starting in the USA in 2008, shows that such catastrophes will ultimately affect other countries as well, as businesses are linked and global trade is the rule.
– Due to increased mobility, diseases like H1N1 ("Swine Flu") or the coronavirus can easily spread all around the globe, developing into a pandemic.
– The refugee crisis in Europe (peaking in 2015) can partly be seen as connected to globalisation: People from all over the world want to participate in growing economic wealth. Many of those from poor countries want to find a better future and leave their homes – just like people have always done over the centuries (e. g. emigration to America in the last two centuries). At the same time, civil and other wars as well as climate change force people to emigrate. As more and more countries close their borders, problems in many regions are growing. Among these problems are huge refugee camps and people drowning and starving during dangerous journeys (cf. also p. 50).

- Terrorism has become an ongoing global threat, which has led to a growing feeling of insecurity in many societies. In some countries (e. g. Israel) terrorist attacks have been permanent aspect of everyday life for six or seven decades. In most Western, as well as Middle Eastern countries, what we know as Islamist terrorism (Al-Qaeda, the "Islamic State") began with the "9/11" attacks on the World Trade Center in New York and the Pentagon in Washington on 11 September 2001. This led to the controversial „War on Terror" on the part of the USA and its allies. Since then, the world has seen a large number of terrorist attacks connected with Islamist ideology (e. g. in France, England, Nigeria and Germany) or with the ideology of white supremacy (e. g. in Christchurch in New Zealand or Utøya in Norway).

Aspects of Globalisation

Progress

- The development of planes, fast ships and trains made quick transportation of goods from one country to another possible.
- New means of communication, especially the internet, have made the collaboration of business partners much easier.
- Multinational companies have branches all over the world, and cost-effectiveness is a decisive factor when new production sites are set up.

Economic challenges

As today's customers wish to buy products at the best cost/performance ratio, the global market has become very **competitive,** with the following (and related) consequences:
- While global players consider efficiency, speed, flexibility and profits as most important, employees are increasingly unable to defend their rights.
- More and more jobs are being outsourced or off-shored to cut down production costs, thereby severely damaging local labour markets.
- When jobs are outsourced to low-wage countries, the workers often work in so-called **"sweatshops"** for long hours at a stretch, earning only minimum wages and under working conditions that are often inhumane. Safety measures in sweatshops are by no means comparable to western standards. Sadly, the lack of efficient safety measures often results in catastrophes. On 24 April 2013, a building housing several garment factories near Bangladesh's capital Dhaka collapsed, resulting in the death of more than 1,000 workers. Despite the fact that factory owners had previously been warned about deep cracks which appeared in the building's structure and had been ordered to evacuate the building, workers were sent in to work. Two weeks after the tragedy, a fire broke out in another clothing factory, killing several people.
- Critics like the Canadian journalist Naomi Klein accuse multinational companies of exploiting the poor and indirectly supporting child labour for their own profit.
- Workers often assemble products which they will never be able to afford or do not know how to use, e. g. computers.

- People in developing countries often live in poor conditions, without a decent education or access to new means of communication. Therefore they cannot reap the benefits of globalisation.
- Advocates of sweatshops claim that these factories provide work for the poor, enabling them to provide for their families. They also say that critics of sweatshops argue from a western point of view without considering the actual situation of people in developing countries. In order to reduce the number of sweatshops, fair trade is becoming increasingly important. Its aim is to ensure that workers and small-scale producers in poor countries are paid a fair price for their work and products.
- Despite these attempts, a growing number of experts and laypeople alike fear that the gap between the rich and the poor is widening.
- The close links and collaboration between companies all across the globe is both a blessing and a curse.

Ecological Challenges and Sustainable Lifestyles

Environmental pollution is growing rapidly. The following factors in particular create global problems:
- Particularly in developed nations, rampant consumerism is still increasing **energy consumption and waste gases** from factories.
- Over the last decades the number of **vehicles** on the roads has steadily increased. Cars are no longer found only in industrialised countries. The number of people travelling by **plane** is also greater than ever, due to the fact that plane tickets have become affordable for a larger number of people. Short-haul **flights** have become particularly popular.
- **food miles:** Whereas some years ago many people bought fruit and vegetables locally and ate seasonal products, they now want to eat strawberries and cherries in December. Hence more goods are air-freighted. Ecologically conscious customers ask themselves whether it is better to buy local products than food (even fair trade) which has been flown across continents. The non-sustainable production of meat and dairy foods is another critical factor in global warming.
- **Greenhouse gases** such as carbon dioxide (CO_2) and methane cause chemical damage to the atmosphere (e. g. ozone hole) as well as global warming.

Global warming and its consequences

- As Al Gore explains in his film *An Inconvenient Truth,* greenhouse gases form a layer around the earth trapping heat and thereby causing the temperature on the ground to rise ("global warming").
- There are many consequences of climate change. Principally, extreme weather phenomena increase in strength and intensity, resulting in, for example, floods, heavy rainfall in some regions and drought in others as well as melting polar ice caps.
- Biodiversity is likewise threatened, as many plants, flowers and animals die out. Desertification (see below) is an increasingly frequent phenomenon today: Due to

overgrazing[1], over-extraction of groundwater, unwise use of water resources, e. g. diverting rivers for industrial use or human consumption, deforestation ("slash-and-burn farming") and rising soil salinity (amount of salt in the ground), vast areas of land in relatively dry areas deteriorate and become useless (desertification).

Attempts to reduce global warming
- Environmental sustainability is on the agenda of many governments and has been an important topic at various summits to date. Significant results are nonetheless still rare.
- The **Kyoto Protocol** from 2005 aimed to reduce the emission of greenhouse gases by an annual 5.2 % by the year 2012, taking 1990 levels as a basis for most countries.
- **Paris UN Climate Change Conference (2015):** A global agreement on the reduction of climate change (Paris Agreement) has been reached and adopted by 195 countries. Among the decisions made was the resolution to limit the long-term increase of global average temperature to well below 2°C above pre-industrial levels. The agreement went into effect on 4 November 2016, as enough countries ratified it. The USA withdrew their consent to the agreement under President Trump.
- On his first day in office, President Biden fulfilled a promise he made during his election campaign and returned to the Paris Climate Agreement.
- **Glasgow UN Climate Change Conference (2021):** In the face of urgently needed action, COP 26 failed to implement significant policies. Participants agreed on reducing coal mining, phasing out cars that run on fossil fuels (a resolution Germany was notably absent from) and halting deforestation. These pledges, however, remain first tentative steps. More significantly perhaps, there was strong disagreement on how developed nations should offer financial compensation for their long-standing contributions to climate change.

Fridays for Future
- In August 2018, Greta Thunberg, a then 16-year-old Swedish student, started protesting outside the Swedish parliament in Stockholm in order to raise awareness of the dangers of climate change.
- According to Thunberg, politicians are not taking enough action against climate change, which is putting our planet's future at risk. Thunberg's solitary school strikes soon caught the attention of the media in countries all over the world.
- Up to May 2019, an estimated 1.4 million teenagers and young adults worldwide followed her example by going on strike from school every Friday and protesting against climate change. This movement, known as "Fridays for Future", was seriously hampered by the COVID-19 pandemic.
- Greta Thunberg has delivered several public speeches in which she has put pressure on politicians and world leaders to combat climate change more swiftly and resolutely. She spoke at various important global meetings, e. g. the United Nations Climate

---

[1] One speaks of "overgrazing" if the number of cattle on a piece of land is too high to be sustainable (in the long term).

Change Conference in Katowice, Poland in December 2018 and at the 2019 UN Climate Action Summit, to which she arrived by boat.

- The speed of the reaction and the immense sums of money provided by governments during the COVID-19 crisis seem to prove Fridays for Future's point: Immediate global action is possible, but the governments all over the world do not seem to regard an effective fight against global warming as a top priority.

Conflict between economic and ecological aspects of globalisation

- Companies face global competition: cost-effectiveness and profits seem more important than ecological issues.
- Some governments are hesitant to set up strict laws to protect the environment, as this might drive away multinational companies that offer employment.
- As environmental pollution does not stop at borders, international cooperation is crucial – and will become even more so in future.

Sustainable lifestyles

- There is a growing awareness among consumers that due to various global challenges our current lifestyles have to change to more sustainable ones. Some of these changes can be put into action by each individual himself/herself, others have to be initiated and carried out by governments, e. g. reforming urban life by planning cities according to citizens' needs.
- Some of the changes everyone can implement individually are:
  - Eating fewer animal products:
  Large amounts of water are needed to produce animal-based food, while the animals' manure pollutes the groundwater. The more meat we eat, the more industrial factory farming is booming. Prices for meat are relatively low compared to the prices for other groceries. Ethical questions also have to be considered when it comes to the consumption of animal-based food. In addition, working conditions in meat factories are often questionable, with workers barely making minimum wage and working overtime.
  - Buying regional products:
  Supporting local shops and producers instead of merely resorting to online shopping reduces the ecological cost of transportation. Additionally, buying fruit and vegetables when they are in season makes it more likely that these are not sourced in from distant countries. In addition, food waste can be reduced by only buying the groceries one needs instead of buying in bulk and running the risk of food going bad.
  Using public means of transport, car sharing, bikes, etc. to get from A to B is a quick way to fight CO_2 production.
  - Producing less waste:
  This sound fairly straightforward but can make a huge difference. It really is that simple: The less waste one produces, the less of it can cause environmental pollution.

- Buying less but better:
  If one buys less or buys products second-hand, one actively helps to minimise electronic and textile waste. In many cases, defective items can be repaired. In case of clothing, the idea of a "capsule wardrobe", where a person possesses a limited number of good-quality key items that can be mixed and matched with one another, becomes more and more popular. Studies have shown that lots of pieces of clothing in our wardrobes are never or seldomly worn. Why not swap unwanted but wearable pieces of clothing with other people? Or why not consider buying second-hand? Gadgets which one only temporarily needs, e. g., electric power drills or other tools, can also rented or shared with others.

There are many more things each one of us can change about our lifestyles to transform them from a consumption-orientated to a more sustainable one. Basically, all these changes aim at reducing one's carbon footprint. Of course, not everything works for everyone, but even minor changes make a difference.

Corona – a virus that changed the world

- COVID-19 (Coronavirus disease 2019) is a highly infectious disease with symptoms usually similar to those of the common flu, e. g. fever, cough and shortness of breath. In more severe cases, it impacts on a wide variety of organs, including the heart and lungs, possibly resulting in chronic health issues or even death. People with a weakened immune system as well as older persons run a higher risk of experiencing severe symptoms, in worst cases multi-organ failure, but most cases only exhibit light symptoms.
- Due to intense and efficient research, several vaccines against COVID-19 were developed, but the availability in different countries varies, as does the vaccination strategy. Most countries, e. g. Germany, prioritised certain population groups regarded as vulnerable before vaccinating other sections of the population.
- The number of people having received at least one vaccination against COVID-19 is growing rapidly. The WHO (World Health Organisation) reports that, as of 15 April 2023, a total of 13 billion vaccine doses had been administered.
- COVID-19 was first identified in Wuhan, China in December 2019. It is thought to have been transmitted from animals to humans at a seafood and animal market. On 31 December 2019, Chinese authorities informed the WHO of the outbreak of a new form of pneumonia. Since then it has spread across the world.
- On 12 January 2020, the WHO named this previously unknown form of the coronavirus disease COVID-19, and on 20 March 2020, it was officially declared a pandemic.
- As of January 2024, almost 775 million cases and 7 million deaths had been reported.

How countries and governments attempted to tackle the virus

- Governments all across the globe encouraged the public to take up basic protective measures for the sake of both themselves and others, e. g. frequently washing one's hands, avoid touching one's face, practise respiratory hygiene, social distancing, wearing face masks.

- In most countries wearing a mask or covering your mouth and nose with a piece of cloth is/was obligatory while out in public. Shops and service providers with in-person contact are/were required to limit the number of people inside and/or to ascertain that all customers are fully vaccinated or recently recovered from an infection. Getting tested and/or providing negative test results in writing several times a week was mandatory for German teachers and students. The so-called „Corona-Schutzmaßnahmen" eventually expired on 7 April 2023 and there were no more restrictions in place in Germany.
- In order to "flatten the curve", i. e. restrict the number of new infections so that health services could still cope, many countries imposed restrictions at some point during the pandemic: closing schools, kindergartens, restaurants and shops not necessary to fulfil basic needs, restricting or banning visitors from hospitals and nursing homes and imposing travel restrictions, e. g. closing borders or imposing quarantine on people crossing national borders. People wishing to enter Germany temporarily faced a test obligation and were only allowed to enter the country if they could provide proof of a negative test result no older than 48 hours.
- Businesses were required to allow their employees to work from home to limit personal contacts. Events that attract large crowds, such as concerts, theatre performances and festivals were often cancelled.
- Hospitals and clinics in some countries have faced difficulties meeting the increasing demand for intensive care due to COVID-19.

Consequences of these governmental measures

- Economic: Closing shops put severe strain on shop owners and employees. Many governments, including that of Germany, have installed programmes that offered some financial compensation. It was feared that many companies would not survive the restrictions during the pandemic.
- Personal: The number of people working from home has increased drastically due to changes in the organisation of the workplace and as a result of schools and kindergartens closing frequently. Many parents struggle to balance childcare and work. Governments encouraged families not to visit grandparents and family members at risk or even forbade visits, which can lead to isolation and loneliness. Digital media have therefore played an important role in keeping in touch with one another while being physically apart.
- Neighbourly help has become more important, e. g. doing grocery shopping for those at risk and checking regularly on those affected by the virus.
- On 24 February 2022, the UK released the "Living with Covid-19" plan. It focuses on everyone's personal responsibility to keep the virus in check. While legal restrictions were lifted, UK citizens are still encouraged to become fully vaccinated and to act sensibly to avoid spreading the virus.

International Relations

The UN

- 24 October 1945: A group of 51 countries founded the United Nations (UN) as a replacement/successor for the League of Nations.
- The UN headquarters is located in New York City and the current Secretary General is António Guterres.
- The UN has 193 member states (April 2024).
- It defends human rights and fundamental freedoms.

Five of six **main organs** of the UN (General Assembly, Security Council, Economic and Social Council, Trusteeship Council and Secretariat) are located in New York City, while the International Court of Justice is in The Hague in the Netherlands.
There are **various programmes** and funds affiliated to the UN. Two of the best known are UNICEF (United Nations Children's Fund) and the UNHCR (Office of the United Nations High Commissioner for Refugees). The latter deals with the needs of refugees and displaced persons in post-conflict countries, e. g. Djibouti.

Aims of the UN

- to preserve international peace and security
- to promote friendly relations between member countries
- to support international cooperation with regard to economic, social and cultural as well as humanitarian issues
- Apart from **peacekeeping** and **peacemaking** operations, **peacebuilding** has become more and more important.
- The UN and its affiliated organisations work to equip national groups with the necessary skills in conflict management and to ensure that lasting peace can be established.
- Currently (April 2024), the UN is involved in eleven peacekeeping operations, e. g. in Cyprus, Mali and the Democratic Republic of the Congo.
- **Humanitarian aid** is also of major importance, e. g. providing relief for people affected by either man-made or natural disasters and helping refugees and displaced persons.
- Other main concerns of the UN are **international law and development**, e. g. sustainable development, agriculture, international trade.

The EU

- Currently 27 states belong to the European Union (EU). The newest members are Bulgaria and Romania, which both joined the EU on 1 January 2007, and Croatia, which became a member on 1 July 2013.
- After the Second World War there was a desire for a united Europe in order to prevent extreme forms of nationalism. The European Coal and Steel Community, the European Economic Community (EEC) and the European Atomic Energy Community (Euratom) were merged into the European Community (EC) in 1967.

- The EU as we know it came into existence in 1993, when the Maastricht Treaty – which, among other things, initiated the euro as common currency – was ratified. The individual member states came to be regarded as a single global player.
- At present the EU faces the challenge of maintaining its unity – and indeed remaining a union at all – in the face of the refugee crisis, to which EU countries have very differing attitudes. The current Russian invasion of Ukraine will likely also put the unity within the EU to the test.
- In 2020, the United Kingdom left the EU ("Brexit", cf. p. 32).
- On 24 February 2022, the Russian army invaded Ukraine. This aggression is condemned by the EU and other countries worldwide. EU countries agreed on swift political, financial and humanitarian support for Ukraine and imposed severe sanctions on Russia. While the war's immediate effect on the Eurozone was to cause heavy inflation, it is likely to have more significant political consequences. Whereas support for Ukraine has been wide-ranging across European countries as well as America, people in nations such as China and India prefer an immediate end to the war, even at the cost of Ukrainian territory.

Aims of the EU

- to promote prosperity and social progress with European citizenship for its peoples while still keeping their diversity alive
- to promote friendly relations between member countries
- to guarantee freedom and justice for the European peoples
- to internationally represent the member states with a single voice, tackling the various challenges of globalisation as well as respecting human rights

When it comes to defence, the individual member countries are sovereign. However, there is military cooperation in peacekeeping missions.

The three main groups which make up the EU are the **Council of Ministers,** the **European Parliament** and the **European Commission.**

Although the EU has no capital, the official seat of the European Commission, the Council of the European Union and the second seat of the European Parliament are located in Brussels, Belgium.

International peacekeeping

International peacekeeping is one of the aims of the UN:
- Once peace has been established in a country or region, peacekeepers are sent to the country or region in question to oversee the peace process.
- This can be done by supervising elections, providing reconstruction aid and managing the withdrawal of combatants.
- Very often, UN peacekeepers are soldiers, but they can also be police officers or other civilian personnel.
- The UN Security Council authorises peacekeeping missions, which are then carried out by the international community.

- Many of these missions are organised and led by the UN, even though the UN itself has no army. While the troops acting as peacekeepers are under the control of the UN, they still belong to the armed forces of their country of origin. The UN itself is controlled by the Security Council and the UN Secretariat. This reduces the risk that one peacekeeping party only follows its own interests.
- Regional organisations (e. g. NATO) can be authorised by the UN to lead peacekeeping missions. These regional organisations can also organise peacekeeping missions of their own.

Migration – a global challenge

- Migration has been a worldwide phenomenon since the beginning of human history.
- People have had a number of reasons for leaving their places of origin: poverty and the dream of a better life elsewhere, climatic reasons, wars and civil unrest or religious persecution, to name only the most important.[1]
- One has to distinguish between migrants and refugees:
- **Migrants** leave their countries of origin for a limited period of time or permanently, usually for economic reasons. They might have job offers in a different country or they might have heard of good opportunities. Examples of this are emigration from European countries to the USA in the 19th century, immigrants from Poland to the Ruhr district (also during the 19th century), migrant workers inside Europe today, for example to help on farms, as carers for elderly people or to work in hospitals, and people from Africa trying to find better living conditions in Europe.
- **Refugees** usually flee their homes in order to escape persecution or wars. Unlike migrants, refugees are forced to leave their home countries. Examples of this at present are the Ukrainians fleeing the Russian invasion and Syrian or Afghan people fleeing to Europe. An important example from the past are the Jews from Germany and other countries, who had to flee from the Nazis.
- The International Migration Report of the UN from 2022 states that migration has increased worldwide, with most migrants going to Europe, Asia and North America. The countries with the most immigrants are the USA, Germany and Saudi Arabia. According to the UN, as of 2022, there were about 281 million people living in countries other than the ones they were born in.
- The UNHCR (United Nations refugee agency) states in its statistical report covering trends and developments up to the end of 2021 that the world is now witnessing the highest levels of displacement on record. 108.4 million people around the world have been forced to leave their homes. Among them are nearly 35.3 million refugees. 63 million are internal refugees, i. e. they flee from one part of the country to another (e. g. Nigeria). There are 5.4 million asylum seekers worldwide. However, 70 % of refugees stay in neighbouring countries: Syrian refugees mainly flee to Turkey, Jordan

---

[1] Information based on:
https://worldmigrationreport.iom.int/wmr-2022-interactive/; https://www.unhcr.org/figures-at-a-glance.html; https://www.unhcr.org/refugee-statistics; https://www.refugeesinternational.org/ (all websites accessed on 1 April 2024)

and other countries close by. More than half the refugees worldwide at present come from Syria, Afghanistan and Ukraine.

- In 2023, Iran hosted the largest refugee population worldwide, with 3.4 million refugees and asylum seekers, followed by Türkiye (3.4 million), Germany (2.5 million), Colombia (2.5 million) and Pakistan (2.1 million). Most refugees come from Syria (6.5 million), Afghanistan (6.1 million) and and Ukraine (5.9. million).
- There are also millions of stateless people who have been denied nationality and access to basic rights such as education, healthcare, employment and freedom of movement.
- More than 1 percent of the world's population have fled their homes.
- Nearly 1 person is forcibly displaced every two seconds as a result of conflict or persecution.
- The fact that most refugees seek help in neighbouring, not always wealthy countries can cause major problems there: The population of these countries has to share access to education, healthcare and jobs with the refugees. Compared to rich nations like Germany, countries like Jordan or the Lebanon find it far more difficult to cope with the situation. Colombia is another example of these conflicts, as it only just beginning to overcome the effects of a civil war. Recently it has also been the destination of over 1 million refugees from Venezuela.
- On the other hand, migration always also means enrichment: The destination country will, with time, integrate the new arrivals. Their culture, beliefs and customs will become part of the country, thus leading to a more diverse culture in general.
- Many migrants and refugees wish to return to their home countries if the situation allows them to. Seasonal migrants, for example, usually leave their families behind and return when their work has finished for the year, and refugees often want to return to their old home after the end of a war. Others would like to stay in their new home and build a new life there.

Glossary – Globalisation

Americanisation	Amerikanisierung
anti-globalist	Globalisierungsgegner/-in
backwardness	Rückständigkeit
company philosophy	Geschäfts-/Firmenphilosophie
competition to be competitive	Konkurrenz(kampf)/Wettbewerb konkurrenzfähig sein
corporate identity	Firmenimage
crop diseases	Krankheiten von Pflanzen/Saatgut
debt relief	Schuldenerlass, Entschuldung
desertification	die Desertifikation/Wüstenbildung, das Vordringen der Wüste

developing countries	Entwicklungsländer
development aid	Entwicklungshilfe
driving forces of globalisation	die Antriebskräfte der Globalisierung
drought	Dürre, Dürreperioden
earth's atmosphere	die Erdatmosphäre
economic growth	Wirtschaftswachstum
economic prosperity	ökonomischer Wohlstand
emerging markets	Schwellenländer
environmental commitment	Umwelteinsatz
environmental damage	Umweltzerstörung
environmentally friendly	umweltfreundlich
expansion of capitalism	Ausbreitung des Kapitalismus
fair trade	fairer Handel
floods	Hochwasser, Überschwemmungen
global interconnection	globale Querverbindungen
global marketplace	globaler Marktplatz
global player	Weltfirma
global super power	globale Supermacht
global warming	Erderwärmung
greenhouse gases	Treibhausgase
human rights	Menschenrechte
human-generated greenhouse gases	durch Menschen produzierte Treibhaus-gase
to increase profit margins	die Gewinnspanne erhöhen
Industrial Age	das Industriezeitalter
industrial nations	Industrieländer/-nationen
interdependence of economy and eco-logy	gegenseitige Abhängigkeit/Verflechtung von Ökonomie und Ökologie
international stock markets	internationale Börsenmärkte
investment climate	Investitionsbedingungen
labour laws	Arbeitsgesetze
labour market	Arbeitsmarkt
long-range goals	langfristige Ziele
low-wage countries	Niedriglohnländer
mass communication; mass media	Massenkommunikation; Massenmedien
mass tourism	Massentourismus
melting of glaciers	das Schmelzen von Gletschern

micro-credits	Kleinkredite
NGO (non-governmental organisation)	Nichtregierungsorganisation
outsourcing	Produktionsverlagerung
political turmoil	politischer Aufruhr, politische Turbulenzen
pollution	Verschmutzung
population overshoot, overpopulation, excess of population	Überbevölkerung
poverty	Armut
reduce greenhouse gas emissions	den Ausstoß von Treibhausgasen reduzieren
reduce the cost of production	die Produktionskosten senken
rise in global temperature	weltweiter Temperaturanstieg
robotised production	computergesteuerte Produktion/Fertigung
short-haul flights	Kurzstreckenflüge
surface transport	Bodentransport
supremacy	Vormachtsstellung, Überlegenheit
sustainability	Nachhaltigkeit, Zukunftsfähigkeit
sweatshop	ausbeuterischer Betrieb
trade	Handel
trademark policy	Markenpolitik
undernutrition; malnutrition	Unterernährung; Mangelernährung
unemployment	Arbeitslosigkeit
working conditions	Arbeitsbedingungen

Visions of the Future: Utopia and Dystopia

> **Keywords**
>
> **Utopian literature:** a fictional text dealing with an ideal (future) society
>
> **Dystopian literature:** a fictional text dealing with a future society in which human freedom is severely limited. A dystopia often criticises our present-day society by exposing trends and tendencies towards totalitarian control.
>
> **Extrapolation:** here: fictitious description of elements of a future society on the basis of present day phenomena and developments. The writer criticises his or her own society by demonstrating what certain trends may lead to or what point society has already reached.

School classics – background knowledge

The three novels presented here are so well known in and outside of English-speaking countries that you may encounter references to any one of these works in numerous texts. They will be presented here in the order of their first publication.

Aldous Huxley: *Brave New World*

written in 1931; set in the distant future (26th century)

Generally known elements

- total control of society by in-vitro fertilisation, artificial breeding of humans, "cloning" of work force and conditioning
- society strictly divided into Alpha, Beta, Gamma, Delta and Epsilon people with Alphas constituting the ruling class and Epsilons constituting a slave-like work force
- natural reproduction outlawed, sex as pure entertainment, monogamy regarded as unnatural and immoral
- people kept happy by means of a drug called "soma"
- religion replaced by a strong belief in technology and science

Extrapolation of developments of 20th century society in *Brave New World*

- ardent belief in science, technology and progress
- misuse of science
- political and economic control and manipulation
- mass production and mass consumption
- decline of religious and moral values
- decline of educational standards
- drugs
- mass entertainment
- sensationalism

George Orwell: *Nineteen Eighty-Four*

written in 1948; set in the relatively near future

Generally known elements

- **Big Brother:** constant surveillance, "Big Brother is watching you"
  (origin of the name of the popular, present-day TV show)
- **Newspeak:** invention of a new, simplified form of the English language to manipulate
  thought; complex (i. e. critical) thinking cannot be put into words anymore
  Examples:
  - words like *goodthink, oldthink, crimethink:* simplify expressions of thought, make
    them imprecise, one-dimensional, eventually devoid of meaning
  - euphemisms like *Miniluv, Minipax, Minitrue:* sound positive, conceal their true mean-
    ing (Ministry of Love = police; Ministry of Peace = organises the military; Ministry
    of Truth = produces and spreads propaganda)
- **rewriting of history:** books and newspapers are manipulated

Extrapolation of elements of 20th century society in *Nineteen Eighty-Four*

precursors in Nazi Germany and Soviet Uniun under Stalin:
- intrusion in people's privacy, spying on people
- propaganda, misuse of mass media
- psychological torture

21st century relevance

- electronic surveillance and digital tracking
- fake news
- nationalism
- censorship

Ray Bradbury: *Fahrenheit 451*

written in 1953; set in 2049

Generally known elements

- **451 degrees Fahrenheit:** the temperature at which paper starts to burn
- society marked by entertainment, speed, restlessness and superficiality: extremely
  fast driving; multi-screen television with very shallow programmes, usually set at high
  volume; constant exposure to sound and advertising (individually by the wearing of
  ear-plugs or collectively by loudspeaker announcements)
- critical thought impeded as books are forbidden
- the firemen's job: to burn books

Extrapolation of elements of 20th century society in *Fahrenheit 451*

- burning of books (Nazi Germany)
- atomic bomb (Hiroshima)
- rise of television and audio media, effect on reading
- acceleration in all areas of life: transport, communications, work, production, consumption
- dominance of entertainment
- decline of education

Science Fiction

Science fiction is a genre of fiction dealing with imaginary content set in the future, with particular focus on science and technology.

As opposed to fantasy, its imaginary elements are largely possible within scientifically postulated laws of nature.

The settings for science fiction are often contrary to known reality, but most science fiction relies on potential scientific explanations or solutions to various fictional elements. There is no magic involved.

Elements of science fiction

- a setting in the future
- a setting in outer space (e.g. spaceflight), in other worlds or in remote regions of the earth (underground, bottom of the sea)
- characters that include aliens, mutants, androids or other types of artificial intelligence (AI)
- technology that is futuristic (e.g. ray guns, teleportation machines, humanoid computers, space ships, artificial planets, independent AI)
- scientific principles that are new and have overcome known laws of nature, for example time travel, wormholes or faster-than-light travel
- new and different societies, especially post-apocalyptic worlds
- paranormal abilities such as mind control, telepathy and telekinesis

There is considerable overlap between utopia/dystopia and science fiction. However, one may say that science fiction is a lot more concerned with futuristic science and technology, which is central to the story, whereas utopian/dystopian narratives rather put their focus on social aspects. The element of extrapolation therefore plays a greater role in dystopian films and novels.

As an example, the films *Star Wars* or *Alien* do not essentially extrapolate from today's society. The novels *Fahrenheit 451* and *Brave New World* or productions such as *Gattaca* and *Black Mirror* do so extensively.

Classic science fiction narratives

These classics are so well known in and outside of English-speaking countries that you may encounter references to any one of these works in numerous texts.

Mary Shelley, *Frankenstein; or, The Modern Prometheus* (1818)

Dr Frankenstein brings to life a creature made of dead body parts and is then repulsed by what he has done. The creature becomes lonely and violent after being rejected by its creator and turns against him.

As one of the most easily recognised icons of fantastic fiction, Frankenstein's creature has inspired innumerable works of art, from films to mangas and computer games. "Frankenstein's monster" has become synonymous with things, in particular an invention, that become destructive to its inventor.

H. G. Wells, *The Time Machine* (1895)

In this novel the nameless Time Traveller visits a future in which the human race has evolved into two separate species: the childlike Eloi, leading relatively carefree and happy lives, and the brutal Morlocks, who provide for the Eloi's wealth but also eat them. The Time Traveller is forced to retrieve his machine from the Morlocks before he can return home.

Wells's story has popularised the concept of time travel, using a machine that allows an operator to travel to whatever period of history they want. It has inspired countless science fiction stories, the most popular probably being the Hollywood production *Back to the Future*. The term "time machine", coined by Wells, is now universally used.

H. G. Wells, *The War of the Worlds* (1898)

The War of the Worlds tells the story of a Martian invasion, apparently to harvest humans. As mankind's weapons turn out to be useless against the Martians, the aliens are eventually killed by earthly bacteria.

The story has become particularly famous because of its adaptation in the 1938 radio broadcast by Orson Welles, which allegedly led to widespread panic among listeners who thought the invasion was real. Significantly, the novel also gave birth to the fictional theme of the Martians and their potential invasion.

20th and 21st century science fiction novels and films are so abundant that there is no use listing any of them here. For your final exam, make sure you are familiar with the texts you studied.

Glossary – Utopia and Dystopia

anti-individualist	anti-individualistisch
anti-utopian	anti-utopisch
authoritarian	autoritär
brainwashing to brainwash so.	Gehirnwäsche jmd. einer Gehirnwäsche unterziehen
to dissent dissenter	abweichende Meinung haben Andersdenkender
dystopia	Anti-Utopie, Dystopie
extrapolation	Fortführung, Ableitung
fiction fictitious fictional	Dichtung, erzählende Literatur fiktiv, erfunden erdichtet
future futuristic	Zukunft, zukünftig futuristisch
hierarchy	Hierarchie
imaginary	erfunden
individualist	Individualist, individualistisch
indoctrination	Indoktrinierung
oppression	Unterdrückung
restriction	Einschränkung
surveillance	Überwachung
totalitarian	totalitär
utopia	Utopie

Visions of the Future: Ethical Issues of Scientific and Technological Progress

Artificial Intelligence (AI)

Definition

– Alan Turing (1950): "Can machines think?"
   → **Turing Test** ("imitation game"): a human interrogator tries to distinguish between a computer text and a human text
– "It is the science and engineering of making intelligent machines, especially intelligent computer programs. It is related to the similar task of using computers to understand human intelligence, but AI does not have to confine itself to methods that are biologically observable." (John McCarthy, 2004)
– More differentiated approach (cf. Stuart Russel & Peter Norvig, 2016):
   Human approach:
   – systems that think like humans
   – systems that act like humans
   Ideal approach:
   – systems that think rationally
   – systems that act rationally
   Turing's definition would have fallen under the category of "systems that act like humans".
– In its most basic shape, artificial intelligence is a field which employs computer science and datasets to solve problems.

Milestones

– 1950: Alan Turing proposes the answer to the question "Can machines think?" and introduces the Turing Test to determine if a computer can demonstrate the same intelligence as a human.
– 1956: John McCarthy coins the term "artificial intelligence".
– 1956: Logic Theorist, the first-ever running AI software program
– 1967: first computer based on a neural network that "learned" though trial and error
– 1980s: Neural networks training themselves by means of a backpropagation algorithm become widely used.
– 1997: IBM's "Deep Blue" beats world chess champion Garry Kasparov in a chess match (and a rematch).
– 2015: Supercomputer can identify and categorise images with a higher rate of accuracy than the average human.
– 2023: Large language models (LLMs) such as ChatGPT create an enormous change in the world of communication.

Types of artificial intelligence – weak AI vs. strong AI

– **Weak AI** (also: Narrow AI) is AI that is trained and aimed at performing precisely delineated tasks.

Current every-day applications are virtual assistants such as Siri and Alexa, and autonomous vehicles.
- **Strong AI** (also: General AI) is a theoretical form of AI where a machine would have an intelligence equal to or even surpassing humans. It would have consciousness, the ability to solve problems, learn and plan for the future. Strong AI is still entirely theoretical with no practical examples in use today, but research is being done on it. Examples are to be found in works of science fiction such as 3-CPO and R2-D2 in the *Star Wars* franchise, HAL in *2001: A Space Odyssey*, Ava in *Ex Machina* and Samantha in *Her*.

Deep learning vs machine learning
- Deep learning and machine learning are sub-fields of AI.
  Deep learning is a sub-field of machine learning.
- Classic machine learning needs human intervention to process data and "learn", whereas deep learning does not.
- **Generative AI:** Deep-learning models that can take data and "learn" to generate statistically probable outputs. Generative models have been used for years in statistics to analyse numerical data. Their use has recently been extended to images, speech and other complex data types (e. g. ChatGPT, DALL·E).

Applications
- There are numerous, real-world applications of AI systems today. Below are some of the most common uses:
  - **speech recognition:** speech to text, voice search; known from many mobile devices and texting
  - **customer service:** virtual online agents answer frequently asked questions (FAQs); examples: messaging apps, virtual assistants and voice assistants
  - **computer vision:** enables computers and systems to gather relevant information from visual input such as videos and images and perform specific functions based on these inputs; more than just image recognition; examples: photo tagging in social media, radiology imaging in healthcare and self-driving cars
  - **recommendation engines:** based on their consumption behaviour, AI can make relevant recommendations to customers that buy online

Ethical Issues
benefits
- "solve intelligence, and then use that to solve everything else" (Demis Hassabis, Google)
- numerous applications (see above)

risks
- large collection of data
  - concerns about privacy
  - concerns about copyright

- concerns about misinformation (fake news; images, audio, video and text that are indistinguishable from real photographs, recordings, films or human writing), conspiracy theories and extreme partisan content
  - concerns about "artificial stupidity" (AI mistakes)
  - lack of transparency (AI application may be so complex that nobody knows how it works anymore)
- technological unemployment
- algorithmic bias (see below)
- military AI (e. g. used by US and Israeli military to identify human targets)
- decision making (purely statistical, may be unethical, e. g. in autonomous driving: who to hit in an accident)
- existential risk, irreversible loss of control

Biases in AI systems

- AI systems will be biased if they learn from biased data. Developers may not be aware that the bias exists.
- **Language bias:** Current LLMs are mostly trained on English-language data, thus they may present western views as true.
- **Gender bias:** LLMs may reinforce gender stereotypes, assigning roles and characteristics based on traditional gender norms.
- **Racial bias:** There is often a racial bias with regard to e. g. violence. AI systems may also have a higher fail rate in identifying key factors in minority groups, e. g. AI diagnostic systems in healthcare have a lower accuracy for Black patients than for white patients.
- **Stereotyping:** Apart from gender and race, AI can reinforce stereotypes, including those based on age, nationality, religion or occupation. This can lead to unfair generalisations or caricature of groups of people, which may even be harmful or derogatory.
- Bias and discrimination may remain undetected because developers are mainly white and male: among AI engineers, about 4 % are Black and 20 % are women.

UNESCO recommendations on the ethics of AI

According to UNESCO, four core values should be the basis for all AI systems so that humanity and the environment can be protected. In addition, ten core principles ensure that human rights remain at the centre when considering AI ethics.

Four core values:
I. Human rights and human dignity
    Respect, protection and promotion of human rights and fundamental freedoms and human dignity
II. Living in peaceful, just and interconnected societies
III. Ensuring diversity and inclusiveness
IV. Environment and ecosystem flourishing

Ten core principles:[1]

1. Proportionality and Do No Harm
   AI must only be used where needed and may not cause harm.
2. Safety and Security
   Unwanted harms and security risks should be avoided.
3. Right to Privacy and Data Protection
   Privacy must be protected and data protection must be provided for.
4. Multi-stakeholder and Adaptive Governance & Collaboration
   The use of data must be in accordance with the law. Divers interest groups are to participate in the control of AI
5. Responsibility and Accountability
   Mechanisms should be in place to ensure care and control to avoid conflicts with human rights or the environment.
6. Transparency and Explainability
   Systems must be explainable and transparent without conflicting with other principles like privacy or security.
7. Human Oversight and Determination
   Member States should ensure that AI systems do not displace ultimate human responsibility and accountability.
8. Sustainability
   All technologies must constantly strive to be sustainable, i.e. use a minimum of resources.
9. Awareness & Literacy
   Public understanding should be promoted by means of education and information.
10. Fairness and Non-Discrimination
    Social justice, fairness and non-discrimination must be ensured. Everybody should benefit from AI.

Genetics

> **Keyword**
> **Genetics:** field of study examining the way living organisms inherit certain qualities from their ancestors via DNA. These qualities are called traits. Traits are e.g. a person's eye-colour or height.

- Genetic information is carried by a molecule called DNA, which is copied and passed on across generations.
- DNA is widely known as the "double helix" and looks like a twisted ladder. It is made up of nucleotides, which are the rungs of the ladder. There are four types of nucleotides (adenine, cytosine, guanine and thymine; A, C, G and T). The sequence of the nucleotides determines the genetic code of an organism.

---

[1] Source: UNESCO, https://www.unesco.org/en/artificial-intelligence/recommendation-ethics (accessed on 1 March 2024)

– Genes are segments of DNA which provide information used to encode proteins. They are like sentences spelled out by means of the "letters" of the nucleotide alphabet.
– The complete set of genes in a particular organism is known as a genome.
– Genes are copied each time a cell divides into two new cells. It is through a similar process that a child inherits genes from its parents, when a copy from the mother is mixed with a copy from the father.

Genetic engineering

Altering strings of DNA in a cell can produce a new trait. For example, crop plants can be given a gene from an Arctic fish, so they produce an antifreeze protein in their leaves. This may prevent frost damage. Other crops can be given genes including a natural insecticide, which will protect the plant.

People with genetic disorders can be treated by means of gene therapy. The idea is to replace a malfunctioning gene with one that functions properly.

Important steps in genetic engineering
– 1953: discovery of double helix by Watson and Crick, Cambridge, UK
– 1973: first insertion of foreign DNA into an organism
– 1978: production of human protein insulin
– 1980s: beginning of work with human genes
– 1986: open-air experimentation with genetically modified plants
– 1992: first commercial cultivation of genetically modified plants
– 1996: cloning of mammals (sheep "Dolly")
– 2003: sequencing of the human genome
– 2009: first transgenic primates
– 2013: use of cloning to create human embryonic stem cells
– 2016: cultivation of crops that are modified on a large scale by means of "genetic scissors" is permitted in the US
– 2018: babies modified by means of "genetic scissors" have been allegedly born in China

Designer babies (Reprogenetics)

The colloquial term "designer baby" refers to a baby whose genetic makeup has been artificially selected to ensure the presence or absence of certain characteristics, especially with regard to the sex of the child.

Cloning

Cloning is the creation of an organism that is an exact genetic copy of another. This means that every single bit of DNA is the same between the two.

Dolly (5 July 1996 – 14 February 2003): A female sheep (ewe) was the first mammal to be cloned from an adult body cell. She lived until the age of six, when she developed severe diseases.

Ethics
Biotechnology in agriculture

Pros	Cons
higher productivity	genes can end up in unexpected places
more efficient land use	genes can mutate with harmful effect
more ecological farming (no ploughing, no fertilising, no insecticides, no pesticides)	"sleeper" genes could be accidentally switched on, active genes could become "silent"
solution to problem of famine in the world	loss of farmers' control over material; "terminator" technology prevents sustainable farming → dependence on big corporations
higher quality of food	transfer of allergenic genes
longer shelf life	GM products in the food chain
rehabilitation of damaged land	transfer of antibiotic resistance
	interaction with wild and native plant populations: negative impact on birds, insects and soil

Reprogenetics

Pros (once it is safe)	Cons
parents have a right to choose	technology is not safe yet
moral obligation to give children the best life possible	bioethical codes condemn experiments with human beings
will lead to improvement of the whole species	"super humans" may look down on normal people
	"imperfect" human beings would be discriminated against
	rich people would be at an advantage
	the human gene pool may be damaged
	"New Eugenics": people are designed to suit the needs of society
	people may be thought of as products
	human beings should not play God

Sex selection

Pros (once it is safe)	Cons
parents have a right to choose	preferences in patriarchal cultures lead to demographic imbalance

in some cultures male offspring are important to provide support for old age	members of the unwanted sex may be discriminated against
theory that having sisters (as opposed to brothers) enhances adults' quality of life	the child may not be loved if sth. goes wrong and it is not of the desired sex
	parents fulfil their own wishes, disregarding the rights of the child
	human beings should not be allowed to play God

Human cloning

Pros	Cons
medical reasons: resource of bone marrow or replaceable organs	cloning is inherently evil, an intrusion into human life
infertile couples may have children	a person who wants to clone himself/herself is self-centred
	cloning in order to produce superior beings is discriminatory (eugenics)
	using human beings as a resource for "spare parts" is unethical
	reproduction by means of cloning might have long-term consequences for human relationships
	children may be thought of as products
	Hinduism: What about the person's karma?
	dictators may become immortal

Glossary – Artificial Intelligence

algorithm	Algorithmus
artificial intelligence (AI)	künstliche Intelligenz (KI)
autonomous driving	autonomes Fahren, Selbstfahren
bias	Verzerrung; unproportionale Gewichtung eines Faktors zu (Un-)Gunsten einer Person, Sache oder Idee
big data	große Datenmengen bzw. Firmen/Technologien, die damit arbeiten
computer vision	Computer Vision (Wissenschaft, wie von Kameras erfasste Bilder analysiert und weiterverarbeitet werden können)

data mining	Data-Mining (statistische Auswertung großer Datenmengen hinsichtlich möglicher Trends und Muster)
deep learning	mehrschichtiges/tiefes Lernen (Form des maschinellen Lernens neuronaler Netzwerke)
deepfake	Deepfake (Medieninhalte wie Fotos, Videos und Tonaufnahmen, die auf kaum feststellbare Weise digital erstellt oder manipuliert wurden)
facial recognition	Gesichtserkennung
generate	generieren
LLM, large language model	großes Sprachmodel (künstliches neuronales Netzwerk, das Sprache generieren kann und durch (halb-)autonom überwachtes Training lernt
machine learning	maschinelles Lernen
Natural Language Processing (NLP)	natürliche Sprachverarbeitung
neural networks	neuronale Netzwerke
optimisation	Optimierung
prediction	Vorhersage
robotics	Robotik
speech recognition	Spracherkennung
supervised learning	überwachtes Lernen
test data	Testdaten
training data	Trainingsdaten
unsupervised learning	unüberwachtes Lernen

Glossary – Ethical Issues

achievement of scientists	Errungenschaft/Leistung der Wissenschaftler/-innen
artificial insemination	künstliche Befruchtung
development	Entwicklung
DNA (deoxyribonucleic acid)	DNS (Desoxyribonukleinsäure)
double helix	Doppelhelix
error rate	Fehlerrate
genetic disorders	genetische Funktionsstörung
genetic engineering	Gentechnik, Genmanipulation

genetic fingerprint	genetischer Fingerabdruck
genetic make-up, genetic constitution	Erbgut
genetic modification (GM)	genetische Veränderung
heredity, inheritance	Vererbung
to inherit	erben
insecticide	Insektizid
in-vitro fertilisation	In-vitro-Befruchtung
laboratory	Labor
to modify modification	modifizieren, verändern Modifizierung
molecule	Molekül
to mutate mutation	mutieren Mutation
non-polluting	umweltverträglich
organ donor	Organspender/-in
to pass on	vererben
pesticide	Unkrautvernichtungsmittel, Pestizid
progress (no article, no plural)	Fortschritt
reproductive cloning	Klonen von Menschen
research (into)	Forschung (über)
research facility	Forschungseinrichtung
resistance	Resistenz
stem cell	Stammzelle
technology	Technologie, Technik
test-tube baby	Retortenbaby
therapeutic cloning	therapeutisches Klonen
transgenic	transgen (genetisch verändert)

The Impact of the Media

Roles of the Media:

- information, entertainment and education through
  - news, features and analysis
  - documentaries, dramas, current affairs programmes, public service announcements, magazine programmes
- facilitate social change and shape public opinion
- watchdog role: monitoring the performance of governments

Dangers:

- often strongly biased reporting
- reinforcement of stereotypes (gender, ethnicity, religion, culture)
- manipulation of public opinion
- fake news (see below)

Types of Media

UK

Print Media (newspapers, magazines)

Broadsheets / quality papers

daily	weekly	political orientation
The Daily Telegraph	The Sunday Telegraph	conservative
The Times	The Sunday Times	centre-right
The Guardian	The Observer	centre-left
The Financial Times		centre (focus on business, economy)

Note that there is a strong tradition of reading the Sunday papers in Britain

Tabloids / yellow press
(strongly partisan papers, important role in shaping public opinion)

daily	weekly	political orientation
The Sun	The Sun on Sunday	right-wing conservative
The Daily Express	The Sunday Express	right-wing conservative
The Daily Mail	The Mail on Sunday	right-wing conservative
The Daily Mirror	The Sunday Mirror	centre-left
The Morning Star		left, socialist

Broadcasting: Radio and television

Television
- BBC TV – operates BBC1, BBC2 and digital services, including BBC News channel
- BBC World News – commercially-funded international news channel
- ITV / Channel 3 – commercial network with regional divisions
- Channel 4 – commercially funded but publicly owned national station
- Channel 5 – national commercial channel
- Independent Television News (ITN) – supplier of news to ITV, Channel 4 and other outlets
- Sky –provider of film, entertainment channels and Sky News

Radio
- national radio dominated by the BBC
- numerous local commercial radio stations

US

Print Media (newspapers, magazines)

Traditionally there is no national paper in the USA. **USA Today** has tried to fill this gap, but it is not accepted as a serious newspaper, i. e. libraries do not provide it ("McPaper"). Originally local papers circulate nationwide.

Best known and largest newspapers:
- liberal: The New York Times, The Boston Globe, The Washington Post, San Francisco Chronicle, Los Angeles Times
- neutral: USA Today
- conservative: Chicago Tribune, The Wall Street Journal
- There is no equivalent to the polarising tabloids in Britain. This role is assumed by the television giant Fox News.

Broadcasting: Television and radio

Television:
- NBC – National Broadcasting Company
- CBS – Columbia Broadcasting System
- ABC – American Broadcasting Company
- Fox Broadcasting Company
- Cable Television: CNN – Cable News Network

The Fox Phenomenon:

Republicans take their news from one source more than from any other source. They trust Fox more than any other television outlet. Democrats trust CNN, NBC, CBS, ABC to a similar extent.

Radio:
- no national radio station
- numerous local commercial radio stations

New Media (digital media, websites, apps)
Entertainment: Netflix, Amazon etc.

News:
- online editions of the traditional print and broadcast media
- internet news channels: formal and informal publication of news stories through mainstream media outlets or social media platforms

Social Media:
- most popular: Facebook, YouTube, Instagram, TikTok, X (formerly: Twitter)
- differ from traditional media in many ways
- most important: reach a lot more people than traditional media
- provide user created content (see below)

Impact on politics:
- a lot of people get their political news from social media
  → less well-informed and more likely to be misinformed
- large increase of influence in political campaigns

Impact on society:
- increased visibility of marginal issues, power is shifted to the masses
- "slacktivism": real activism is replaced by social media activism, which increases awareness but may not result in change

Impact on commerce:
- companies use social media to connect with customers
  → stimulation and creation of demand, targeted product offerings, customer feedback to create innovation
- increased attention / reach of a product can reinforce sales
- however: companies/products without such attention may be mistrusted

Impact on the world of work:
- recruiting and hiring: people can create their personal brands on social networks
- job candidates are researched on social media and hired on the basis of the information given there

Negative impact of social media:
- Fear of Missing Out (FOMO):
  - addiction to checking out what other people are doing
  - checking your messages all the time

- feeling that other people are living better lives than you
- cyberbullying
- lack of privacy:
  - stalking, doxxing, identity theft, personal attacks and misuse of information
  - users share content that should not be public

Most important difference to traditional media: individual as content creator
- seen by many as democratic, objective exchange of information
- but: no professional journalism, no control, no code of ethics
- danger: manipulation, fraud, propaganda → **fake news** (false or misleading information presented as news)

Some types of fake news:
- false connection (headlines, captions, pictures do not match and are misleading)
- misleading content (misleading use of information)
- false context information
- manipulated content (e.g. with a manipulated photo)
- fabricated content (100 % false)
- scientific denialism (rejection of undisputed facts like the Holocaust, climate change, Covid-19)

Glossary – The Media

advertisement	Werbung
algorithm	Algorithmus
anchor	Moderator
audience	Publikum
breaking news	Eilmeldung
broadcast	Übertragung
censorship	Zensur
circulation	Auflage
clickbait	Klickköder
commercial	Werbespot
coverage	Berichterstattung
dark web, darknet	Darknet (Netzwerk aus zum Teil manuell erstellten Verbindungen, das größeren Schutz vor Zugriffen bietet, aber auch zur Verschleierung krimineller Machenschaften dient)
editor	Redakteur
editorial	Leitartikel

fact-checking	Faktenprüfung
filter bubble	Filterblase
headline	Schlagzeile
hoax	Falschmeldung
impact, influence	Einfluss
infographic	Infografik
journalism	Journalismus
magazine	Magazin, Zeitschrift
media	Medien
media bias	Medienvoreingenommenheit
newspaper	Zeitung
opinion piece	Meinungsbeitrag
pay-per-click	Pay-per-Click
paywall	Bezahlschranke
press	Presse
press release	Pressemitteilung
propaganda	Propaganda
public relations	Öffentlichkeitsarbeit
publish	veröffentlichen, herausgeben
publisher	Verlag, Verleger
radio	Radio
ratings	Einschaltquoten
reporter	Reporter
source	Quelle
subscription	Abonnement
television	Fernsehen
viewer	Zuschauer
vlog	Videoblog
yellow press	Boulevardpresse

The International World of Work

With the world constantly becoming smaller due to globalisation, it has become much easier to spend some time in a foreign country for educational reasons, both during one's time at school and/or as part of university studies or vocational training.

Benefits for Oneself

- getting a personal insight into other cultures
- improving one's foreign language skills
- experiencing different educational systems
- contributing to personal development, e.g. greater independence and confidence
- making new friends and broadening one's horizon on various levels
- improving one's career opportunities

Studying and working abroad also has benefits for employers. Employees who have studied abroad are said to possess key job skills, e.g. cultural empathy, excellent foreign language skills, self-organisation, adaptability, open-mindedness and flexibility. Some employers therefore consider it an essential aspect of a prospective employee's CV (résumé) to have spent some time abroad, very often in an English-speaking country.

Volunteerism and Voluntourism

In the last couple of years, **volunteerism** has become more popular. It means that a person volunteers their time and skills to contribute to a community for free, e.g. through humanitarian aid or by teaching at a local school in a rural village. An increasing number of people combine being a volunteer with spending some time abroad.
Volunteerism should not be confused with **voluntourism,** which can generally be defined as a combination of volunteering and sightseeing. Voluntourism is a neologism based on the words "volunteer" and "tourism" and has been criticised as counterfeiting the original idea of volunteering. Some of the arguments critics put forward against voluntourism are that it is not truly beneficial for communities, since "voluntourists" only spend a relatively short time in the communities in question and therefore often do not immerse themselves enough in their culture to truly contribute. In addition, voluntourists are said to enjoy all the benefits of an ordinary tourist, e.g. staying in hotels far above the living standards of the community they are helping, and are thus often unprepared for their placement. Whereas in the past charities and NGOs were mostly in charge of matching volunteers with the right projects, some major travel agencies now also specialise in offering placements for "voluntourists" against payment.

English as a *Lingua Franca*

English is a *lingua franca,* which means that it is a language spoken by such a vast number of people all over the world that it enables speakers of different first languages to successfully communicate with each other. These non-native speakers of English have a huge impact on the English language, e. g. when it comes to grammar or pronunciation, for when non-native speakers of English communicate with each other, it is their main intention to communicate a message. As a consequence, grammatical constructions regarded as incorrect by native speakers of English are accepted by both speakers and do not impede the flow of their conversation.

Code mixing and code switching also occur. It means that a speaker uses words, syntax, etc. from his mother tongue as well as English words in the same sentence. In contrast to that, the term code switching is used to refer to a speaker who switches between the vocabulary, syntax, etc. of his or her mother tongue and English, often in the same sentence.

Nowadays English language skills are not considered a special feature but are taken for granted in many areas of life.

The Changing World of Work

Past generations often spent their entire working life with one employer, retiring from the same company with which they started. But, due to globalisation, the world of work has changed rapidly over the last half century. Advances in information technology have made it possible for a company's employees in different countries to work on the same project and to exchange information on the spot. Due to new technological and economic developments, new types of jobs have been created which were unheard of only half a century ago.

Still, finding one's dream job has not become easier, and employees are often expected to show a high level of flexibility and adaptability. Changing jobs and places of residence frequently is not uncommon, as there is high competition in certain jobs.

Nor do the realities of the job market always match one's expectations and wishes. Despite the fact that there is employment growth in the United Kingdom, Germany and the USA, not everyone profits from it. The number of jobs for people with no or low work skills is decreasing and the gap between the rich and the poor is widening all over the world.

Minimum Wage and Living Wage

21 countries of the European Union as well as the USA, have a statutory minimum wage. In 2015, Germany introduced a minimum wage, calculated either on the basis of an hourly rate or as a monthly payment. The minimum wage varies in different fields of work. Being paid a minimum wage means that an employee receives the lowest wage his/her employer is legally allowed to pay. Some of the arguments put forward in favour of the minimum wage are that it prevents people from being exploited by employers, forcing them to rely on social benefits in order to make ends meet.

In the UK some companies and institutions voluntarily pay their employees a "living wage" instead of the legal minimum wage. While a "minimum wage" is calculated in accordance with the development of the job market, a "living wage" is an hourly rate calculated on the basis of the cost of living index (e. g. accommodation, travel, food and drink, costs for heating, water and electricity), which in the UK is adjusted annually. In 2022, the voluntarily paid living wage in the UK was £10.90 an hour, with the exception of London where it is £11.95 an hour, due to higher costs of living. In the same year the compulsory "national living wage" for people aged 23 or older was £9.50 per hour – significantly lower than the living wage calculated by the Living Wage Foundation.

Glossary – The International World of Work

adaptability	Anpassungsfähigkeit
apprenticeship, vocational training	Berufsausbildung, Lehre
charity	Wohlfahrtsorganisation
community service	ehrenamtliche Tätigkeit
compulsory education/schooling	Schulpflicht
CV (curriculum vitae) (BE) / résumé (AE)	Lebenslauf
exchange student	Austauschschüler/-in oder -student/-in
flexibility	Flexibilität
gap year	etwa einjährige Auszeit vor/nach Ausbildung/Studium, oftmals zum Sammeln von Wissen oder Arbeitserfahrung
job advertisement/offer	Stellenanzeige/-angebot
job interview	Bewerbungsgespräch
key qualifications	Schlüsselqulifikationen
minimum wage	Mindestlohn
open-mindedness	Aufgeschlossenheit
placement/internship	Praktikum
scholarship	Stipendium
school exchange	Schüleraustausch
social commitment/skills	soziales Engagement/Kompetenz
study abroad	Auslandsstudium
to apply for (a job)	sich (für eine Stelle) bewerben
to broaden one's horizon	seinen Horizont erweitern
to carve out a career	Karriere machen
to donate/give sth. to charity	etw. an eine Wohltätigkeitsorganisation spenden/weiterleiten
to gain experience	Erfahrungen sammeln
to get an insight into foreign cultures	Einblick in fremde Kulturen erhalten
to speak from one's own experience	aus eigener Erfahrung sprechen
volunteer	Freiwillige/-r

Questions of Identity and Gender

Over the past couple of years, there has been growing public awareness of issues related to the topic of gender and identity. These issues are important in various areas of life: work, family, religion, pop culture and education, to name just a few.

In western societies, traditional and stereotypical concepts, e. g., of what a "real" man or woman should be like, have been questioned. There has been a change in gender roles and the expectations affixed to them, which is due to people breaking with old traditions and concepts. Unlike previous generations, which usually unquestioningly accepted society's often rigid expectations, people today are more inclined to embrace personal and individual notions of what one's life should be like.

Pop culture, e. g. in the form of films like *Barbie*, plays a significant role when it comes to challenging and/or reversing stereotypes. In addition to that, social media has also helped to empower girls and women around the world.

The challenging and ever-changing world of work likewise encourages and forces people to achieve their wishes and expectations in life. Governments paved the way for parental leave for fathers in a growing number of countries, e. g. Scandinavia and Germany. This has helped young families to balance their work and family life. However, challenges persist, as taking parental leave can have a negative impact on one's career advancement. Companies are often biased when it comes to parental leave and exclude those employees that take it from promotion since raising young children is regarded as detrimental to their flexibility and reliability.

Despite increasing support for and acceptance of the LGBTQ+ movement in western societies, there is still a long way to go when it comes to true gender equality. Huge discrepancies between the situation in liberal countries and conservative ones persist, depending on the government and the influence of religious groups.

One should not forget that finding one's place in society requires the freedom to make independent decisions and to express oneself. In countries around the world, women's access to abortions is often restricted or abortions – even if the pregnancy is the result of rape – are sometimes completely forbidden. Doctors who carry out abortions in such countries and women deciding to have one are severely punished. However, in March 2024, France became the first country to make the right to an abortion part of their constitution.

Glossary – Questions of Identity and Gender

abortion	Abtreibung
cisgender	cisgender (Person, deren soziales Geschlecht mit dem angeborenen biologischen Geschlecht übereinstimmt)
discrimination	Diskriminierung
domestic violence	häusliche Gewalt

emancipation	Emanzipation, Selbstbemächtigung
empowerment	Ermächtigung
equal pay	gleiche Entlohnung
femicide	Frauenmord
gender binary	binäres Geschlechtsmodell (ausschließlich männlich und weiblich als eindeutig unterscheidbare, gegenübergestellte Geschlechter)
gender equality	Gendergerechtigkeit, Gleichberechtigung der Geschlechter
gender role	Geschlechterrolle
heteronormativity	Heteronormativität (Konzept, das Heterosexualität als die bevorzugte oder normale sexuelle Orientierung ansieht)
LGBTQIA+	LGBTQIA+, LSBTI* (Lesbian, Gay, Bisexual, Transgender, Queer, Intersex, Asexual/Aromantic/Agender, weitere non-cisgender Personen)
mansplaining	Mansplaining *(man + explain;* Erklärung, bei der die sprechende (männliche) Person deutlich macht, dass sie sich besser auskennt als die zuhörende (weibliche) Person
parental leave	Elternzeit
patriarchy	Patriarchat (gesellschaftliche Strukturen, in denen die männliche physische, soziale und/oder ökonomische Macht über Frauen institutionalisiert ist)
reproductive rights	Recht auf selbstbestimmte Fortpflanzung
sex gender	biologisches Geschlecht soziales Geschlecht
sexual harassment	sexuelle Belästigung

Methoden der Textarbeit

Literarische Texte

Narration

> **Keyword**
> **Narrative texts:** Narrative texts can have many forms, among them short story, novel, fairytale, satire, parable, legend, etc.
> Most relevant for your final exam are the short story and the novel.

When asked to analyse a narrative text, you will have to focus on particular elements that are characteristic of short stories or novels.

Elements of narration
Plot

INFO Elements of a complete plot

exposition → rising action → climax/turning point → falling action → ending

A **plot** need not necessarily be complete (e. g. open ending).

The **sequence** need not necessarily be in chronological order.
There may be foreshadowing or flashbacks or there may be reverse narration (*umgestelltes Erzählen*).
In particular, an excerpt from a longer text, which is the most common sort of text in the final exam, may not contain all the elements of plot.

Certain **key events** within the action of a story will raise the tension; they will create suspense, rising to a climax or turning point. After that there will be falling tension or relief.

INFO Tension curve

rising tension → climax or turning point → falling tension or relief

Theme

The **theme** of a story is always abstract. Themes are e.g. love, poverty, racism, childhood, etc.
The **subject matter** of a story is the concrete realisation of a theme.

Example:
Two stories may have the same theme: racism. The subject matter of the one may be the murder of an African-American, while the other may be dealing with the bullying of a black schoolgirl.

Characters

When asked to characterise a figure from a narrative text, you will have to be aware of different aspects. There are key questions that can guide you.

Direct characterisation
– What does the narrator say about the character?
– What do other characters say about the character?
– What does the character say about himself/herself?
– How objective is what they say? Be aware of words with negative or positive connotations.

Indirect characterisation
– How does the character act?
– What does the character say?
– What kind of language does he/she use?

It might help to fill in a table with the following headings:

Character's outward appearance	Character's language	Character's actions	What the character says	Other characters' statements (or actions)
...	...	...	...	...

Narrator / Point of view

INFO Narrator

The narrator is usually either a first-person or a third-person narrator.
The first-person narrator is NOT the author!

limited point of view	unlimited/omniscient point of view
first-person narrator	third-person narrator (neutral omniscience, God-like knowledge about all facts)
third-person narrator (one character's point of view)	third-person narrator (several characters' points of view)

The narrator always works like a camera operator, taking a point-of-view shot through a character's eyes or looking at the characters from the outside.

Example:
In Alan Sillitoe's novel *Saturday Night and Sunday Morning* (1975), the reader is presented with an episode in a pub (cf. p. 10). When the narrator says, "Brenda and two other women sitting at Arthur's table saw him push back his chair and stand up with a clatter", he takes Brenda's and the women's point of view. Arthur is clearly seen from outside, not by a neutral narrator but through the women's eyes: The women sitting at Arthur's table saw him push back his chair, NOT "Arthur pushed back his chair".
→ limited point of view A

A few lines later the point of view changes: "He felt electric light bulbs shining and burning into the back of his head".
The narrator takes Arthur's point of view, knows what Arthur feels.
→ limited point of view B

If the point of view switches multiple times between various different characters, this usually indicates an unlimited/omniscient point of view.

Mode of presentation
Panoramic presentation (telling) vs. scenic presentation (showing)
There are two modes of presentation to be found in narratives: the **panoramic** and the **scenic** mode.

The **panoramic** mode is employed when the narrator summarises several events, whereas **scenic** mode is used when the narrator describes scenes in great detail.

Interior monologue is a particular kind of scenic presentation, in which the thoughts and feelings passing through a character's mind are depicted. In **reported thought** the thoughts are presented as reported speech.

This is closely connected with the concepts of *narrated time* and *narrating* (or *acting*) *time:*

narrated time longer than narrating time	usually summary of events
narrated time identical with narrating time	e.g. direct speech
narrated time shorter than narrating time	e.g. stream of consciousness, interior monologue, detailed description of a scene, comparable to slow motion in film

INFO Function of mode of presentation and point of view

A neutral, omniscient narrator, who observes the action and the characters from above and who uses a panoramic mode of presentation, is more detached and thus creates a distance between the reader and the action. On the other hand, a narrator who takes a character's point of view creates immediacy and directly involves the reader in what happens.

Setting

The place and time where the action is set is called the setting. It is especially important for *atmosphere* and *symbolism*.

Atmosphere

Atmosphere is created by means of setting, objects, colours, light and darkness but also by reference to a character's mood or the use of language.

Example:
In Kate Chopin's short story "Desirée's Baby", a "yellow stuccoed house" is described with a roof that comes down "steep and black like a cowl" (cowl: *Mönchskutte*). It is surrounded by "big, solemn oaks", the "thick-leaved, far-reaching branches" shadowing "it like a pall" (pall: *Leichentuch*).

colour	black, dirty yellow
light/darkness	shadow of the oaks
language: similes, "like a pall", "like a cowl"	→ connotations of death, darkness, mystery

The atmosphere created here is gloomy, sombre, sinister, threatening and eerie.

Symbolism

Symbols are part of the setting of the narrative.

> **INFO** Established symbols

These are conventional symbols which have long been used and have a certain, traditional significance which everybody knows. Examples of established symbols: rose, cross, the colour white.

> **INFO** Created symbols

Something becomes symbolic within a certain context, because it is closely connected to an event, a situation or a character.

Example:
In the novel *Angela's Ashes* (1996), Angela, the family's mother, vomits over the side of the ship when they leave New York harbour for Ireland and the wind from the Atlantic blows it all over the family (cf. p. 53).
In the course of the novel, the reader will learn how unfortunate the family's decision to leave America will turn out to be and how disastrous the wind from the Atlantic will be for the family. Thus, this passage from the first chapter of the book is symbolic.

> **INFO** Symbols and metaphors

Symbols are NOT metaphors!
Symbols are really there, are part of the story. Metaphors or similes are figures of speech.

Examples:
She was a rose, so beautiful. → metaphor
She was like a rose, so beautiful. → simile/comparison
They fell in love when they first met in her father's rose garden. → symbol

Language and style

In order to determine the style of a text it is necessary to examine aspects such as register, diction (choice of words), tone and also sentence structure.

Register is the level of language used in a particular situation. It may be formal, neutral, informal or vulgar. There may be a lot of slang words, even taboo words, or technical terms or jargon.

The **tone** may be ironic, sarcastic, sad, humorous, serious, playful, angry, etc., depending on the emotional attitude it expresses. This has an effect on the choice of words, level of speech, rhythm, sentence length, etc.

Stylistic devices will be considered at length in the chapters on poetry and non-fictional texts (pp. 86 f., 93 f.).

Poetry

Poetry focuses on the **aesthetic function** of language.
Poetry appeals to the senses. It is usually to be enjoyed for its beauty, its cleverness, its wit or its impact. This is achieved by
- the sound of words,
- the rhythm of the words and phrases,
- the choice of words,
- the structure of the sentences,
- the composition of the poem,
- the visual arrangement of words and lines, and
- the means of imagery.

In your final exams, however, you will be asked not so much to enjoy the poem but to examine its meaning and the effect of the language the speaker uses.

How to proceed

Questions to be asked
- Who is the speaker of the poem?
- Where is the speaker?
- Does the speaker address somebody?
- Does the speaker contemplate something?
- Does the speaker describe something or somebody?
- Does the speaker tell a story?
- Does the speaker explain something?
- Does the speaker argue against or in favour of something?
- What is the speaker's attitude? What is he/she saying?
- How is the poem composed? Is it structured by rhyme scheme, by division into stanzas or by some other device?
- Is there a correspondence between the structure of the poem and the structure of the speaker's thoughts?
- What is the significance of the title?
- What words does the speaker use? What do they mean?
- What is the structure of the sentences? Simple? Complex?
- What poetic devices does the speaker use?
- And what is the effect of all this? What is the experience of reading the poem?

In order to understand and describe poetry you need to be familiar with its most important elements.

Elements of poetry

INFO Speaker and author

The speaker of the poem is NOT the author. Poems may be autobiographical, but you must still refer to the "speaker of the poem".

Poems are composed of **stanzas** and **lines**.
Stanzas may have a certain **rhyme scheme.**

Rhyme
Types of rhyme schemes

rhyme pair	a a b b
alternate rhyme	a b a b
embracing rhyme	a b b a

Types of rhymes

masculine rhyme (stress on final syllable)	kiss/this
feminine rhyme (stress on penultimate syllable)	dreary/weary
true rhyme	kiss/this, dreary/weary
slant rhyme assonance (same vowel) consonance (same consonant)	comb/coat hope/heap

Metre
Lines may also be marked by a certain rhythm. The smallest unit that determines rhythm is the foot, consisting of at least one stressed and one or two unstressed syllables. The pattern of stressed and unstressed syllables is called **metre.**

A sequence of stressed and unstressed syllables is nothing artificial. It is the natural rhythm of the English language. It is the poet's skill to choose words in a way that this pattern will constitute a regular metre.

Types of feet

foot	stresses		example
iamb/iambic	– /	(da-**dum**)	compare
trochee/trochaic	/ –	(**dum**-da)	lovely
spondee/spondaic	/ /	(**dum dum**)	drop dead
anapest/anapestic	– – /	(da-da-**dum**)	lemonade
dactyl/dactylic	/ – –	(**dum**-da-da)	whispering

The number of feet or stressed syllables in a line determines its metre. The most common types are shown here:

number of feet	metre	example
1	monometer	"And **find** / What **wind**" (John Donne, "Song", ll. 7 – 8)
2	dimeter	"Why **dost** thou **thus**" (John Donne, "The Sun Rising", l. 2)
3	trimeter	"**Go**, Soul, the **bo**dy's **guest** / U**pon** a **thank**less **er**rant;" (Sir Walter Raleigh, "The Lie", ll. 1 f.)
4	tetrameter	"**Bu**sy old **fool**, un**ru**ly **sun**" (John Donne, "The Sun Rising", l. 1)
5	pentameter	"If **mu**sic **be** the **food** of **love**, play **on**" (William Shakespeare, *Twelfth Night*, I.i)
6	hexameter	"And **in** your **dread**ful **verse** in**grav'd** the **pro**phe**cies**" (Michael Drayton, "Poly-Olbion", l. 33)

INFO Most important metre in English poetry

Iambic pentameter:
"But **thy** e**ter**nal **sum**mer **shall** not **fade**" (William Shakespeare, Sonnet 18).

Lines

end-stopped lines	The meaning requires a pause at the end of the line.	"Shall I compare thee to a summer's day?" (William Shakespeare, Sonnet 18)
run-on lines (enjambement)	The meaning requires no pause between the lines.	"When yellow leaves, or none, or few, do **hang** **Upon** those boughs which shake against the cold" (William Shakespeare, Sonnet 73)
caesura	The meaning requires a pause in mid-line.	"Let me not to the marriage of true minds Admit **impediments; love** is not love" (William Shakespeare, Sonnet 116)

Imagery

A writer or speaker using language beyond its dictionary meaning makes use of **imagery.** All figurative use of language is imagery. Imagery appeals to all the senses, it is meant to stimulate the reader's or listener's imagination.

> **INFO** Watch out!
>
> The word *imagery* is an abstract noun. There is no plural. You can only talk about single *images.*

Types of imagery

metaphor	A metaphor compares two basically dissimilar things without using the words 'like' or 'as'. Some characteristics of the one are thus transferred to the other in order to illustrate its qualities. "All the world is a stage." (William Shakespeare, *As You Like It*, II.viii)
simile/ comparison	Like a metaphor, a simile draws a comparison, but it explicitly uses the words 'like' or 'as' to do so. "my luve is like a red, red rose" (Robert Burns, "A Red, Red Rose", l. 1)
personification	This is a kind of metaphor in which animals, plants, inanimate objects or abstract ideas are represented as if they were humans or possessed human qualities: "Busy old fool, unruly sun, / Why dost thou thus, / Through windows, and through curtains call on us?" (John Donne, "The Sun Rising", ll. 1–3)
symbol	see examples in previous chapter, p. 82

Other poetic devices

stylistic device	definition	example
alliteration	repetition of a sound (usually a consonant) at the beginning of adjacent words	"From forth the fatal loins of these two foes" (William Shakespeare, *Romeo and Juliet,* Prologue)
onomatopoeia (adj.: onomato-poeic)	the use of words which imitate the sound they refer to	"the stuttering rifles' rapid rattle" (Wilfred Owen, "Anthem for Doomed Youth", l. 3)
anaphora	repetition of one or more words at the beginning of adjacent sentences or lines	"In every cry of every man In every infant's cry of fear In every voice, in every ban" (William Blake, "London", ll. 5–7)
chiasm	reversal of order of the words in the two parts of a sentence	"Fair is foul, and foul is fair" (William Shakespeare, *Macbeth*, I.i)
oxymoron	a combination of contradictory words and meanings	"O heavy lightness, serious vanity, Misshapen chaos of well-seeming forms" (William Shakespeare, *Romeo and Juliet*, I.i)

Drama

When asked to analyse a dramatic text, you will have to focus on particular elements that are characteristic of plays or film scripts.

Elements of drama
Plot

The action is presented to the audience on a stage or on a screen directly. There is no narrator. Yet one can identify the same elements of plot as are found in narration.

> **INFO** Elements of a dramatic plot
>
> exposition → rising action → climax/crisis → falling action → dénouement/catastrophe

In tragedy, the opponents of the hero gain the upper hand in the falling action, which ends in the catastrophe.
Comedy has a happy ending, in which conflicts are resolved (dénouement).

Stage directions

The dramatic text consist of **two kinds of text:** the more important kind of text is **spoken by the characters** (i. e. dialogues, monologues, soliloquys and asides).

The **stage directions** are the second kind of text. They give instructions concerning the stage design, about sounds to be heard, visual effects, the characters' actions and also the way some of the dialogue has to be spoken.

The following visual and acoustic elements will have to be considered in your analysis of stage directions. They will help to characterise, to create a specific atmosphere or they will function as symbols (cf. p. 82).

concerning the actors		concerning the stage	
visual	**acoustic**	**visual**	**acoustic**
size	voice	scenery	music
facial expression	intonation	stage design	noise
gestures	language of the play	lighting	sound
costumes	non-verbal noises	properties/props *(Requisiten)*	

Characters

The characters are not mediated via a narrator but are presented through action, interaction and dialogue and, of course, their outward appearance on stage (see above). There are **flat** characters, types that act in a predictable way, and **round**, lifelike characters that are fully developed and usually go through some form of inner development over the course of the play.

Language/Dialogue/Communication

Analysing the language of a play you have to keep in mind that it works on two levels:
1. the inner system of communication, i. e. the communication among the characters
2. the outer system of communication between the playwright and the audience

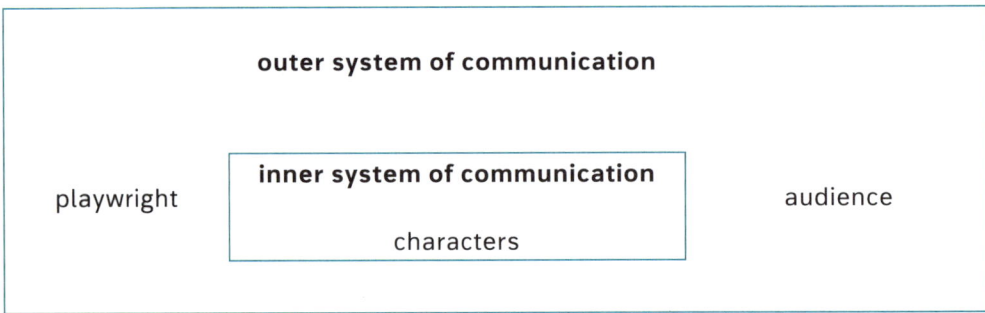

Dramatic irony

Dramatic irony is an important effect that is created by these two levels of communication. It arises when there is a sharp contrast between what the audience knows and what a character knows or utters. Dramatic irony often serves to great comic effect as well. Shakespeare, for example, puts it to great effect in his comedies when he introduces cases of mistaken identity.

Examples:

In Shakespeare's tragedy Macbeth, *King Duncan praises the peaceful atmosphere at Macbeth's castle, whereas the audience knows that Macbeth is planning to murder Duncan.*

In Shakespeare's comedy Twelfth Night, *Viola, disguised as a man, is asked by the Duke, whom she has fallen in love with, to woo Olivia for him.*

Aside

In an aside an actor speaks to the audience in order to provide information on his thoughts and feelings or intentions. The other characters on stage supposedly do not hear what she/he says.

TIPP

As many of Shakespeare's plays are written in verse, you may approach their language in the same way as poetry.

Glossary – Vocabulary for Analysing Literary Texts

the narrator tells of / shows / relates / reveals
the narrator takes xy's point of view
the narrator is omniscient
the story is told in the first/third person
the story is told from the first-person-singular point of view
the narrator uses / employs / makes use of
this metaphor shows / stands for / suggests
the narrator speaks in an ironic/satirical/detached/matter-of-fact/serious tone
the story deals with / treats of / concentrates on / focuses on
the ... atmosphere is created by
tension/suspense is created / built up
the poem is written/composed
the poem is read/spoken/recited
a recital of a poem

the poem is by Shakespeare
it is a song by Genesis
the speaker of the poem / the lyrical "I" / the poetic persona
the poem consists of / is composed of / is arranged in stanzas
the comedy ridicules/mocks/satirises
the exposition sets the action in motion
the action moves towards and culminates in a turning point
the play/film has a simple/complex/tight plot
it has a happy/unhappy ending
there are main/major/minor characters
the protagonist is in conflict with an opponent
the antagonist fights the protagonist
the spectator/audience follows the play
the play is performed/produced/staged
scenery is shifted
actors perform/play/enact
an actor enters / makes an entrance
an actor exits / makes his exit

Sach- und Gebrauchstexte

Argumentative Texts: How to Deal with (Political) Speeches

> **Keyword**
> **(Political) speeches:** aim at convincing *(überzeugen)* the audience of the speaker's position, winning them over to his/her side. Very often, the speaker tries to persuade (überreden) the listener by appealing to his/her feelings. In some cases, the orator may even attempt to manipulate *(manipulieren)* his audience.
> You should always keep in mind that the speaker wants to present his/her opinion / conviction / point of view as positively as possible.

When asked to analyse a political speech, you will have to focus on the topic as well as characteristic features.

How to proceed

Reading the text

1. Read the (political) speech (or, more likely, an extract from it) as a whole, trying to identify the main topic (reading for gist).
2. Re-read the (political) speech or extract several times, paying close attention to certain characteristic features of such speeches. Mark words or phrases in the text and take notes (intensive reading).

Pay special attention to

- key words and phrases
- references to historical events
- use of symbols, key words, slogans
- references to famous people
- references to works of literature
- stylistic devices (see below)

Questions to be asked

When it comes to analysing a (political) speech, you should always ask yourself the following questions:

- What is the main topic of the speech?
- What is its political, historical and social context?
- What do I know about the speaker (biography, political orientation)?

Elements of a (political) speech
Structure

(Political) Speeches can usually be divided into **introduction**, **main part** and **conclusion**. These parts serve different purposes:

INFO Introduction to a speech

In the introduction the orator announces the topic/purpose of the speech and explains why it is of major importance. He/she also wants to attract the audience's attention so that they will follow the speech closely and accept his/her opinion.

There are several ways to make listeners interested:
- The speaker can open by telling the audience **something about their personal history/recent experiences**, thereby underlining the fact that the topic of the speech is of personal importance to them. By relating a **little story** to the audience, the speaker will also appear more human and less flawless.
- Another common way of starting a speech is to **open it with a question** that refers to the main topic and which will be answered later in the speech. By asking the audience a question, the speaker actively involves them, indirectly asking them to think more deeply about an issue.
- A speaker may also **present visuals to the audience**, e.g. pictures, concrete objects or a short extract from a film. This also helps to attract the audience's attention: listeners will become curious about how the object or visual is related to the content of the speech.

INFO Main part of a speech

In the main part of the speech the orator needs to keep the audience interested and to make sure that they can follow the train of thought.

Again, there are several ways to do this. The following techniques are particularly effective:
- **using short and simple sentences**, developing the argumentation step by step and ensuring that the audience can follow,
- quoting reliable sources/experts, referring to statistics and **providing the audience with facts and necessary background information**, which shows that the speaker is well-informed and has researched the subject ,
- **pointing out problems** but also providing solutions for them, thus showing that the speaker is competent, and
- **including personal experiences** and vivid, specific events, again aiming for a personal relationship to the audience, **often using personal pronouns like "we", "us", "our".**

Towards the end of a speech the speaker might
- take up a question posed at the beginning of the speech,
- appeal once more to both the audience's heads and hearts,
- ask for support, giving the listeners the feeling that their support is important, and
- develop a vision for the future.

Argumentative comments use the same stylistic means as political speeches.

Language and style

There are certain stylistic devices, which are often used in (political) speeches. They aim at making the speech more lively and interesting.

Important stylistic devices

analogy	A resemblance is established between things which are dissimilar.
simile	This is a direct comparison using the words "like" or "as", e.g. *He fought like a lion in the battle.*
metaphor	This is an indirect comparison without using the words "like" or "as", e.g. *He was a lion in battle.*
alliteration	A consonantal sound of two or more adjacent words is repeated, e.g. *We will win; "We must understand that ties of trade bind nations in closest intimacy"* (Warren G. Harding: Inaugural address, 4 March 1921).
repetition	Repeating certain words or phrases puts emphasis on the meaning of the words and phrases in question, e.g. *"The answer to the slavery question was already embedded within our Constitution – a Constitution that had at its very core the ideal of equal citizenship under the law; a Constitution that promised its people liberty, and justice "* (Barack Obama: *A More Perfect Union*).
parallelism	Two or more parts of a sentence (or two or more sentences) have the same (or similar) syntactical structure. Like repetition, parallelism puts stress on the parts of the sentence in question, intensifying the force of the statement and encouraging the audience to think about its meaning, e.g. *"Let us be our sister's keeper. Let us find that common stake we all have in one another, and let our politics reflect that spirit as well."* (Barack Obama: *A More Perfect Union*)
antithesis	Two ideas are opposed to one another, using a parallel syntactical structure to reach the desired effect, i.e. establishing a contrast, e.g. *"It's a story that hasn't made me the most conventional candidate. But it is a story that has seared into my genetic makeup the idea that this nation is more than the sum of its parts – that out of many, we are truly one."* (Barack Obama: *A More Perfect Union*)

rhetorical question	A rhetorical question is one to which no answer is expected; instead, the listener is asked to think about the question and its relevance, e. g. *How long should this suffering continue?*
irony	Words or phrases are used to mean something different, often the opposite of their literal meaning. This is often done for rhetorical or humorous effect.

Glossary – Vocabulary for Analysing Speeches

By telling the listeners something about his personal history he attempts to establish a personal relationship with his audience.	Er bemüht sich, eine persönliche Beziehung zu seinen Zuhörern aufzubauen, indem er seinem Publikum etwas über seine persönliche Geschichte erzählt.
She attempts to win her listeners over to her side.	Sie versucht, das Publikum auf ihre Seite zu ziehen.
He draws a comparison between ... and ...	Er zieht einen Vergleich zwischen ... und ...
He puts emphasis on the meaning of his words by using a parallelism/repetition in line X.	Durch den in Zeile X verwendeten Parallelismus / die in Zeile X verwendete Wiederholung verleiht er seinen Worten Nachdruck.
He refers to well-known historical events such as ...	Er bezieht sich auf allgemein bekannte historische Ereignisse wie z. B. ...
He wants to call/draw the audience's attention to the fact that ...	Er möchte die Aufmerksamkeit des Publikums auf die Tatsache lenken, dass ...
His frequent use of rhetorical questions is intended to show that ...	Sein häufiger Gebrauch rhetorischer Fragen soll verdeutlichen, dass ...
His metaphorical use of language is intended to make his speech more lively and interesting.	Sein metaphorischer Sprachgebrauch soll seine Rede interessanter und lebendiger machen.
In lline X he directly criticises his political opponents.	In Zeile X kritisiert er offen seine politischen Gegner.
The frequent use of personal pronouns such as "we", "us" and "our" gives the audience the impression that he does not regard himself as superior to them but as one of them.	Der häufige Gebrauch der Personalpronomen „wir", „uns" und „unser" soll dem Publikum das Gefühl geben, dass er sich als einer von ihnen und nicht als eine höher gestellte Person sieht.
The speaker appeals to the audience's emotions by ...	Der Redner / Die Rednerin spricht die Gefühle des Publikums an, indem er/sie ...
The speaker begins by ...	Der Redner / Die Rednerin beginnt mit ...

The speaker makes frequent use of metaphors/similes/symbols/examples to point out / to underline that …	Der Redner / Die Rednerin macht regen Gebrauch von Metaphern/Vergleichen/Symbolen/Beispielen, um herauszustellen / zu unterstreichen, dass …
The speaker tries to convince his audience of his point of view by …	Der Redner / Die Rednerin versucht sein/ihr Publikum von seinem/ihrem Standpunkt zu überzeugen, indem er/sie …
The speaker aims to convince/persuade/manipulate the audience.	Es ist das Anliegen des Redners / der Rednerin, das Publikum zu überzeugen/überreden/manipulieren.

Expository Texts: How to Deal with Essays

Keyword
Essay: There are various kinds:
a) essays which reflect the author's opinion on a certain topic (**comment**)
b) essays in which the author weighs the pros and cons of a particular subject (**argumentative essay**)
c) essays in which a topic is presented in a clear and logical way and which do not contain the author's opinion (**expository essay**)

How to proceed

First you have to find out which kind of essay you are asked to analyse.

TIPP Argumentative comments

Argumentative comments use the same stylistic means as political speeches.

For details on how to analyse **comments** you can refer to the section on **political speeches** above.
Here we will focus on the **argumentative essay.**

Structure

– In the **introduction** the author expresses the main idea of the essay. Instead of giving a personal opinion, she/he might choose to provide the reader with some background information, or start with a question which will serve as a guideline and be answered in the course of the essay.
– For the **main part** of the essay, the author can decide on a dialectical or an enumerative approach.
– In an **enumerative approach** the author will enumerate all the aspects of the subject in a neutral way. A **dialectical approach** can either present all the arguments in favour of a position before focusing on the counterarguments (or vice versa), or it can present the pros and cons alternately. The latter is usually considered more skilful.

- Each **new aspect** is usually presented in a new paragraph. The various **arguments** can be backed with examples from real life, established facts, an expert opinion or other reliable sources. These pieces of evidence are very important, as they enable the author to make his/her argument convincing and thus to persuade the reader.
- In the **conclusion** the author sums up the arguments, frequently also restating his/her own opinion and giving an outlook on the future.

Glossary – Vocabulary for Analysing Essays

The author discusses the pros and cons of …	Der Verfasser / Die Verfasserin diskutiert die Vor- und Nachteile von …
The author gives his/her personal opinion on the problem of …	Der Verfasser / Die Verfasserin äußert seine/ihre eigene Meinung zum Thema …
He/She believes / is convinced / presumes that …	Er/Sie glaubt / ist überzeugt davon / nimmt an, dass …
She/He wants to persuade the reader …	Sie/Er möchte die Lesenden überreden …
One can easily follow his train of thought.	Man kann seinen Gedankengang leicht nachvollziehen.
At the end of her essay she draws / comes to the conclusion …	Am Ende ihres Berichts kommt sie zu dem Schluss …
His/Her arguments are (not) convincing/well-chosen.	Seine/Ihre Argumente sind (nicht) überzeugend / gut gewählt.
The main topic of the essay is …	Das Thema des Berichts ist …
The tone of this essay is humorous/neutral/ironic/serious.	Der Ton des Berichts ist humorvoll/neutral/ironisch/ernst.
The author uses real examples to convince her/his readers.	Die Verfasserin / Der Verfasser verwendet reale Beispiele, um ihre/seine Leserschaft zu überzeugen.
The author's choice of words shows/underlines that he/she is for/against …	Die Wortwahl des Verfassers / der Verfasserin zeigt/unterstreicht, dass er/sie für/gegen … ist.
In the introductory paragraph of her/his essay, he/she asks a rhetorical question which serves as a thread for the whole text.	Im einleitenden Abschnitt seines/ihres Berichts stellt er/sie den Lesenden eine rhetorische Frage, die sich wie ein roter Faden durch den Text zieht.
The author uses adjectives with a positive/negative connotation to support his/her point of view.	Der Verfasser / Die Verfasserin verwendet Adjektive mit einer positiven/negativen Konnotation, um seinen/ihren Standpunkt zu verdeutlichen.
Her attempt to persuade the readers backfires / works very well.	Ihr Versuch, die Lesenden zu überreden, misslingt/gelingt.

Narrative Texts: How to Deal with Reports

> **Keyword**
> **Report:** This is a special kind of newspaper article.
> It provides answers to the five "W" questions *(Who? What? Where? When? Why?),* as well as the *How* question. Its aim is to inform its readers and NOT to manipulate or influence them.
> A report deals with current events and only contains facts.

Sometimes students have problems when it comes to differentiating between a *report* and an *article,* which might also deal with current events but which is usually a mixture of both fact and opinion.

The style of an **article** is usually more personal and its main aim is to entertain the reader. This is ensured by using many adverbs and adjectives to make the article lively and by addressing its readers directly, often by asking them a hypothetical question, e.g. *How would you feel if you discovered that someone had stolen your brand-new car?* The main characteristics of a **report** are outlined below.

Elements of a report
Structure

- To arouse the reader's curiosity, reports have **headlines** containing basic information without providing too much detail.
- The basic information is generally provided in the first paragraph, which serves as an **introduction.**
- The **main body** of a report consists of different paragraphs, which contain one piece of information each.
- The last paragraph serves as a kind of **conclusion.**

Language and style

- A report is written in a factual style and neither reflects the author's personal opinion nor contains any kind of speculation.
- Individual paragraphs are relatively short and consist of short sentences, which aim to ensure that the reader understands the information presented.
- Experts – or people who have first-hand experience of the topic in question – are often quoted, but no authorial comment is given about what they say.

Glossary – Vocabulary for Analysing Reports

The report [title] written by [author] deals with / is about / relates / describes ...	Der Bericht [Titel] von [Verfasser] beschäftigt sich mit / handelt von / berichtet von / beschreibt ...
The theme(s) of the report is (are) ...	Das Thema / Die Themen des Berichts ist/sind ...
In the introduction the reader learns about / gets to know ...	In der Einleitung erfährt der Leser / die Leserin ...
The report can be divided into ... paragraphs.	Der Bericht kann in ... Absätze gegliedert werden.
The report consists of ... paragraphs.	Der Bericht besteht aus ... Absätzen.
It is the author's aim to inform the reader about ...	Es ist das Anliegen des Autors / der Autorin, den Leser / die Leserin über ... zu informieren.
The 2nd/3rd paragraph contains information on ...	Der 2./3. Absatz enthält Informationen über ...
The author quotes an eye-witness/expert who says that ...	Der Autor / Die Autorin zitiert einen Augenzeugen/Experten, der sagt, dass ...
The author describes how ...	Der Verfasser / Die Verfasserin beschreibt, wie ...
The author does not give his/her personal opinion on the subject/problem/question but merely relates facts.	Der Verfasser / Die Verfasserin äußert nicht seine/ihre eigene Meinung zum Sachverhalt / Problem / zu der Frage, sondern gibt Fakten wieder.
The factual style of writing shows that it is the author's aim to inform the reader and not to entertain him/her.	Der sachliche Sprachgebrauch verdeutlicht, dass es das Anliegen des Autors / der Autorin ist, die Lesenden zu informieren und nicht, sie zu unterhalten.

How to Deal with Cartoons, Diagrams and Statistics

Keywords:
Cartoons are visual images aimed at criticising, ridiculing or commenting on current events or ideas.
Diagrams and statistics: intend to present information by comparing different items and their relations to each other. Diagram types include pie charts, bar charts, tables and line graphs.
In written exams cartoons, diagrams and statistics will always be accompanied by a text.

Dealing with cartoons

Taking a closer look: What is shown?
Describe all the important elements of the cartoon in detail and point out the relation between them:
- start with the foreground and end with the background; of course, you can also proceed from top to bottom or from left to right, but make sure that your reader can easily follow your train of thought,
- indicate the key features of each object or character, including captions and speech bubbles.

Analysing the message: What is the cartoonist's intention?
Explain what the artist wants to express by
- examining the use of colours if the cartoon comes in colours,
- focusing on the relation of the objects and characters presented in the cartoon (e. g. size, situation and role within the cartoon),
- interpreting the meaning of the caption or speech bubble (if the cartoon has these features).
In written exams cartoons will not have to be analysed alone but always in combination with a text. Therefore, one should always pay close attention to the respective task.
It might also be necessary to consider the political, historical or social context and to refer to one's background knowledge.
Here it is also important to look at the task once more (What is the connection between cartoon and text?).

Evaluating the cartoon: Does the cartoonist get his/her message across?
Is the cartoon effective?
After having described and analysed the cartoon, you should evaluate whether it is effective or not. You are free to give your own opinion, but do not forget to give reasons for it.

Dealing with Diagrams and Statistics

Taking a closer look:
What is the diagram about? / What are the statistics about?
First state what kind of diagram (table, pie chart ...) you are describing and what it is about.
Diagrams or statistics usually come with a heading, which includes necessary information about what is being described, referred to or compared, as well as the source the information is taken from. Do not forget to mention this.

Analysing the diagram/statistics:
What can be concluded from the diagram/statistics?
Describe the relation between the different items (e.g. in bar charts and pie charts) and/or the development shown (e.g. in line graphs).
Then it is time to draw your conclusions from what is shown. In written exams you should also point out the connections between the diagram/statistics and the text.

Glossary – Vocabulary for Analysing Cartoons, Diagrams and Statistics

pie chart	Tortendiagramm
bar chart	Säulendiagramm
table	Tabelle
line graph	Kurvendiagramm
per cent / percentage	Prozent / prozentualer Anteil
The cartoon / pie chart shows / depicts / presents / is about ...	Der Cartoon / Das Tortendiagramm stellt ... dar / zeigt ... auf / handelt von ...
The cartoon/diagram is taken from ...	Der Cartoon / Das Diagramm stammt von/aus ...
The artist mainly uses light/bright/dark colours to achieve the desired effect.	Der/Die Künstler/-in verwendet überwiegend helle/strahlende/dunkle Farben, um den gewünschten Effekt zu erzielen.
The cartoonist wants the spectator to ...	Der/Die Karikaturist/-in möchte, dass der/die Betrachtende ...
The artist intends to ...	Der/Die Künstler/-in beabsichtigt ...
The message of the cartoon is that ...	Die Botschaft des Cartoons ist, dass ...
In the foreground/background of the cartoon one can see ...	Im Vorder-/Hintergrund des Cartoons kann man ... sehen.
In the top left-hand corner / in the bottom right-hand corner ... is shown.	In der linken oberen / der rechten unteren Ecke wird ... gezeigt/dargestellt.
The bar chart compares the development of ... and ...	Das Säulendiagramm vergleicht die Entwicklung von ... und ...

The pie chart is divided into ... slices, each slice representing ...	Das Tortendiagramm ist in ... Stücke aufgeteilt, von denen jedes ... darstellt.
Looking at the size of the different slices of the pie chart / at the height of the different bars of the bar chart, one can conclude that ...	Wenn man die Größe der verschiedenen Stücke des Tortendiagramms / die Höhe der verschiedenen Balken des Balkendiagramms betrachtet, kann man erkennen / darauf schließen, dass ...
The bar chart describes the relation between ... and ...	Das Säulendiagramm beschreibt die Beziehung zwischen ... und ...
The line graph shows the population development in ... from (month/year) to (month/year).	Das Kurvendiagramm stellt die Bevölkerungsentwicklung in ... von (Monat/Jahr) bis (Monat/Jahr) dar.
Over the period of time covered by the line graph, the population of ... increased/decreased from ... to ... / the number of inhabitants remained constant.	In dem Zeitraum, der durch das Kurvendiagramm abgedeckt wird, hat sich die Bevölkerung in ... von ... auf ... vergrößert/verrringert / ist die Zahl der Einwohner/-innen in ... gleich geblieben.
The horizontal axis of the line chart shows ..., while the vertical axis represents ...	Die horizontale Achse (x-Achse) des Kurvendiagramms zeigt ..., während die vertikale Achse (y-Achse) ... abbildet.
The number of ... in ... is compared in the pie chart / bar chart.	Das Tortendiagramm/Balkendiagramm vergleicht die Anzahl von ... in ...
All figures are given in per cent.	Alle Zahlen werden in Prozent angegeben.

Sprachmittlung

In der Aufgabe zur Sprachmittlung, werden Sie dazu angehalten, die wesentlichen Inhalte von authentischen deutschen Texten sinngemäß und zusammenfassend in englischer Sprache wiederzugeben. Dabei ist es wichtig, dass Sie darauf achten, Ihren Text zielgruppengerecht und situationsangemessen zu verfassen.

Eine Sprachmittlungsaufgabe gibt immer eine fiktive Situation vor, die eine Mittlung des deutschen Ausgangstextes verlangt. Im Gegensatz zu einer Übersetzung, die die wörtliche Übertragung eines Textes in die andere Sprache mitsamt aller möglicherweise vorhandenen Untertöne, Bildhaftigkeit, Ironie etc. erfordert, geht es bei der Sprachmittlung nur um die sinngemäße Übertragung in die Fremdsprache.

Je nach Aufgabenstellung geht es entweder um eine Zusammenfassung des Textes, häufiger jedoch um das „Herauspicken" relevanter Informationen. Die Methodik für die inhaltliche Bearbeitung der Aufgabe gleicht also der Methodik für die Erstellung von Inhaltsangaben.

Beim Schreiben des englischen Textes berücksichtigt man die verschiedenen Aspekte der Sprachmittlung, wie sie hier in einer Übersicht dargestellt werden:[1]

sinngemäß	– keine wortwörtliche Übersetzung – keine Übernahme von Stilmitteln oder Ton – ggf. implizierte Inhalte – nur die Inhalte des Textes, kein eigenes Wissen
situationsangemessen	– angemessener Stil – Beachtung der vorgegebenen Textform
zielgruppengerecht	– passendes Register (Freund? Professor? Gastmutter?) – Erläuterung von sprachlichen und kulturellen Eigenheiten[1]
zusammenfassend	– wesentliche Inhalte – ggf. wesentliche Details – nicht detailliert – nicht kommentiert (d. h. keine eigene Meinung)

TIPP zum Punktesammeln

Beachten Sie – wie immer – genau die Aufgabenstellung! Anders als bei der kreativen Teilaufgabe im Klausurteil zu Schreiben/Leseverstehen müssen Sie möglicherweise nicht den kompletten Zieltext erstellen, sondern nur den Teil, den die Sprachmittlung ausmacht. So kann die Aufgabenstellung z. B. lauten: "Write the part of your email that is based on …" oder "Write the part of your article that deals with …".

---

[1] Viele Eigennamen oder Konnotationen werden sich dem fremdsprachlichen Adressaten nicht erschließen. Sie bedürfen daher einer Erklärung oder Umschreibung (z. B. *Rosenmontag, Abigag, BILD-Zeitung*).

Zieltextformate

In der anwendungs-/produktionsorientierten Teilaufgabe *re-creation of text* des Klausurteils Schreiben/Leseverstehen werden die in diesem Kapitel behandelten Textformate vorausgesetzt:

- *letter/email, letter to the editor*
- *speech script: talk, public/formal speech, debate statement*
- *newspaper/internet article, blog entry*
- nur im Leistungskurs: *(written) interview*
- Ausgestaltung, Fortführung oder Ergänzung eines literarischen Ausgangstextes: narrative Texte; zusätzlich im Leistungskurs: dramatische Texte, *film script*

In der Sprachmittlung wird Vertrautheit mit den folgenden Zieltextformaten vorausgesetzt:

- *letter/email*
- *newspaper/internet article, blog entry*

Letter/Email

Formal Letter (förmlicher Brief)
Äußere Form
Adresse:
- eigene Adresse: anders als in Deutschland oben rechts, üblicherweise ohne Namen
- Empfänger: darunter auf der linken Seite

Datum:
unter der Anschrift entweder rechts oder links, Monat als Wort

persönlich bekannter Empfänger:
Anrede:
Dear Mr/Mrs/Miss/Ms/Dr/Professor/...
(Ms ist die neutrale Form, um *Mrs* bzw. *Miss* zu umgehen)

Schlussformel:
Yours sincerely / Kind regards

unbekannter Empfänger:
Anrede:
Dear Sir / Dear Madam,
Dear Sir or Madam,

Schlussformel:
Yours faithfully

Unterschrift:
– persönliche Unterschrift
– darunter Name in Druckschrift

Inhaltliche Gliederung

Einleitung:
Bezug und Zweck des Briefes

Hauptteil:
relevante Informationen, klar und logisch dargelegt, keine Schnörkel und Abschweifungen

Ende:
Erwartung an den Empfänger, üblicherweise als Bitte oder Aufforderung

Sprache
förmlich, **keine** *informal language*, d. h. **vermeiden** Sie
– *short forms* wie *it's, would've, can't*
– Interjektionen und Füllwörter wie *well, alright, okay, I see, you know*
– *question tags (isn't it, don't you, etc.)*

Benutzen Sie Wendungen wie
– *With reference to your letter of May 13th …*
– *Thank you for your letter of …*

– *I am writing to apply / to enquire about / to inform you / to lodge a complaint regarding …*
– *I should be delighted if …*
– *I would be very glad if …*
– *It would be very convenient if …*
– *Please find enclosed …* (In der Anlage finden Sie …)

– *I should very much appreciate it if …*
– *Please note that …*

– *Thank you very much in advance.*

Die Regeln für die äußere Form gelten für eine E-Mail nicht. Die Form wird ja im Browser oder Client vorgegeben. Sprachlich gelten dieselben Regeln.

Letter to the Editor (Leserbrief)

Ein Leserbrief ist eher ein Zeitungsartikel als ein förmlicher Brief.
Zur sprachlichen und inhaltlichen Gestaltung siehe *Comment* (S. 109).

Äußere Form

Anrede:
Sir, oder *Madam,* – kein *Dear* (gilt nicht bei einer Schülerzeitung)

Unterschrift:
Name, Stadt, ggf. Land/US-Staat

Personal Letter (persönlicher Brief)

Äußere Form

Adresse und Datum:
– eigene Adresse: anders als in Deutschland oben rechts, üblicherweise ohne Namen
– Datum darunter

Anrede:
Dear …

Schlussformel:
Yours (nicht: *your*) / *Best wishes* / *All the best* / *(Lots of) Love* (nicht: *in love*) / *Your friend …*

Unterschrift:
Vorname

Inhaltliche Gliederung

Einleitung:
Bezug zum Ausgangstext, Grund des Schreibens

Hauptteil:
z. B. Erzählung, Erklärung, Erläuterung, relevante Informationen

Ende:
z. B. Fragen, Vorschläge, Ausblick

Sprache
– freundlicher Ton
– *informal language*, d. h.:
  – *short forms* wie *it's, would've, can't*
  – Interjektionen und Füllwörter wie *well, alright, okay, I see, you know*

- *question tags (isn't it, don't you* etc.*)*
- weitgehend einfache Satzgefüge
- Alltagsvokabular, thematisches Vokabular

Speech Script (Rede)

Denkbar – und in den vergangenen Jahren im Abitur als kreative Teilaufgabe vorge-kommen – sind verschiedene Formen der Rede wie *talk* (Vortrag), *public/formal speech* (öffentliche/formelle Rede) oder *statement* (Erklärung).

Talk (Vortrag)

Einleitung:
- Begrüßung der Zuhörerschaft
- ggf. Vorstellung der eigenen Person
- Anknüpfung an den Ausgangstext
- Zusammenfassung von Inhalt und Zielen des Vortrags
- ggf. vorgesehene Gliederung

Hauptteil:
richtet sich nach dem Zweck des Vortrages:
- etwas mitteilen
- Interesse für ein Thema wecken
- für Publikation, Produkt, Dienstleistung werben
- einen Standpunkt verteidigen
- Zuhörer überzeugen
- Diskussion anregen

Strukturieren Sie ihren Hauptteil inhaltlich stringent! Ein inhaltlicher Aspekt folgt dem anderen, Argumente und Beispiele unterstreichen die einzelnen Aspekte.

Ende:
- Zusammenfassung
- Appell
- Ausblick
- Dank an die Zuhörer

Public/Formal Speech

Die öffentliche Rede ist meist politischer Art und dient der Überzeugung der Zuhörerschaft.

Einleitung:
weniger sachlich als der Vortrag, d. h.:
- keine Zusammenfassung von Inhalt und Zielen
- keine Vorstellung der Gliederung
- keine persönliche Vorstellung

Begrüßung der Zuhörer
- Anknüpfung an den Ausgangstext
- provokative oder plakative Hinführung zum Thema
- Problemstellung (und evtl. Lösung in Aussicht stellen)

Hauptteil:
- klare Argumentation
- Kausalketten beachten
- Belege durch logische Argumente, Beispiele, Expertenmeinungen, Verweis auf Autoritäten (Regierung, Kirche, Wissenschaft)

Ende:
- Zusammenfassung
- Appell

Statement

Ein Statement wird gewöhnlich im Vorfeld einer Debatte abgegeben, um die Fronten zu klären. Ziel eines Statements ist es, einen Standpunkt zu verteidigen oder gar die Zuhörenden zu überzeugen. So wird es den objektiven Ton eines Vortrages mit den Zielen der öffentlichen Rede verbinden.

Anrede:
Unbedingt der vorgegebenen Situation anpassen, z. B.
- *Dear Students / Dear Listeners / Dear Members of ... (talk)*
- *Fellow Citizens / Friends / Dear Citizens of ... (public speech)*
- *Ladies and Gentlemen*
- bei Anwesenheit hochrangiger Personen oder auch nur Gastgeberinnen/Gastgebern:
  Mr President / Your Majesty / Prime Minister / Mr Chairman / Mr Jones

Hinführung:
- plakative Aussagesätze
- weitgehend einfache Satzgefüge
- Fragen

public speech:
- rhetorische Fragen
- Anspielungen
- Ironie

Hauptteil:
talk/statement:
- klare, weitgehend einfache Aussagesätze
- sachlicher, objektiver Stil

public speech:
emphatische Mittel: Parallelismen, Aufzählungen, Wiederholungen
(s. „Methoden der Textarbeit", S. 78 ff.)

Ende:
appellative Strukturen:
- *We must / We have to / We should ...*
- *It is imperative that ...*
- *Let us ...*

> **TIPP** zum Punktesammeln
>
> Überfrachten Sie Ihre Rede nicht mit Metaphern und emphatischen Mitteln! Das kann albern wirken.

Dank:
- *Thank you.*
- *Thank you for your attention.*

Newspaper Article / Internet Article

Report

Ein *report* ist ein Bericht beziehungsweise ein objektiver, sachlicher Artikel, dem eine Begebenheit oder eine Geschichte zugrunde liegt. Damit handelt es sich um einen narrativen Text. Sie können einen *report* in einer kreativen Aufgabe erwarten, wann immer eine Geschichte zu erzählen ist, insbesondere dann, wenn der Ausgangstext gerade kein Zeitungsartikel ist.
Dramen oder Gedichte bieten häufig Stoff als Grundlage für einen Bericht.

Beachten Sie die Merkmale eines Berichtes, wie sie im Kapitel „Methoden der Textarbeit" zusammengefasst werden (S. 97 f.).

Comment

Ein *comment* ist die Textform, die Sie besonders häufig als Sachtextvorlage Ihrer Analyseaufgabe finden. Als kreative Aufgabe sind verschiedene *comments* vorstellbar:

- ein Artikel aus Ihrer persönlichen Sicht
- ein Artikel aus der persönlichen Sicht einer Figur des Ausgangstextes
- ein Artikel aus der persönlichen Sicht des lyrischen Ichs eines lyrischen Ausgangstextes
- ein Artikel aus der persönlichen Sicht einer Figur aus Werken, die Sie im Unterricht behandelt haben

Sollten Sie die Aufgabe mit engem Bezug zum Ausgangstext gewählt haben, so stellen Sie sicher, dass Sie Ihre Erkenntnisse aus den Teilaufgaben 1 und 2 heranziehen, um die Aufgabe optimal zu lösen! Der Schlüssel zu Ihrer persönlichen Stellungnahme, aber auch zur fiktiven Person einer Verfasserin bzw. eines Verfassers und deren/dessen persönlicher Meinung liegt genau darin.

Sprache und Aufbau

Beachten Sie die Merkmale eines Essays, wie sie im Kapitel „Methoden der Textarbeit" (s. S. 95 f.) zusammengefasst werden! Für den Sprachgebrauch orientieren Sie sich an der Rhetorik der öffentlichen Rede (s. S. 91–95)!

(Written) Interview (nur LK)

Auch im Interview geht es um eine persönliche Stellungnahme, allerdings nicht um Ihre persönliche Meinung, sondern um die eines fiktiven Gesprächspartners.

> **Achtung, häufiger Fehler:**
> Schreiben Sie nur in Dialogform! Schreiben Sie keinen Erzähltext, in dem wörtliche Rede nur anteilig enthalten ist!

Struktur

Beginn:
- Aufnahme der situativen Vorgabe der Aufgabenstellung
- Begrüßung, Vorstellung
- Anknüpfung an den Ausgangstext
- Hinführung zum Thema, ggf. Vorstellung des Anliegens

Hauptteil:
- Frage/Antwort in sinnvoller Verknüpfung
- Argumente und Beispiele

Schluss:
- Abrundung, z. B.:
  - Zusammenfassung
  - Witz
  - Ausblick
    - Dank
    - Verabschiedung

Sprache
- freundlicher Ton
- *informal language*, d.h.:
  - *short forms* wie *isn't, I'm, should've*
  - Interjektionen und Füllwörter wie *well, alright, okay, I see, you know*
  - *question tags (isn't it, don't you* etc.)
  - weitgehend einfache Satzgefüge
- Alltagsvokabular, thematisches Vokabular

- rhetorische Mittel: Wiederholungen, Aufzählungen, Anaphern, aber keine ausgefeilten Stilfiguren
- Grußformel: *Good morning/afternoon/evening Mr/Mrs Jones / Sir / Ma'am*
- Schlussformel: z. B. *Thank you for your time, goodbye ..., Thank you very much for the interview. Goodbye ...*

Literarische Texte

Narrative Texte

Im Abitur werden Ihnen narrative Ausgangstexte meist als Roman- oder Kurzgeschichtenauszug begegnen. Folgende Varianten einer kreativen Aufgabenstellung sind denkbar:

- Lücken füllen (d.h. Begebenheiten, die im Ausgangstext nur erwähnt werden oder die der/die Lesende nur aus dem Handlungsverlauf erschließen kann, sollen kreativ ausgestaltet werden),
- ein Ende oder eine Fortsetzung schreiben,
- ein alternatives Ende schreiben,
- Perspektivwechsel.

Übernehmen Sie – falls die Aufgabenstellung es nicht ausdrücklich anders verlangt – die Erzählperspektive des Ausgangstextes!
Beachten Sie, dass Figuren sich weiterhin so verhalten, wie es ihrem Charakter entspricht, auch in ihrer Sprache!

> Schreiben Sie keine neue Story mit einem vollständigen *plot* und einem neuen Höhepunkt. Es geht nicht um die Erfindung einer spannenden oder besonders originellen Handlung, sondern um eine logisch-konsequente Ausgestaltung des Ausgangstextes.

Sprache

Übernehmen Sie, soweit es geht, den Stil des Ausgangstextes.

Übernehmen Sie das Tempus des Ausgangstextes. In der Regel werden narrative Texte im *past tense* erzählt. Beachten Sie die Tempora der Vergangenheit.

Beispiel:
*The ground **was** wet because it **had been raining** all morning and although the rain **had stopped** and the sun **was shining** now, it **would be** difficult to find the track. On dry ground it **would have been** easy.*

was wet – Erzähltempus
it had been raining – vorzeitig; andauernd bis hin zum Erzählzeitpunkt; Betonung der Dauer/Kontinuität einer Situation
had stopped – vorzeitig; Situation zum Erzählzeitpunkt abgeschlossen; Betonung der Beendigung / des Effekts einer Situation
was shining – gerade ablaufende Hintergrundhandlung
it would be difficult – Zukunft aus der Sicht der Vergangenheit
it would have been easy – reine Hypothese in der Vergangenheit

Wechsel der Textform

Sollte die Aufgabenstellung eine vollständige Erzählung z. B. auf der Grundlage eines Gedichtes oder eines Zeitungsartikels verlangen, so achten Sie auf einen plausiblen inhaltlichen Bezug. Für die Ausgestaltung Ihrer Erzählung beachten Sie die Erzählelemente, wie sie im Kapitel „Methoden der Textarbeit" (S. 78–83) vorgestellt werden.

Dramatische Texte (Schauspiel / Film)

Folgende Varianten einer kreativen Aufgabenstellung sind denkbar:
Bei einem dramatischen Ausgangstext:
- Lücken füllen (d. h. Begebenheiten, die im Ausgangstext nur erwähnt werden, sollen kreativ ausgestaltet werden)
- ein Ende oder eine Fortsetzung schreiben
- ein alternatives Ende schreiben

Bei anderen Ausgangstexten (z. B. Erzählung, Zeitungsartikel, Gedicht):
- Wechsel der Textform

Beachten Sie, dass Figuren sich so verhalten, wie es ihrem Charakter entspricht, auch in ihrer Sprache.

Sprache
Dialogtext:
- gesprochene Sprache, d. h.
  - *short forms* wie *isn't, I'm, should've*
  - Interjektionen und Füllwörter wie *well, alright, okay, I see, you know*
  - *question tags (isn't it, don't you* etc.*)*
  - weitgehend einfache Satzgefüge
- Alltagsvokabular, thematisches Vokabular

stage directions:
- in Klammern
- stichpunktartig
- *present tense*

Achtung, häufiger Fehler!
Erzählen Sie keine Geschichte mit wörtlicher Rede! Schreiben Sie ein Bühnenstück mit Dialogen und Regieanweisungen!

Hörverstehen

Beispielaufgabe 1: „Do We Need a Monarchy?"

Thematischer Bezug gemäß KLP (Soziokulturelles Orientierungswissen):
Das Vereinigte Königreich im 21. Jahrhundert – Selbstverständnis zwischen Tradition und Moderne: *Tradition and change in politics and society – the UK in the European context*

Quellenangaben:
"The Today Debate: Do we need a monarchy?", *BBC Sounds*, 25 April 2023, https://www.bbc.co.uk/sounds/play/p0fjs1j8 (00:05–03:55) (accessed on 1 April 2024)

You can listen to the audio file by scanning this QR code:

Aufgabe

You will hear a radio programme called *Best of Today,* dealing with the future of the royal family. While listening, tick the right answer (a, b, c or d). Do not tick more than one answer. You will hear the recording twice. You have two minutes to look at the task. You will have 30 seconds to finalise your answers after the second listening.

1. The host wonders whether
a) we should celebrate the coronation of the king. ☐
b) historical periods should be named after their monarchs. ☐
c) the monarchy links us to our past. ☐
d) royal children are strange. ☐

2. The audience
a) are invited to join in the debate. ☐
b) didn't know what the topic of the debate would be. ☐
c) boo some of the people on the stage. ☐
d) had to book their places far in advance. ☐

3. Billy Bragg doesn't regard himself as
a) a left-winger. ☐
b) an anti-monarchist. ☐
c) a Republican. ☐
d) an anti-Republican. ☐

4. Juliet Samual points to the beauty of the monarchy in
a) the symbolism of the rose and the thistle. ☐
b) the allegory "The Pilgrim's Progress". ☐

c) the painting of the unicorn and the magician. ☐
d) every-day experiences such as traffic jams and call centres. ☐

5. What has the *Guardian* recently been investigating?
a) the uselessness of the British monarchy ☐
b) the power of the monarchy ☐
c) fake stories about the British monarchy ☐
d) the wealth of the British monarchy ☐

6. Charles Moore claims that Queen Elizabeth was a role model for
a) good management. ☐
b) ceremony. ☐
c) leadership. ☐
d) restraint. ☐

7. What topic does Jason Arday not work on?
a) education ☐
b) gender ☐
c) race ☐
d) inequality ☐

8. According to Jason Arday, Britain doesn't need a monarchy because
a) some aspects are not appropriate any more. ☐
b) it is useless in 21st-century society. ☐
c) it isn't affordable any more. ☐
d) it doesn't make a difference in today's society. ☐

Lösung

1. c	2. b	3. c	4. a
5. d	6. c	7. b	8. c

Beispielaufgabe 2: „How to Survive the Digital Age"

Thematischer Bezug gemäß KLP (Soziokulturelles Orientierungswissen):   Medien in ihrer Bedeutung für den Einzelnen und die Gesellschaft: *The impact of the media – information, entertainment, manipulation*   Fortschritt und Ethik in der modernen Gesellschaft: *Ethical issues of scientific and technological progress*
Quellenangaben: „BBC Trending: How to survive the digital age", *YouTube*, 2 July 2019, https://www. youtube.com/watch?v=l-ZJNGuEP4U (01:10–04:37) (accessed on 1 April 2024)

You can listen to the audio file by scanning this QR code:

Aufgabe

You will hear a podcast dealing with recent technological developments and the rise of social media. While listening, complete the table below. Write your answers in the boxes. You do not have to write complete sentences. There is one example answer (0). You will hear the recording twice. You have 90 seconds to look at the table. You will have 2 minutes to finalise your answers after the second listening.

0	Douglas Rushkoff can be called ...	*an intellectual of the digital world.*
1	"Team Human" is a book about what Rushkoff calls ...	
2	Rushkoff wrote his book after ...	
3	Other scientists argue that human beings had to accept that ...	
4	In what way are humans special, according to Rushkoff? (Give two examples)	*a)* *b)*
5	According to Rushkoff, human beings get their power from ...	
6	Rushkoff fears that the digital world we are creating ...	
7	The problem for social media companies was that ...	
8	In order to grow fast enough, social media companies ...	

Lösung

1. anti-human machinery.
2. he spoke on a panel (with a famous transhumanist).
3. we will be succeeded by technology.
4. social; able to deal with ambiguity and paradox; able to experience liminal/transitional states
5. connecting with one another.
6. isolates us. / prevents us from connecting with each other.
7. they needed too much money.
8. became manipulative. / manipulated their users.

Beispielaufgabe 3: „Plastic Fantastic"

Thematischer Bezug gemäß KLP (Soziokulturelles Orientierungswissen):
Chancen und Risiken der Globalisierung: Ecological challenges and sustainable life-styles   Globale Herausforderungen und Zukunftsvisionen: Globalisation and global challenges – *economic, ecological and political issues*
Quellenangaben:
"Plastic Fantastic: What's the Solution", *BBC Sounds,* 29 May 2018, https://www.bbc.co.uk/sounds/play/b0b42z8k (01:11–05:05) (accessed on 1 April 2024)

You can listen to the audio file by scanning this QR code:

Aufgabe

You will hear a podcast dealing with the topic of solutions to the plastic pollution. While listening, complete the table below. Write down your answers in the boxes. You do not have to write complete sentences. There is one example answer (0). You will hear the recording twice. You have 90 seconds to look at the table. You will have 2 minutes to finalise your answers after the second listening.

1	Why it is not realistic to go plastic-free?	
2	More environmentally friendly forms of plastic currently aren't a good solution because …	
3	Plastic bottles shouldn't be recycled but …	
4	The government is discussing the introduction of …	
5	Which two economic systems is Purnell talking about?	
6	What is the key aspect of the economy Purnell wants to transition to?	
7	The main problem of designers is that they feel …	

Lösung

1. Because everything around us is plastic.
2. we don't have the right infrastructure. / it isn't recycled/composted properly.
3. reused.
4. a deposit return scheme for bottles.

5. linear and circular
6. Products return to the value they had before they were used.
7. that they have no sense of responsibility.

Mediation

Beispielaufgabe 1: „Warum finden alle Berlin so toll – außer den Berlinern?"

Thematischer Bezug gemäß KLP (Soziokulturelles Orientierungswissen):
allgemeiner lebensweltlicher Bezug

Quellenangaben:
Lorenz Maroldt, „Image der deutschen Hauptstadt. Warum finden alle Berlin so toll – außer den Berlinern?", *Tagesspiegel*, Berlin, 22.04.2018, https://www.tagesspiegel.de/berlin/image-der-deutschen-hauptstadt-warum-finden-alle-berlin-so-toll-ausser-den-berlinern/21200348.html (Zugriff: 01.04.2024, gekürzt) (534 W.)

Aufgabe

During an exchange visit at an English school, you are doing an e-zine project in class on views people hold on various metropolises in the world. Your class comes across many English articles on Berlin. You are asked to write a short article for the e-zine on what an insider's view on Berlin is like. Write your article based on Maroldt's article.

Image der deutschen Hauptstadt. Warum finden alle Berlin so toll – außer den Berlinern? *Lorenz Maroldt*

Exzellent organisiert, erschwinglich, cool: Eine neue Begeisterung für die deutsche Hauptstadt wächst in der Welt. In Berlin dagegen überwiegt der Ärger über alltägliche Mängel. Wie passt das zusammen?

Kaum zu fassen, was da gerade so alles über Berlin geschrieben wird, vor allem in Großbritannien und den USA. Das soll unsere Stadt sein? Wir zwängen uns in übervolle Busse, quälen uns durch den Schienenersatzverkehr, lernen auf dem Bahnsteig wartend immer neue Arten von Betriebsstörungen bei der S-Bahn kennen – und lesen in der Londoner „Times": „Excellent public transport." What?

Wir erleben stark steigende Mieten und Wohnungspreise, spüren den Druck von Immobilienspekulanten, fürchten, uns die eigene Stadt nicht mehr leisten zu können – und bekommen gesagt: „Berlin is very affordable". Really?

Wir wissen nicht, wohin mit den Kindern, stehen vor gesperrten Spielplätzen, hören, dass stadtweit 500 davon demoliert sind – und lesen sprachlos in der „New York Times": „Berlin is a playground paradise." Wir stolpern über wild abgestellten Sperrmüll, lesen von Rattenalarm in heruntergekommenen Häusern, erkennen unter Tonnen von Tüten, Pappen und Flaschen

117

nach den Wochenenden unsere Parks nicht mehr – und lassen uns von New Yorks Ex-Bürgermeister Rudy Giuliani sagen: „Berlin ist eine sehr saubere Stadt."

Die Stadt ist nicht die aus den Netflix-Serien

Haben wir, die ewigen Nörgler, eine Wahrnehmungsstörung? Finden wir nicht heraus aus unserer folkloristischen Meckerattitüde? Oder übersehen die Gäste bei ihren Stippvisiten, berauscht von was auch immer, was hier wirklich läuft – oder vielmehr: was nicht? Verwechseln sie gar die echte Stadt mit der, die in Serien von Sky, Netflix und Amazon in mehr als hundert Ländern der Welt gezeigt wird? Allein die Zahl der in Berlin lebenden US-Amerikaner ist in den vergangenen zwei Jahren um 9,6 Prozent gestiegen. 46.600 sind es jetzt, dazu kommen noch die Botschaftsangehörigen.

Auch der Blick von außen aufs große Ganze verblüfft. Im „Economist" erscheint unter dem Titel „Cool Germany" eine Hymne auf unser Land, das doch eigentlich erschöpft ist: von der Pflege-, Diesel- und Flüchtlingskrise, der quälenden Regierungsbildung, vom Aufmarsch der Rechtspopulisten, der außenpolitischen Orientierungslosigkeit. Aber auf dem Titel der „Times" steht, zu einem Bild der Hauptstadt Berlin: „A Titan of Europe".

Schließen wir mal aus, dass es eine virtuelle Parallelwelt gibt, die Berlins Stadt-marketingprofis bei Bedarf präsentieren. Woran liegt es dann, dass andere so begeistert sind von diesem Ort, Ordnung loben, wo wir Chaos sehen, Modernität erkennen, wo wir mit der Verwaltung nur analog in Kontakt treten können? Dass sie unsere Internationalität so anziehend finden, aber wir einen polyglotten belgischen Theaterintendanten nicht mal ein Jahr lang ertragen können?

[...]

In Berlin erleben wir das weitgehend klassenlose Zusammenleben zwar als spannend, aber auch als Anstrengung. Wir sind stolz auf unsere Toleranz, aber die ist stressfrei kaum zu haben. Andererseits stimmt ja auch: Wenn hier alles nur so schrecklich wäre, wie wir uns oft gegenseitig in geselliger Runde versichern, wären wir längst woanders. Die Kunst, das Theater, die Musik, Bars und Restaurants, Markthallen, die Food-Szene, relaxen an den Ufern der Spree und den zwei großen Seen – so ertragen wir das Bürgeramt, die Verkehrslenkung. Und wer an das Londoner U-Bahnnetz gewöhnt ist, wo das Schild „No Service on Victoria Line" zur Ausstattung gehört, oder die maroden, unzuverlässigen New Yorker Züge kennt, empfindet das Angebot der BVG schon eher nachvollziehbar als „excellent", relativ gesehen.

[...]

Bearbeitungsschritte und Beispiellösung

Vergegenwärtigen Sie sich die Prinzipien der Sprachmittlung, wie wir sie auf Seite 101 dargestellt haben. Für den vorliegenden Text beachten wir konkret:

Zieltext: *Article* (vgl. Zieltextformate, S. 108 ff.)
Für eine knappe Wiedergabe gehen Sie wie bei einer Zusammenfassung vor. Der Text ist bereits vorstrukturiert – fassen Sie nur noch die einzelnen Aspekte zusammenfassen:

- die positive Sicht auf die Stadt in der angloamerikanischen Presse hinsichtlich ÖPNV, Lebenshaltungskosten, Kinderfreundlichkeit und Sauberkeit;
- die Reflexion, ob die Wahrnehmung der Berliner/-innen oder jene der Besucher/-innen gestört ist: Berliner/-innen als notorische Meckerer, Reisende, die die wahren Zustände übersehen, Beeinflussung durch Netflix etc.;
- der verblüffend positive Blick auf Deutschland als *cool Germany* und *Titan of Europe,* ungeachtet der derzeitigen Krisen: Pflegenotstand, Flüchtlingskrise, Dieselskandal, Rechtsextremismus, Regierungsbildung, außenpolitische Orientierungslosigkeit;
- die Erklärung, die die Klagen der Einheimischen relativiert: Unzulänglichkeiten bei Infrastruktur und Verwaltung werden wettgemacht durch Kunst, Theater, Musik; Gastronomie; Flair; Entspannung an Fluss und Seen; einen Vergleich des Berliner ÖPNV mit den U-Bahnen in New York und London.

Zielgruppenorientiertung

In Ihrer fiktiven Situation als Teilnehmer/-in an einem Kurs in einer englischen Schule müssen Sie dafür sorgen, dass Ihr Artikel zielgruppengerecht gestaltet wird. Wörter wie „Schienenersatzverkehr" oder „Betriebsstörungen", die wir unweigerlich mit nervigem Bus- und Bahnfahren assoziieren, müssen angemessen umschrieben werden beziehungsweise am besten in einer verallgemeinerten Beschreibung aufgehen. Das gleiche gilt für „ewige Nörgler", „Wahrnehmungsstörung" und „folkloristische Meckerattitüde". Einer kurzen Erklärung bedürfen die politischen Anspielungen, weil eine bloße Übersetzung den fiktiven britischen Mitschülern nichts sagen würde. Einer Erklärung bedarf wohl nicht das Wort „Food-Szene". Ganz schlecht ist eine Übernahme eines Wortes in Anführungsstrichen (z. B. „BVG"). Anführungsstriche helfen des Deutschen unkundigen Menschen gar nicht beim Verständnis.

Hier eine mögliche Umsetzung:

<u>Views on Berlin</u>

It's astonishing how positive the view on Berlin is in the British and American Press. We read about "excellent transport" in The Times, whereas Berliners feel that buses are crammed and many trains do not run for all kinds of reasons. It is said that "Berlin is very affordable", whereas Berliners feel that due to rising rents and property prices, they can't afford their own city anymore.

The "New York Times" writes that Berlin is a "playground paradise", whereas Berliners experience more and more closed-down and vandalised playgrounds, and the former mayor of New York, Rudy Giuliani, calls Berlin a clean city, whereas Berliners hear of houses full of rats and see their streets and parks full of rubbish.

So, whose perception is skewed? Do Berliners notoriously complain about everything or are the visitors so impressed by whatever aspect that they don't see the downsides? Or is the image influenced by the way Berlin is presented by series on Netflix, Sky or Amazon? Even Germany as a whole is presented as "cool Germany" or the "Titan of Europe" despite a catastrophic shortage of hospital staff, the arrival of many refugees from the Middle East and fierce controversy on their acceptance, a worldwide scandal on manipulated Diesel cars, a renaissance of the extreme right and a government seemingly unfit to rule.

Yet, it's true, Berlin cannot be that terrible. Otherwise, people would have left. What makes up for administrative failure and insufficient infrastructure is the large variety of theatre, art and music events, pubs and restaurants, market halls and the food scene as well as the river and the lakes, where people can relax. Even the public transport system is not too bad, if you compare it to London or New York.

Beispielaufgabe 2: „Von Geburt an Multikulturalist"

Thematischer Bezug gemäß KLP (Soziokulturelles Orientierungswissen):
Das Vereinigte Königreich im 21. Jahrhundert – Selbstverständnis zwischen Tradition und Moderne: *Tradition and change in politics and society – the UK in the European context*
Chancen und Risiken der Globalisierung: *Globalisation and global challenges: economic, ecological and political issues*

Quellenangaben:
Tanja Dückers, „Von Geburt an Multikulturalist", *ZEIT online,* Hamburg, 06.02.2015, http://www.zeit.de/gesellschaft/zeitgeschehen/2015-02/europa-identitaet-migrationeinwanderung/komplettansicht (Zugriff: 01.04.2024, gekürzt) (497 W.)

Aufgabe

At your British host school, notions like "freedom", "independence" and "identity" used by Brexiteers are irritating you. You strongly agree with the view on European identity Tanja Dückers puts forward in *ZEITonline*. Write a short article for the school magazine based on Tanja Dückers's article.

Von Geburt an Multikulturalist *Tanja Dückers*

[...]

Was Europa derzeit fehlt, ist ein neuer Identitätsbegriff. Bislang haben wir unsere europäische Identität in erster Linie über Abgrenzung konstruiert: Wir sind nicht wie die Amerikaner, die Russen oder die Afrikaner. Statt sich zu einer Identität zu bekennen, haben sich Europäer nur gegen andere Nationen, Kulturen und zum Teil auch pauschal gegen nicht-christliche Religionen gerichtet.

Erinnern wir uns nur an die peinliche Leitkultur-Debatte. Sie hat es Migranten nicht leicht gemacht, sich diesem merkwürdigen, sich ständig selbst spiegelnden Goethe-und-Dieter-Bohlen-Land in der Mitte Europas zugehörig zu fühlen. Dabei wurden Trennlinien zwischen Christen und Muslimen gezogen, ungeachtet der Tatsache, dass in Deutschland mittlerweile fast die Hälfte der Menschen keiner der beiden großen christlichen Kirchen angehört. In Berlin leben mehr Muslime als Katholiken.

Viele Menschen beklagen zwar, dass die Binnenkräfte, die Europa zusammenhalten, vor allem ökonomischer Natur seien. Sie haben aber, nach ihrem Identitätsverständnis von Europa befragt, selber wenig zu bieten. Dass die Europäer sich schwer damit tun, eine europäische Identität festzulegen, ist verständlich. Zu viele Einflüsse haben historisch den Kontinent geprägt.

Der Kontinent war zwar schon immer geprägt von regem Handel und Austausch – aber auch von vielen Kriegen. Es gibt keine Region in der Welt, in der so viele von der Fläche her kleine Länder eng beieinanderliegen und keine, deren Geographie so kleinteilig und ineinandergreifend ist. Europa müsste sich jetzt auf seinen Platz in der Welt als Drehkreuz zwischen Ost und West berufen.

Denn Europa kann sich eigentlich nur als regen Marktplatz der Welt, als Vielvölkerstaat mit zahllosen kulturellen, linguistischen und ökonomischen Verbindungen zur außereuropäischen Welt verstehen. Der Europäer ist, wenn er diese Offenheit zulässt, qua Geburt ein Multikulturalist. Es war der kürzlich verstorbene deutsche Soziologe Ulrich Beck, der als einer der ersten den Europäer als Kosmopolit gedacht hat. Doch für Beck bedeutete Europa nicht das Ende der alten Nationalstaaten. Das neue Europa könne vielmehr das alte in sich bergen und zugleich sanft verändern.

Das eine – die transnationale Identität – schließt nämlich das andere – die Herkunftsidentität – nicht aus. Mit dieser Einsicht können wir die große Angst vor einem transnationalen Identitätsbegriff besiegen, die in vielen Regionen Europas geschürt wird, erst recht vor einem, der außereuropäische Fremde miteinschließt. Die Angst ist verständlich, denn es scheint zunächst schwer vorstellbar, dass die Erweiterung eines Identitätsbegriffs nicht gleichzeitig einem Verlust an anderer Stelle gleichkommt.

Berlinerin, Atheistin, Europäerin

Unsere Aufgabe ist es deshalb, einen facettenreichen, multidimensionalen Identitätsbegriff zu etablieren. Einer Identität, die sich gleichwertig aus einem nahen Herkunftsbereich („Berlinerin") speist, einer soziokulturellen und religiösen Zugehörigkeit („atheistische Schriftstellerin") und einem geographisch weitergefassten Bereich („Zugehörigkeit zu einem sich als heterogenes Staatengebilde verstehenden Europa"). Was bislang eher als exkludierend empfunden wurde, könnte in Zukunft integrierend verstanden werden. Wenn europäische Bürger sagen: Ich stamme aus einem Kontinent, in dem ich nicht nur jeden Tag Deutsch höre, nicht nur Nachbarn mit meiner Hautfarbe habe. Zu meiner Identität gehört es dazu, mehrere Sprachen zu sprechen und viele Sprachen ein wenig zu verstehen.

Ich lebe in einem Kontinent, der sich dem keineswegs toten, sondern von 500 Millionen Menschen täglich gelebten Multikulturalismus verschrieben hat.

Bearbeitungsschritte und Beispiellösung

Vergegenwärtigen Sie sich die Prinzipien der Sprachmittlung (siehe Seite 101).
Für eine knappe, sachliche Wiedergabe gehen Sie wie bei einer Zusammenfassung vor.

Zielgruppenorientierung

In Ihrer fiktiven Situation als Gastschüler/-in an einer britischen Schule müssen Sie Ihren Artikel zielgruppengerecht gestalten. Häufig müssen Begriffe oder Eigennamen, die es im Englischen so nicht gibt, erläutert werden. In diesem Text sollte man sich überlegen, wie man mit der Erklärung der verschiedenen Identitäten umgeht. Die Erklärung der Autorin (Berlinerin, Atheistin, Schriftstellerin) zu übernehmen, wird in dem neuen Kontext merkwürdig erscheinen, denn Sie stellen die Autorin ja nicht explizit vor. Auch das Wort „Drehkreuz" in diesem übertragenen Sinne kann nicht einfach so wie im Deutschen benutzt werden. Insbesondere die Begriffe „Leitkultur" und „Goethe-und-Dieter-Bohlen-Land" könnten Probleme bereiten. In der Beispiellösung gehen sie einfach in der Zusammenfassung auf.

Hier eine mögliche Umsetzung:
<u>Our identity ought to be European</u>
Unlike Americans, Russians or Africans, we Europeans don't have a common notion of identity. Instead of acknowledging one common European identity, Europeans have always defined themselves against other nations, other cultures or non-Christian religions, even though in Germany, for instance, half of the population are not members of the Church and in Berlin there are more Muslims than Catholics.
People complain a lot about Europe being just an economic union, yet they find it hard to define a European identity. Of course, European history has always been ambivalent. There has always been internal as well as external trade but also many wars. There's no other region in the world where so many countries share a relatively small geographical area. Today, Europe should really see itself as a crossroads between East and West.
Europe's self-image should be that of an international marketplace, a multi-ethnic place with cultural, linguistic and economic ties with the rest of the world. A European is multicultural by birth. This doesn't mean that we have to give up our national identities. If we understand that transnational identity doesn't exclude national identity, we will overcome the fear that is being fuelled in many European countries and regions, especially if this notion includes non-European immigrants.
We have to establish a multidimensional notion of identity, which includes identity of origin, of sociocultural background and religion as much as being part of a wider geographical area. In my case this would mean being German from the Rhineland, a Catholic high-school student and multicultural European. To sum up, European identity should be multilingual, multiracial and multicultural.

Beispielaufgabe 3: „Warum es immer noch so wenige Frauen im MINT-Bereich gibt"

Thematischer Bezug gemäß KLP (Soziokulturelles Orientierungswissen):
Lebensentwürfe, Studium, Ausbildung, Beruf international – Englisch als *lingua franca: Questions of identity and gender*   Chancen und Risiken der Globalisierung: *The international world of work*
Quellenangaben:
Petra Maier, „Allein unter Männern. Warum es immer noch so wenige Frauen im MINT-Bereich gibt", in: *DER SPIEGEL,* Hamburg, 29.08.2019, zitiert nach: https://www.spiegel.de/karriere/mint-faecher-warum-frauen-so-oft-allein-unter-maennern-bleiben-a-1281877.html (Zugriff: 01.04.2024; gekürzt) (586 W.)

Aufgabe

Your friend from America has asked you about differences between men and women in university education in Germany. Write an email based on what you have read in the article from *Spiegel*.

Warum es immer noch so wenige Frauen im MINT-Bereich gibt

Petra Maier

[...]

„Komm, mach MINT"

Schon im Jahr 2008 beschloss das Bundesministerium für Bildung und Forschung den Nationalen Pakt für Frauen in MINT-Berufen, „Komm, mach MINT". Ziel des millionenschweren Vorhabens: ein bundesweites Netzwerk aufbauen, technisch interessierte Schülerinnen fördern, mehr junge Frauen für ein MINT-Studium begeistern, mehr Führungspositionen weiblich besetzen.

So entstand eine bundesweite Initiative, an der sich mehr als 300 Partner aus Politik, Wirtschaft und Wissenschaft beteiligten. Auf der Website sind rund tausend Projekte verzeichnet. Daneben sollen seit Jahren zahlreiche Initiativen wie der Girl's Day oder Mentorinnen-Programme wie CyberMentor den MINT-Bereich für junge Frauen attraktiver machen.

Und das zeigt offenbar Wirkung: Seit 2008 habe es erhebliche Fortschritte gegeben, sagt Barbara Schwarze, Professorin für Gender und Diversity Studies an der Hochschule Osnabrück und Vorsitzende des Kompetenzzentrums Technik – Diversity – Chancengleichheit. Sie führt das durchaus auf die verschiedenen Initiativen zurück.

MINT-Fächer: Die Mehrheit bleibt männlich

Eine Veränderung ist jedenfalls messbar: Wie aus einer Erhebung der Bundesagentur für Arbeit hervorgeht, ist die Zahl der Studentinnen im MINT-Bereich seit 2008 um 75 Prozent gestiegen. Trotzdem sind Männer in MINT-Fächern noch deutlich in der Überzahl: [...] Auch in der Berufswelt bleiben Frauen – allen Fortschritten zum Trotz – im MINT-Bereich deutlich unterrepräsentiert. Hier sind von 7,7 Millionen Beschäftigten bisher nur 15,2 Prozent weiblich, wie aus einer Berechnung des Statistischen Bundesamtes hervorgeht.

Dabei klagt die Branche über einen teils dramatischen Fachkräftemangel und müht sich nicht nur im Sinne der Frauenförderung, sondern auch purer Personalnot um weiblichen Nachwuchs. Aber das läuft zäh.

Nerd-Image: „Das schreckt Mädchen ab"

An mangelnder Qualifikation der Frauen liege es jedenfalls nicht, sagt Schwarze. Das größte Problem seien sich hartnäckig haltende Stereotype in den Köpfen vieler Menschen – insbesondere bei Eltern, Lehrern und Beratungskräften. Beispiel: Es gebe immer noch die Vorstellung, dass Technik allgemein schweißtreibend und nichts für Frauen sei, sagt Schwarze.

Berufen rund um Informatik wiederum hafte das Image des Nerdigen an, sagt Ursula Köhler, Sprecherin der Frauenfachgruppe in der Gesellschaft für Informatik. Und Katharina Gryc, Hauptansprechpartnerin für Mentorinnen bei CyberMentor, beklagt, dass dagegen auch wenig getan werde. Die ein oder andere populäre Serie sei auch nicht gerade hilfreich, um Vorurteile aufzubrechen. Bei „The Big Bang The-

70 ory" würden MINT-Frauen zum Beispiel als unattraktiv und nerdig dargestellt. „Das schreckt Mädchen ab."

Susanne Peter, die an der Hochschule Bremen das Projekt Mentoring MINT lei-
75 tet, hat festgestellt: „Interessiert sich eine Schülerin für Technik, wird das als etwas Besonderes betrachtet und stets kommentiert – sowohl positiv als auch negativ", sagt sie. „Bei Jungen dagegen finden andere
80 ein Interesse an Technik normal."

Dazu kommt: Mädchen trauen sich weniger zu, in MINT-Fächern glänzen zu können. „Bei gleichen Leistungen schätzen sich Mädchen in der Schule viel schlechter
85 ein als Jungs", sagt Peter. Und sie zweifelten daran, ob sie gut genug seien, ein MINT-Studium zu schaffen. Selbst während des Studiums hätten Studentinnen „wesentlich größere Selbstzweifel" als ihre Kommilito-
90 nen.

„Als Frau bleibst du mehr im Kopf"

Rebecca Dahm sagt, Mathematik und Physik seien ihr in der Schule leichtgefallen, hätten Spaß gemacht – da sei es klar gewesen, in diese Richtung zu gehen. Letzt- 95 endlich entschied sie sich für Maschinenbau. Im Bachelor in Konstanz fand sie sich nach ihrem Eindruck durchaus in einer Sonderrolle wieder: „Als Frau bleibst du mehr im Kopf", findet sie. Sie sei eher mal 100 berücksichtigt worden, es sei aber auch sofort aufgefallen, wenn sie bei einem Laborversuch gefehlt hätte.

So erleben es oft auch andere Frauen in MINT-Bereichen, sagt die Informatikerin 105 Köhler. „Man ist immer auf dem Präsentierteller." Viele Frauen wechselten deshalb nach ein paar Jahren in andere Berufsfelder: „Weil es sehr anstrengend ist, sich in so einer männlich konnotierten Arbeitswelt 110 zu behaupten." […]

Bearbeitungsschritte und Beispiellösung

Bei der Sprachmittlung dieses Textes sollten Sie vor allem die Kunst des Weglassens einüben. Ihr Text ist kein wissenschaftlicher Text, der Quellen nennen muss. Der vorliegende Zeitungstext hingegen nennt eine Vielzahl von Akteuren. Ihrem amerikanischen Freund ist es egal, wer welche Studie durchgeführt hat und wer in welcher Funktion welche Aussage getroffen hat. Das Bundesministerium für Bildung und Forschung kann einfach als „the government" bezeichnet werden. Ergebnisse von Studien benennen Sie einfach als Fakten, genau wie die Aussagen der Interviewten.

Was Begriffe angeht, so gibt es das englische „STEM" für MINT, wobei jedoch eine Erklärung, wofür es steht, nicht schaden kann. „Girl's Day" und „CyberMentor" sind zwar englische Begriffe, aber nicht selbsterklärend. Hier bietet sich auch eher an, sie in Ihrem Text wegzulassen, denn eine umfassende Erklärung der Begriffe erscheint an dieser Stelle unverhältnismäßig.

Hier eine mögliche Umsetzung:
RE: Men and women
Hey Doug,
In your email you raised the issue of gender bias in university education. This is indeed an issue in Germany too. As early as 2008, the government started a campaign to support women in the so-called STEM professions (science, technology, engineering and mathematics). It is aimed at building up a network, promote girls who are interested

in technology, encourage more women to take up STEM studies and fill more executive positions with women. Hundreds of projects and initiatives were created to make science and technology more attractive to women. Apparently, there has been a lot of progress. The number of female students in STEM subjects has increased by 75 percent. Yet, the majority is still male. The same is true for the workforce: only 15.2 % of those working in science and technology are women, in spite of the shortage of skilled labour.

The biggest problem is the still prevalent stereotype among parents, teachers and counsellors that technology is inappropriate for women and computer science is for nerds. This image is even supported in "The Big Bang Theory" and it deters women.

Women who show an interest in technology are regarded as an exception. For boys, however, it is normal. In addition, girls are a lot less confident to excel in STEM subjects and doubt their ability to succeed in school or university a lot more often than their male counterparts. Women feel they are a lot more visible in the male-dominated field of science and technology, which is exhausting in the long run. Therefore, a lot of women quit their jobs in favour of other occupational fields.

So much for the situation in Germany. What do you think?

Talk to you soon,

xxx

Beispielaufgabe 4: „Tiktoker nimmt in kurzen Videos deutsche Sitten aufs Korn"

Thematischer Bezug gemäß KLP (Soziokulturelles Orientierungswissen):
allgemeiner lebensweltlicher Bezug
Lebensentwürfe, Studium, Ausbildung, Beruf international – *Englisch als lingua franca: Questions of identity and gender*

Quellenangaben:
Anna Ross, dpa, „Tiktoker nimmt in kurzen Videos deutsche Sitten aufs Korn", in: *Aachener Zeitung,* Aachen, 29. Januar 2024, zitiert nach: https://www.aachener-zeitung.de/digital/tiktoker-nimmt-in-kurzen-videos-deutsche-sitten-aufs-korn/7684233.html (Zugriff: 01.03.2024). ©dpa (657 W.)

Aufgabe

Write an article for *GAPP-Magazin,* the magazine for the participants of the German-American Partnership Program, in which you sum up the social media trend of presenting German clichés, based on the article from *Aachener Zeitung.*

Tiktoker nimmt in kurzen Videos deutsche Sitten aufs Korn

Anna Ross, dpa

Stoßlüften, Pfandflaschen wegbringen oder Müll trennen – mehr oder weniger typisch deutsche Gewohnheiten sind auf Social Media ein Hit. Ein britischer Tiktoker, hat

5 *vor drei Jahren sein erstes Video dazu hochgeladen.*

Liam Carpenter steht vor seinem Handy, es klemmt in einem Stativ. Er überprüft kurz die Einstellungen, geht seinen Text

10 durch, dann geht es los. Der gebürtige Brite drückt auf Play und sagt mit deutschem Akzent: „In Germany we don't say". Ein Satz, der Liam in den vergangenen drei Jahren rund 2,2 Millionen Follower auf Tiktok

15 beschert hat.

Der 27 Jahre alte Influencer beschäftigt sich in seinen 30- bis 60-sekündigen Videos mit Themen wie Stoßlüften, Pfandflaschen wegbringen oder Müll trennen. Kurzum:

20 Mit deutschen Gewohnheiten, die für Ausländer oder Ausländerinnen nicht immer einleuchtend sind. Ein Klischee über Essverhalten und Sparsamkeit der Deutschen? „In Germany we don't say: ‚Wow, that is de-

25 licious'", sagt Liam im Video dazu. ‚We say: Für den Preis kann man nicht meckern'."

Sein erstes Video hat Carpenter im Februar 2021 hochgeladen. „Fast eine Million Aufrufe für das erste Video. Das war so ein

30 Adrenalinkick, dass ich einfach weitermachen musste." Inzwischen ist Liam hauptberuflich sogenannter Content Creator. In seinen Beiträgen schlüpft er in unterschiedliche Rollen. Immer dabei: der Kli-

35 scheedeutsche im grauen Jogginganzug mit einer schwarzen Kappe, mit Bauchtasche und Schuhen von Birkenstock. Seine Videos lädt er auch auf Social-Media-Kanäle wie Instagram oder YouTube hoch.

40

Der Social-Media-Trend

Carpenter ist Teil eines Social-Media-Phänomens: Influencer und Influencerinnen nehmen deutsche Gewohnheiten aufs

45 Korn – und das, obwohl oder gerade weil sie meist gar nicht aus Deutschland kommen. Liam ist überzeugt, dass das Format vor allem deswegen so gut funktioniert: „Es passt, weil ich meinen Content über die

50 Unterschiede über englische und deutsche Sachen mache."

Das spiegelt sich in den unzähligen „In Germany we don't say..."-Videos (deutsch: „In Deutschland sagen wir nicht ...") und

55 den Reaktionen darauf wider. Auch Influencer aus den USA wie beispielsweise Zac Ryan oder Zack Bachelor, die seit ein paar Jahren in Stuttgart leben, thematisieren in ihren Videos, an welche deutschen

60 Sitten sie sich inzwischen gewöhnt haben: der „Verdauungsspaziergang", die „Es gibt kein schlechtes Wetter, nur die falschen Klamotten"-Mentalität oder das „Liegen-Reservieren" im Urlaub. Auch deutsche

65 Influencer greifen den Trend auf und nehmen sich dabei selbst nicht zu ernst.

Das Erfolgskonzept hinter dem Trend

Die Kommunikationswissenschaftlerin am Center for Advanced Internet Studies (CAIS, Bochum), Josephine B. Schmitt,

70 sieht den Grund für den Erfolg dieses Social-Media-Trends vor allem in dem Gefühl, das bei den Nutzern entsteht: „Solche Angebote schaffen das Gefühl von Zugehörigkeit und betonen die eigene soziale Identi-

75 tät." Es würden Dinge porträtiert, die viele Menschen auf unterschiedliche Art und Weise kennen.

Die humorvolle Darstellung sei ein entscheidender Faktor, da so Distanz entstehe: „So muss man sich nicht notwendigerweise mit dem Klischee oder den Eigenheiten identifizieren. Man kennt aber bestimmt Personen im Umfeld, auf die das zutrifft."

Liam ist sich bei seiner Arbeit über des schmalen Grats zwischen Belustigung und Beleidigung bewusst. Warum der 27-Jährige überwiegend positive Rückmeldungen seiner oft auch deutschen Follower bekommt, erklärt er sich so: „In meinen Videos ist der Brite ja der größte Dummkopf, nicht der Deutsche. Der Deutsche zeigt ihm, wie es geht. Deswegen glaube ich, dass es eine gute Balance ist."

Dass dieses Format vor allem auf Tiktok so erfolgreich ist, liegt nach Auffassung der Kommunikationswissenschaftlerin unter anderem daran, dass die Videos unterhaltsam und leicht zugänglich sind. „Das führt dann auch dazu, dass sie schneller verbreitet, geteilt, zitiert und kommentiert werden", sagt Schmitt.

„Gut eingedeutscht"

Der frühere Basketballprofi Liam, eigentlich aus England, wohnt inzwischen in Crailsheim (Kreis Schwäbisch Hall) mit seiner Frau und zwei Hunden. In seinen mittlerweile zehn Jahren in der Wahlheimat sind deutsche Gewohnheiten nicht spurlos an ihm vorbei gegangen: „Ich bin so gut eingedeutscht. Manchmal fühle ich mich eher in England wie ein Outsider. Zum Beispiel warte ich immer an der Ampel, bis es grün wird. Meine Freunde fragen mich dann: „Was machst du? Was ist los mit dir?""

Bearbeitungsschritte und Beispiellösung

Die Herausforderung bei diesem Text ist vor allem der Umgang mit dem Vokabular, das deutsche Klischees beschreibt. Während „Müll trennen" ein auch in USA bekanntes Konzept ist, „Pfandflasche" ohnehin „returnable bottle" heißt und Birkenstock auch im Ausland bekannt ist, bedürfen das Stoßlüften, der Verdauungsspaziergang und das Reservieren von Liegen einer Erklärung. Stoßlüften lässt sich überhaupt nicht verständlich übersetzten, und eine einfache Übersetzung als „digestive walk" oder „deck chair reservation" ließe den amerikanischen Leser verständnislos zurück.

Für die Optimierung der eigenen Textstruktur bietet es sich an, Carpenters übernommene Angewohnheiten zusammen mit den anderen zu benennen, so dass man einen stimmigen Schlussteil erhält.

Hier eine mögliche Umsetzung:

Scrutinising Stereotypes

An article in *Aachener Zeitung* reports on the influencer Liam Carpenter, who amiably satirises German habits.

Originally from England, he has lived in Germany for ten years and has been very successful on TikTok with his short videos. He takes on different roles, his main character being the stereotypical German in a grey jogging suit, a black baseball cap, a bumbag and Birkenstock sandals, and he pokes good-natured fun at those habits that are often strange to foreigners. A cliché of German eating and spending habits, e.g., is revealed by contrasting the rather British statement "Wow, that is delicious" with the German "You can't complain at this price".

Other examples of typical German habits are sorting waste, returning bottles and opening doors and windows wide for fresh air regardless of the outside temperature. The concept seems to work especially because an outsider's view is taken. In fact, there are several American influencers living in Germany who show habits in their videos which they have already got used to. Examples are the after-dinner walk (supposedly good for your digestion), placing towels on hotel deck chairs to claim them for the day and the saying "there is no bad weather, there is only inappropriate clothing". Carpenter himself has adopted many of these habits and sometimes feels like an outsider in Britain, e. g. when waiting for the green light at a pedestrian crossing.

Scholars see the reason for the success of these videos in the feeling they give to viewers. It creates a sense of belonging and stresses one's own social identity. The humorous presentation of those habits creates distance. Thus, you need not identify with the cliché, but everybody knows somebody for whom it is true. The videos are entertaining and easily available, which explains their particular success.

Beispielaufgabe 5: „Fördert endlich mal die Väter!"

Thematischer Bezug gemäß KLP (Soziokulturelles Orientierungswissen):
Lebensentwürfe, Studium, Ausbildung, Beruf international – Englisch als *lingua franca: Questions of identity and gender*
Quellenangaben:
Anne Jeschke, „Fördert endlich mal die Väter! ", in: *Zeit online,* Hamburg, 23. Mai 2023, zitiert nach: https://www.zeit.de/arbeit/2023-05/elternzeit-vater-karriere-gleichstellung (Zugriff: 01.04.2024) (542 W.)

Aufgabe

Your American friend is interested in the role of fathers when it comes to taking paid parental leave in Germany. Write an email to your friend based on Anne Jeschke's comment, presenting the reasons why many fathers believe that taking paid parental leave puts a stop to their careers and why swift action by both the government and employers is needed to convince them otherwise.

Fördert endlich mal die Väter!   *Anne Jeschke*

Jeder Zweite glaubt, dass die Elternzeit Vätern beruflich schadet. Das Schlimme ist: Das stimmt – und muss dringend verhindert werden.

Die Hälfte der Deutschen glaubt laut der neuen Vermächtnisstudie, dass es der Karriere von Männern schadet, wenn sie Elternzeit nehmen. Nun ist das zwar eine eher theoretische Sorge: Gerade mal zehn Prozent der Väter in Deutschland gehen überhaupt länger als zwei Monate in Elternzeit, mehr als die Hälfte gar nicht.

Und doch ist die Angst berechtigt. Wer sich für eine längere Elternzeit entscheidet, gefährdet seine Karriere. Unternehmen und die Politik sollten das dringend ändern – und Männer fördern, die sich dafür entscheiden. Nur dann kann eine Gesellschaft entstehen, in der Väter mehr Aufgaben im Haushalt übernehmen und in der Paare sich die Sorgearbeit fair teilen.

Dass die meisten Väter, wenn überhaupt, nur zwei Monate in Elternzeit gehen, liegt an den gesetzlichen Vorgaben. Diese beiden sogenannten Partnermonate sind nötig, damit Paare das volle Elterngeld bekommen. Daran muss sich etwas ändern: Das volle Elterngeld sollte es nur geben, wenn beide sich die Elternzeit gleichberechtigt aufteilen. Das ließe sich am einfachsten erreichen, indem man die Partnermonate erhöht, zum Beispiel von zwei auf sechs Monate.

Das wäre ein erster Schritt, doch darüber hinaus sollte sich auch in den Unternehmen etwas tun. Wenn sich Väter davor fürchten, nach der Elternzeit keine Karriere machen zu können, müssen Vorgesetzte das entkräften. Chefinnen und Chefs, die im drohenden Fachkräftemangel attraktive Arbeitgeber sein wollen, müssen fortschrittlich denken. Es zeugt von schlechter Führung, wenn sie Schwangerschaften abschätzig kommentieren oder genervt reagieren, wenn jemand eine Elternzeit ankündigt.

Mütter können nur müde lachen

In vielen Unternehmen kommen diese Chefinnen und Chefs aber leider immer noch vor. Sie drohen Frauen wie Männern, nach der Elternzeit erst mal „einen Gang runterschalten zu müssen", oder empfehlen ihnen, „Aufgaben am besten abzugeben". Sie wollen nicht garantieren, dass man nach der Elternzeit befördert wird. Damit schrecken sie viele Menschen ab, sich für diese Familienzeit zu entscheiden. Vor allem Väter, die sich zusätzlich noch Kommentare von Kolleginnen und Kollegen anhören müssen und die, anders als Mütter, oft noch die Wahl haben, ob sie Sorgearbeit übernehmen oder eben nicht.

Spätestens wenn die Generation Z auf den Arbeitsmarkt kommt, sollten Arbeitgeber das Thema Elternzeit als selbstverständlich ansehen. 73 Prozent von ihnen gaben in einer Untersuchung an, dass ihnen familienfreundliche Personalmaßnahmen wichtig sind. Fast genauso viele von ihnen wünschten sich darin, für Kinderbetreuung auf Teilzeit wechseln zu können.

Vorgesetzte sollten mit Männern und Frauen, die in Elternzeit gehen, vorab Ziele und Aufgaben für danach bestimmen. Sie sollten festlegen, mit welchem Gehalt, auf welcher Position und mit welchen Aufgaben man aus der Elternzeit zurückkommt. Verbindlich – am besten mit Unterschrift. Im Idealfall wäre das sogar gesetzlich vorgeschrieben.

Noch mehr Förderung für Männer? Falls Sie eine Frau sind, sind Sie jetzt möglicherweise wütend angesichts dieser Forderung. Zu Recht. Schließlich ist das Problem mit

129

der fehlenden Vereinbarkeit in diesem Land
85 noch vor allem eines der Mütter. Sie werden dauerhaft beruflich benachteiligt, weil
sie lange Elternzeit machen oder jahrelang
in Teilzeit arbeiten. Das ist erwiesen.

Und genau deshalb wäre es wichtig, für
90 alle und immer zu verhindern, dass das ge-

schieht. Denn eines ist klar: Männer haben
nur Angst vor dem beruflichen Abstieg
nach der Elternzeit, weil sie ihn seit Jahrzehnten bei Frauen beobachten.

Beispiellösung

Dear Deborah,

To be honest, before you asked me, I didn't know much about the role of fathers when it comes to taking paid parental leave in Germany, but I came across a commentary by Anne Jeschke in *ZEITonline*. As the article is in German, I'll try to outline its line of argument in English to make sure that you can understand it.

Jeschke starts her commentary by stating that there is statistical evidence for what 50 % of all Germans believe to be true: Taking paid parental leave in Germany truly harms the fathers' careers. Only 10 % of all fathers take parental leave for more than two months, while 50 % of all those who could take parental leave don't take any at all. To increase the number of fathers taking parental leave, both politicians and employers need to support these fathers and contribute to allay their fears about missing out career-wise. The reason most fathers who decide to take paid parental leave in Germany only stay at home for two months is that these two so-called "partner months" are required for families to get the complete payout assigned by the government. According to Jeschke, the number of fathers deciding to take paid parental leave could easily be increased if the government raised the number of "partner months" required from two to six.

Employers should also change their attitudes towards fathers who decide to take parental leave. Instead of scaring employees by threatening them that it wouldn't be possible for them to return to their former position in the company if they take parental leave, companies should establish a mindset that regards employees taking parental leave as the rule, not the exception. Employees and employers should collaborate to establish individual guidelines that enable them to make a smooth transition from work to taking parental leave and vice versa. Jeschke points out that companies will sooner or later have to adapt to the fact that a growing number of employees regards parental leave for both sexes as "normal" and that more and more parents wish to split childcare equally, while at the same time enabling both partners to pursue their respective careers.

Jeschke ends her article by stating another important reason for fathers to refrain from taking parental leave: They can see the detrimental effect working part-time and taking a longer leave of absence from work has on women's careers.

Please let me know what the situation is like for fathers and families in the USA.

Talk to you soon,

XXX

Leseverstehen/Schreiben

Die Beispielaufgaben sind vom Umfang und vom Schwierigkeitsgrad her teilweise für Leistungskurse, teilweise für Grundkurse konzipiert. Für Grundkurse gilt eine maximale Wortzahl von 800 Wörtern, für Leistungskurse von 1000 Wörtern. Der deutsche Text für die Sprachmittlungsaufgabe umfasst in beiden Kursen zwischen 450 und 650 Wörtern. Für ein Prüfungstraining spielt die Zuordnung keine entscheidende Rolle.

Um den verschiedenen Vorgaben für die beiden Kursarten gerecht zu werden, wurden überwiegend Texte ausgewählt, die den Vorgaben beider Kursarten entsprechen.

Beispielaufgabe 1: Chimamanda Ngozi Adichie, „Americanah"

Thematischer Bezug gemäß KLP (Soziokulturelles Orientierungswissen): Postkolonialismus – Lebenswirklichkeiten in einem weiteren anglophonen Kulturraum: *Voices from the African Continent: Focus on Nigeria*
Auszüge aus einem englischsprachigen literarischen Text (437 W. und 411 W.)
Quellenangaben: Chimamanda Ngozi Adichie, *Americanah,* London, 2013, pp. 3–4, pp. 385–386

Aufgabe

1. Describe Princeton and Lagos as presented in the excerpts. *(Comprehension)*
2. Examine the way the narrator presents Princeton and Lagos respectively. Consider the narrative point of view, atmosphere, characters and the language used. *(Analysis)*
3.1 Comment on the narrator's presentation of Lagos and Ranyinudo. Assess to what extent it represents Nigeria's as well as Africa's social, cultural and economic situation. *(Evaluation: Comment)*
3.2 Ifemelu and Ranyinudo apparently often talk about the situation in Nigeria as compared to the Western world (ll. 100–105). Write a dialogue between them considering aspects hinted at in the texts as well as aspects discussed in class. *(Evaluation: Re-creation of text)*

Americanah *Chimamanda Ngozi Adichie*
(excerpt from chapter 1)

Princeton, in the summer, smelled of nothing, and although lfemelu liked the tranquil greenness of the many trees, the clean streets and stately homes, the deli-
5 cately overpriced shops and the quiet, abiding air of earned grace, it was this, the lack of a smell that most appealed to her, perhaps because the other American cities she knew well had all smelled distinctly. Philadelphia
10 had the musty scent of history. New Haven smelled of neglect. Baltimore smelled of brine, and Brooklyn of sun-warmed garbage. But Princeton had no smell. She liked taking deep breaths here. She liked watch-
15 ing the locals who drove with pointed courtesy and parked their latest model cars outside the organic grocery store on Nassau Street or outside the sushi restaurants or outside the ice cream shop that had
20 fifty different flavours including red pepper or outside the post office where effusive staff bounded out to greet them at the entrance. She liked the campus, grave with knowledge, the Gothic buildings with their
25 vine-laced walls, and the way everything transformed, in the half-light of night, into a ghostly scene. She liked, most of all, that in this place of affluent ease, she could pretend to be someone else, someone specially
30 admitted into a hallowed American club, someone adorned with certainty.

But she did not like that she had to go to Trenton to braid her hair. It was unreasonable to expect a braiding salon in Princeton – the few black locals she had seen here 35 so light-skinned and lank-haired she could not imagine them wearing braids – and yet as she waited at Princeton Junction station for the train, on an afternoon ablaze with heat, she wondered why there was no place 40 where she could braid her hair. The chocolate bar in her handbag had melted. A few other people were waiting on the platform, all of them white and lean, in short, flimsy clothes. The man standing closest to her was 45 eating an ice cream cone; she had always found it a little irresponsible, the eating of ice cream cones by grown-up American men, especially the eating of ice cream cones by grown-up American men in pub- 50 lic. He turned to her and said. "About time," when the train finally creaked in with the familiarity strangers adopt with each other after sharing in the disappointment of a public service. She smiled at him. The grey- 55 ing hair on the back of his head was swept forward, a comical arrangement to disguise his bald spot. He had to be an academic, but not in the humanities or he would be more self-conscious. A firm science like chemis- 60 try, maybe.

[...]

Americanah *Chimamanda Ngozi Adichie*
(excerpt from chapter 44)

[...]

At first, Lagos assaulted her; the sun-
65 dazed haste, the yellow buses full of squashed limbs, the sweating hawkers racing after cars, the advertisements on hulk-

ing billboards (others scrawled on walls – PLUMBER CALL 080177777) and the heaps of rubbish that rose on the road- 70 sides like a taunt. Commerce thrummed too defiantly. And the air was dense with exaggeration, conversations full of over-protestations. One morning, a man's body lay on Awolowo Road. Another morning, The Island flooded and cars became gasping boats. Here, she felt, anything could happen, a ripe tomato could burst out of solid stone. And so she had the dizzying sensation of falling, falling into the new person she had become, falling into the strange familiar. Had it always been like this or had it changed so much in her absence? When she left home, only the wealthy had mobile phones, all the numbers started with 090, and girls wanted to date 090 men. Now her hair braider had a mobile phone, the plantain seller tending a blackened grill had a mobile phone. She had grown up knowing all the bus stops and the side streets, understanding the cryptic codes of conductors and the body language of street hawkers. Now, she struggled to grasp the unspoken. When had shopkeepers become so rude? Had buildings in Lagos always had this patina of decay? And when did it become a city of people quick to beg and too enamoured of free things?

"Americanah!" Ranyinudo teased her often. "You are looking at things with American eyes. But the problem is that you are not even a real Americanah. At least if you had an American accent we would tolerate your complaining!"

Ranyinudo picked her up from the airport, standing by the Arrivals exit in a billowy bridesmaid's dress, her blusher too red on her cheeks like bruises, the green satin flowers in her hair now askew. Ifemelu was struck by how arresting, how attractive, she was. No longer a ropy mass of gangly arms and gangly legs, but now a big, firm, curvy woman, exulting in her weight and height, and it made her imposing, a presence that drew the eyes.

"Ranyi!" Ifemelu said. "I know my coming back is a big deal but I didn't know it was big enough for a ball gown."

"Idiot. I came straight from the wedding. I didn't want to risk the traffic of going home first to change."

They hugged, holding each other close. Ranyinudo smelled of a floral perfume and exhaust fumes and sweat; she smelled of Nigeria. [...]

Annotations

Princeton – elite university in the US

plantain – kind of banana

Americanah – *Nigerian:* emigrant to America

Bearbeitungsschritte und Musterlösungen

Anforderungsbereich I (Teilaufgabe 1)

1. Describe the places and people presented in the excerpts. *(Comprehension)*

Der Operator „describe" verlangt eine gewisse Ausführlichkeit, anders als „outline" oder „sum up". Eine solche Aufgabe bietet sich an, wenn die Textvorlage selbst sehr deskriptiv ist oder wenn es keine wirkliche Handlung gibt. Wenn Sie einen Blick auf die zweite Teilaufgabe werfen, so sehen Sie, dass auch die Analyse sich mit der Beschreibung der beiden Städte befasst. Beachten Sie die Trennschärfe zwischen den beiden Aufgabenstellungen! Charaktere und sprachliche Besonderheiten, Bildhaftigkeit und Erzähltechnik gehören erst in die zweite Teilaufgabe. Princeton und Lagos werden im engeren Sinne jeweils nur im ersten Textabschnitt beschrieben. Der Mann auf dem Bahnsteig in Princeton und Ranyinudo in Lagos tragen dann als Charaktere zu der Darstellung der jeweiligen Stadt bei. Dieses sollte in Teilaufgabe 2 Erwähnung finden.

Das Isolieren von Schlüsselwörtern ist eine unabdingbare Methode, profundes Textverständnis zu erlangen. Dies geschieht normalerweise durch Markierungen und Notizen im Text. Hier werden wir sie auflisten. Danach sollten sie in einen Sinnzusammenhang gebracht werden.

paragraph	keywords	→
Text 1, paragraph 1 (note: p. 3, i.e. beginning of the novel)	"Princeton" (l. 1)	place, location
	"had no smell" (l. 13)	sensation
	"tranquil greenness" (l. 3) "many trees" (l. 3) "clean streets" (l. 4) "stately homes" (l. 4) "delicately overpriced shops" (ll. 4 f.)	visual appearance
	"locals" / "pointed courtesy" (ll. 15 f.)	people's behavior
	"latest-model cars" (l. 16) "organic grocery store" (l. 17) "sushi restaurants" (l. 18) "ice cream shop" (l. 19)	visual appearance
	"effusive staff bounded out to greet them" (ll. 21 f.)	people's behaviour
	"campus" (l. 23) "Gothic buildings" (l. 24) "[no] braiding salon" (l. 34)	visual appearance
Text 2, paragraph 1	"Lagos" (l. 64)	place, location
	"sun-dazed haste" (ll. 64 f.) "sweating hawkers" (l. 66) "heaps of rubbish" (l. 70) "air dense with exaggeration, conversations full of over-protestations" (ll. 72–74)	sensation
	"buses full of squashed limbs" (ll. 65 f.) "sweating hawkers" (l. 66) "heaps of rubbish" (l. 70) "advertisements on hulking billboards, (others scrawled on walls [...])" (ll. 67 f.)	visual appearance

"a man's body " (l. 74) "flooded" (l. 76)	visual appearance
"shopkeepers become so rude" (l. 95)	behaviour
"patina of decay" (ll. 96 f.)	visual appearance
"quick to beg" (l. 98)	behaviour

Vor dem Verfassen des Textes rufen Sie sich die Prinzipien der Inhaltsangabe ins Gedächtnis:

Gliederung des Textes / Textverständnis:
– Text in Sinnabschnitte unterteilen – meist helfen bereits Absätze des Textes
Schreiben:
– eigene Formulierungen
– einleitender Satz
– Antwort auf die geforderten W-Fragen (hier: Wo, Was und Wer)

Bei Ihrer Sammlung von Schlüsselwörtern sollten Sie prüfen, ob Inhaltsaspekte sich wiederholen (siehe Spalte 3). Ihren eigenen Text sollten Sie dann nicht anhand der Textchronologie, sondern anhand der Inhaltsaspekte strukturieren.

TIPP zum Punktesammeln

Reduzieren Sie Ihre Inhaltsangabe auf das Wesentliche (keine Ausschmückung durch besondere Adjektive, keine kleinen Details, keine Zitate, keine Metaphorik). Lassen Sie aber auch keine Merkmale, die die beiden Städte ausmachen, weg! Beschreiben Sie nur die Städte, nicht die Charaktere!
Verweisen Sie nicht auf Abschnitte oder Zeilen im Ausgangstext! Zitieren Sie nicht! Nehmen Sie keine Wertung vor!
Grundtempus ist das *simple present*.

Hier eine mögliche Umsetzung:
Chimamanda Ngozi Adichie's novel "Americanah", which was published in 2013, begins with a description of Princeton as perceived by Ifemelu, apparently the main character of the novel. Unlike other American cities, Princeton has no smell, which is the most appealing feature to Ifemelu. It is presented as very green and clean, with stately houses and expensive shops, fancy restaurants, ice-cream parlors and an extravagant post office but no braiding salon. The campus is marked by its Gothic buildings.
In a later chapter of the novel, Lagos, Nigeria, is described, also as perceived by Ifemelu, who is evidently from Lagos and comes back after her stay in America. Lagos is hot and moist, people are sweating, and buses are overcrowded. There are large advertising billboards and informal adverts simply scribbled on walls. The roadside is full of rubbish, buildings seem to be decaying. Hawkers try to sell their merchandise to drivers, and everybody has a mobile phone. Shopkeepers seem unfriendly, and there are a lot of beggars. One day there is a dead body in the street, another day the city is flooded.

Anforderungsbereich II (Teilaufgabe 2)

2. Examine the way the narrator presents Princeton and Lagos respectively. Consider the narrative point of view, atmosphere, characters and the language used.
   (Analysis)

Prinzipiell geht es im Anforderungsbereich II immer um Struktur und/oder Sprache des Textes oder um die Analyse von Erzählelementen wie *character* oder *point of view*, nicht mehr um Inhalt, wenngleich dieses Prinzip leider nicht immer gewahrt wird.

Die Aufgabenstellung spezifiziert ausdrücklich *point of view, atmosphere, characters* und *language* (d. h. *choice of words, imagery* und *stylistic devices*). Sie sollten dies somit sehr genau nehmen und diese Anweisung als Checkliste benutzen. Mit einer Analyse der Textstruktur sollte man sich also auch nicht aufhalten.

Passagen, in denen die Erzählperspektive *(point of view)* eine besondere Wirkung erzielt, sind ebenso im Text zu markieren wie die für die Atmosphäre relevanten Beschreibungen des *settings* und der Charaktere sowie Besonderheiten der Sprachverwendung.

Im Zieltext muss dann nicht zwingend jeder einzelne Beleg zitiert werden; Verweise auf die entsprechenden Zeilen sollten jedoch in jedem Fall erfolgen. Wir werden im Folgenden die zu unterstreichenden Elemente benennen.

quotation	narrative technique/ element of narration/	aspect of language	function/ effect
Text 1			
"tranquil greenness" (l. 3) "many trees" (l. 3) "clean streets" (l. 4)	setting, atmosphere	choice of words: "tranquil", "green", "clean", "stately", "deli-cately", "pointed, "courtesy"	positive connota-tion: pleasant, lovely
"stately homes" (l. 4), "de-licately overpriced shops" (ll. 4 f.), "locals" / "pointed courtesy" (ll. 15 f.), "latest-model cars" (l. 16), "orga-nic grocery store" (l. 17), "sushi restaurants" (l. 19), "ice cream shop […] fifty different flavours" (ll. 19 f.), "effusive staff bounded out to greet them" (ll. 21 f.), "[no] braiding salon" (l. 34) "grave with knowledge", (ll. 23 f.), "affluent ease" (l. 28)	setting, atmosphere		people's lifestyle: luxurious, cosmo-politan, ecological → high class, bourgeois, aca-demic, wealthy, quiet, white-dominated, tradi-tional

"the lack of a smell, that most appealed to her" (ll. 6 f.)	point of view		character's thoughts
"she knew well" (ll. 8 f.)			character's experiences
"She liked [...] She liked [...] She liked" (ll. 13–27)		anaphora	emphasis
"she could pretend" (ll. 28 f.)			character's thoughts
"hallowed American club" (l. 30)		choice of words/ imagery	exclusiveness of Princeton University
"But she did not like" (l. 32)		antithesis	emphasis
"It was unreasonable to expect" (ll. 33 f.)			character's reasoning
"She could not imagine" (ll. 36 f.), "she wondered" (l. 40)			character's thinking
"she had always found" (ll. 46 f.)			character's thoughts
"He had to be" (l. 58)		reported thought	
"short, flimsy clothes" (ll. 44 f.), "greying hair [...] swept forward, a comical arrangement" (ll. 55–57), "academic" (l. 58)	character		fitting in with the setting
Text 2			
Beschreibung des setting, *wie für Teilaufgabe 1 unterstrichen*	setting, atmosphere	choice of words: "assault", "sun-dazed", "squashed", "sweating", "hulking", "exaggeration", "dense", "heaps", "overprotestation"	atmosphere of being exposed to too much of everything: climate, population; activity: lively, diverse, overwhelming, threatening
"Lagos assaulted her" (l. 64)	point of view	personification	threat
"she felt" (l. 77)			character's feeling

137

"cars became gasping boats" (ll. 76 f.), "a ripe tomato could burst out of solid stone" (ll. 78 f.)	setting/ atmosphere	personification/ imagery	Lagos as dynamic, unpredictable, amazing
"she had the dizzying sensation of falling" (ll. 79 f.)	point of view		
"Had it always been …?" (ll. 82–84)		reported thought	insight
"When had …?" (l. 94)			
"And when did …?" (l. 97)			
"was struck" (l. 111)	point of view		character's per-ception
"billowy […] dress" (ll. 107 f.), "blusher too red […] like bruises" (ll.108 f.), "big, firm, curvy" (ll. 113 f.), "exulting […] imposing" (ll. 114 f.)	character	choice of words imagery	fitting in with Lagos
"Ranyinudo smelled of … she smelled of" (ll. 124 f.)	point of view		character's sen-sation

Es ergibt meist wenig Sinn, die Texte rein chronologisch zu beschreiben. Dies braucht viel zu viel wertvolle Arbeitszeit und Energie und führt zu Wiederholungen sowie einem unübersichtlichen und viel zu umfangreichen Zieltext. Viel eleganter ist es, den Zieltext inhaltlich anhand der vorgegebenen Formelemente und sprachlichen Mittel zu strukturieren und nicht Zeile für Zeile des Ausgangstextes zu behandeln. Jeder Ihrer Sinnabschnitte erhält dann aussagekräftige Zitate und ergänzende Textverweise. Wichtig sind Aussagen zur Funktion der Elemente, selbst wenn diese in der Aufgabenstellung nicht ausdrücklich genannt wird. Es reicht z. B. nicht, eine Metapher zu finden und zu benennen, man muss sie auch erläutern.

Die Aufgabenstellung verlangt die Untersuchung der Romanelemente *point of view*, *atmosphere* und *character*. Es bietet sich an, diese Elemente auch nacheinander zu untersuchen und dabei die Sprachverwendung im Blick zu behalten.

Da die Vorgaben einen zusammenhängenden Zieltext fordern, sollte man Teil II elegant an Teilaufgabe 1 anbinden. Ein erneuter Einleitungssatz wäre genauso unglücklich wie eine Formulierung wie „Now I am going to analyse …" gefolgt von einer Paraphrase der Aufgabenstellung. Es wäre ein regelrechter Bruch, keine kohärente Anbindung. Eine solche Formulierung strukturiert allenfalls einen mündlichen Vortrag, nicht jedoch einen Aufsatz. Meist ist gar keine Überleitung nötig. Wichtig ist nur Textkohärenz.

Hier eine mögliche Umsetzung:

The atmosphere created in the narrator's description of Princeton contrasts starkly with the atmosphere of Lagos. Princeton, home to one of America's elite universities, appears as an extremely pleasant place with its many trees and clean streets. Positively connoted words like "tranquil", "green" and "clean" (ll. 3 f.) suggest a pleasant, even graceful town. It is a wealthy environment with an atmosphere marked by people's upper-class lifestyle as it is revealed in "stately homes", "delicately overpriced shops", "latest model cars" and "fifty different flavors" in the "ice cream shop" (ll. 4 f., 15–20). People live an upper-class, academic lifestyle of "affluent ease" (l. 28), buying ecologically in "organic grocery store[s]" (l. 17) and feeling cosmopolitan by eating in "sushi restaurants" (l. 18). The lack of a braiding salon shows that Princeton society is almost exclusively white. Princeton University is referred to as a "hallowed American club", "grave with knowledge" with its "Gothic buildings" and "vine-laced walls" (ll. 23–30), which again expresses the exclusiveness and venerability of this place, even at night, when it becomes a "ghostly scene" (ll. 27).

All this is presented to the reader from Ifemelu's point of view. We participate in her perception right from the beginning, when we are told that "Princeton [...] smelled of nothing" (ll. 1 f.). We are also told how much she likes the appearance of the place. The anaphorical repetition of "She liked" supports this as much as the antithetical phrase "But she did not like" (ll. 13–27, 32). The reader also gets an insight into her thinking and reasoning throughout the passage: "she could pretend to be" (ll. 28 f.), "It was unreasonable to expect" (ll. 33 f.), "she could not imagine" (ll. 36 f.), "she wondered" (l. 40) and "she had always found" (ll. 46 f.).

The characters on the platform fit in with the setting and support the atmosphere. "[S]hort, flimsy clothes" (ll. 44 f.) and ice cream suggest pleasant temperatures, and especially the man described by Ifemelu fits in with the academic environment. With the "comical arrangement" of his "greying hair" (ll. 55–57), he has the typical appearance of a university scientist. Again, this is observed from Ifemelu's point of view: she "had always found it a little irresponsible" to eat ice cream in public (ll. 46–51). She supposes he is an academic, expressed by the narrator by means of reported thought ("He had to be", l. 58).

Like Ifemelu's fondness for Princeton, her bewilderment when she returns to Lagos is expressed by the narrator's taking the third-person, limited point of view: She feels "assaulted" by Lagos (l. 64). Unlike Princeton, the atmosphere created here is unpleasant, threatening, overwhelming. There is too much of everything, which is expressed in the first three sentences. The atmosphere is hectic, people are in "haste", and hawkers are "racing after cars" (ll. 66 f.). The yellow buses, which are as characteristic of the traffic of Lagos as the yellow cabs are of New York, are full of "squashed limbs", an amorphous mass of body parts rather than people. The signs of commerce like billboards, writing on the walls, and heaps of rubbish overwhelm the observer. This idea of 'too much' is also expressed in lines 64 to 79: The noises of commerce defying poverty, the noise of conversations and exaggeration in general. Adjectives like "sun-dazed" (ll. 64 f.), "squashed", "sweating" (l. 66), "hulking" (ll. 67 f.) and "dense" (l. 72) give the impression that breathing is hard in Lagos. Even the cars, which metaphorically turn into boats when part of Lagos is flooded, are personified as "gasping" (ll. 76 f.). With the image "a ripe tomato could burst out of solid stone" (ll. 78 f.) the narrator expresses how dynamic, unpredictable, amazing and even uncanny Lagos can be.

As said above, the reader perceives this through Ifemelu's thoughts and feelings. We are told she "felt anything could happen" (ll. 77 f.). She is immersed into the familiar but strange culture she is coming back to. She has a "dizzying sensation of falling" (ll. 79 f.), with the word "falling" repeated twice (l. 81), which suggests suddenness and speed but also duration. Her thinking is again expressed by reported thought when she ponders the changes that have occurred since she left, the mobile phones, communication, the people's behavior and the condition of the buildings in Lagos (cf. l. 84–99).

The character of Ranyinudo fits in with this appearance of and atmosphere in Lagos and supports it. Her appearance, too, seems to be exaggerated in a "billowy" dress and her cheeks "too red", with her blusher compared to bruises (ll. 107–109). Ifemelu perceives her as a "big, firm, curvy woman, exulting in her weight and height". With Ifemelu, the reader perceives her intense smell when they hug, which – to Ifemelu – is the smell of Nigeria (cf. ll. 125 f.).

Anforderungsbereich III (Teilaufgabe 3.1)

> 3.1 Comment on the way Lagos and Ranyinudo are presented. Assess to what extent it represents Nigeria's as well as Africa's social, cultural and economic situation.
> *(Evaluation: Comment)*

Der Operator „comment" verlangt eine persönliche Stellungnahme zum Ausgangstext, in diesem Fall nur zu Text 2. Im Unterricht erworbene Kenntnisse sind hier hilfreich. Ihre Sammlungen zu den Anforderungsbereichen I und II geben hinreichend Anlass zur Betrachtung der soziokulturellen Situation Nigerias bzw. Afrikas. Sie können am Anfang der Stellungnahme ganz knapp darauf Bezug nehmen. Wiederholen Sie aber ja nicht konkret alles, was Sie bereits geschrieben haben! Im Hinblick auf die Anforderungen des Anforderungsbereichs III geht es hier um Verallgemeinerung. Gegebenenfalls könnten Sie diese Aspekte durch weitere Aspekte, die Sie aus dem Unterricht kennen, erweitern. Ein eleganter Bezug kann auch zum letzten Satz des Textauszuges hergestellt werden, der in der Beispiellösung ja auch am Ende von Teilaufgabe II erwähnt wird.

aspects mentioned in the texts	generally true of Nigeria
"Lagos assaulted her"	general impact of African megacity
"sun-dazed haze"	climate
"exaggeration, conversations, over-protestations", "yellow buses full of squashed limbs", "sweating hawkers" "shopkeepers [...] rude", "mobile phone"	people, growing population, noise, young population, modern, affinity to modern media, class differences
"a man's body", "flooding", "patina of decay", "quick to beg"	problems: crime, infrastructure, poverty, gap between rich and poor

"advertisements on hulking billboards", "others scrawled on the wall", "heaps of rubbish", "mobile phone"	economic situation, commerce, environmental awareness, lifestyle
"Ranyinudo [...] clothes [...] smell	exuberance
"Ifemelu [...] Americanah	problems of migration

Die Stellungnahme schließt sich ebenso nahtlos an die Analyse an, wie diese sich an die Inhaltsangabe anschließt. Wichtig ist, dass ein Bezug hergestellt wird zum bisherigen Zieltext. Da die Formulierung der Aufgabenstellung so nicht im Text erscheint, darf auf sie nicht z. B. mit Pronomen Bezug genommen werden. Ganz schlecht ist auch der sofortige Einstieg mit „I think" oder „In my opinion", denn auch die eigene Meinung erfordert eine Hinführung.

Hier eine mögliche Umsetzung:
Bearing the "smell of Nigeria", Ranyinudo is indeed a representative not only of Nigeria but of Africa, at least sub-Saharan Africa. She completely fulfills the cliché of the full-figured black lady, clothed in a colorful traditional dress and talking with a big smile and bright white teeth, giving the cliché of exuberance a lot of truth.
More than just a cliché is the appearance of Lagos and its people. The passage reveals the socio-economic problems of African megacities. It hints at class differences, the large gap between rich and poor, the poor infrastructure, which is vulnerable to natural disaster, and the decay of large parts of the inner cities.
Like any African megacity, Lagos assaults the visitor as the urban nightmare that it is: the buzzing, bustling, fast-paced life of overpopulated African cities trying to come to terms with capitalist achievements and aspirations. Business, trading and advertising play an important part. Making money has become people's main concern and has infected them with selfishness and greed, some even having lost their dignity. Huge billboards and hand-scribbled adverts on the wall witness the predominant role of commerce. Nigeria is Africa's biggest economy. Lagos attracts millions of people who want to get their slice of the cake. Many of them only get a very small slice or none, as few get the lion's share. Nigeria has more millionaires and billionaires than any other African country, while half of the population lives in extreme poverty.
Crime is a serious problem of African cities. The body that is mentioned in the text hints at this omnipresence of crime but also at the negligence of the authorities, the police even, which is also mirrored by the piles of trash in the streets. Indeed, there are enormous sanitary problems in African cities not only concerning rubbish but also sewage, water shortage and poor drainage. This last problem, too, is hinted at in the text when the narrator refers to flooding.
Ifemelu, as a so-called "Americanah", a Nigerian emigrant to America, represents the millions of Africans who try to find a better life abroad. Apparently, Ifemelu, who has got as far as Princeton University, has succeeded. She is only teased about her accent, which does not seem to be properly American. Very often, however, Africans coming back to their home countries are despised as failures, as losers, people who got nowhere – an attitude that makes the problem of migration even bigger.

Nigeria's (and Africa's) population is young; 40 % in sub-Saharan Africa are younger than 15. Therefore, people are up-to-date, using modern media extensively. As in many countries, mobile phones have become an indispensable accessory used in all walks of life. Unfortunately, the text does not hint at many more positive features of Africa, apart from the presentation of Ranyinudo as a likeable person. It may slightly hint at tradition and fashion, which both play an important role in Nigeria and even Africa. Thus, the text does not do much against the negative view of African cities most of us may hold.

Anforderungsbereich III (Teilaufgabe 3.2)

3.2 Ifemelu and Ranyinudo apparently often talk about the situation in Nigeria as compared to the Western world (ll. 100–105). Write a dialogue between them considering aspects hinted at in the texts as well as aspects discussed in class.
(Evaluation: Re-creation of text)

Für die kreative Aufgabe ist zu beachten:

Perspektivwechsel
– Wie ist die zusätzliche Sicht der Dinge aus der Perspektive Ranyinudos?
– Was für eine Art Sprache benutzt sie?

Inhaltliche Anknüpfung an Teilaufgaben 1 und 2 durch einleitenden Satz.
Inhaltlicher Bezug zu Teilaufgaben 1 und 2, z. B. durch:
– Vergleich (Ähnlichkeiten/Unterschiede)
– Kritik
– Wertung
– Gegendarstellung
Eine textkohärente Anknüpfung an Teilaufgabe 2 ist in diesem Fall nicht möglich, denn die Textform ist eine völlig andere.

Hier eine mögliche Umsetzung:
Ifemelu: Ranyinudo, I don't know what has become of Nigeria, what has become of Lagos. As if it was not hot enough in Africa, people have to squeeze into these little yellow buses; they can hardly breathe there. And the hawkers are really getting on my nerves, they harass me.
Ranyinudo: You're looking at all this with American eyes. You are not even a real Americanah, because you haven't got the accent.
Ifemelu: Oh, come on, I may not have the accent, but I really got used to living in the States and to the American way of life. This hassle and this noise is something I can't get used to.
Ranyinudo: Hey, you can't compare Lagos to your beloved Princeton. Princeton is a rich university town, people living there are privileged anyway.

Ifemelu: Yes, you're right. Princeton isn't the place that compares with Lagos, but look at New York City. I've been to New York many times. It's just around the corner from Princeton. New York is as big as Lagos. But it's organised a lot better, a lot less chaotic.

Ranyinudo: Is it?

Ifemelu: I'm sure there must be the same number of people but half the amount of noise. It's clean – at least Manhattan is –, there are no piles of rubbish and people don't throw litter on the streets. Sure, there's a lot of crime, but you don't see dead bodies lying around for days. And the sewage system works. There's never any flooding.

Ranyinudo: Yes, I see your point. There's a lot which is not perfect in this country. But what do you expect? Lagos has become so popular among all kinds of people that they literally flock here. Lagos's infrastructure was not built for this. The city is trying hard to cope with it and to improve – for example – public transport. The sewage system and the waste management are important tasks that we have to tackle. And you know, corruption has always been a problem, and it hasn't changed that much. Petty corruption has declined somewhat thanks to measures taken by the government, but big corruption is still increasing. The bigger the project, the greater the opportunity to divert cash. So a lot of money doesn't get where it's supposed to go.

Ifemelu: Yes, but what about the people? They've changed so much. Everybody seems to have a mobile phone.

Ranyinudo: Yes, but isn't this a phenomenon that we see all over the world? Don't tell me it's not like this in the States. And if it isn't, look at Europe. Texting is what young people do all the time. And Nigeria is extremely young. There aren't so many old people like in Europe or America. And of course, that's why it's a lot more lively.

Ifemelu: But all this commerce everywhere. Everybody seems so greedy, everyone is chasing after money, and shopkeepers are so unfriendly.

Ranyinudo: What do you expect? People have learned the lesson of democracy; people have learned the lesson of free enterprise and competition. This is based on your American Dream – a Nigerian Dream, Ifemelu. Look at the things that Nigeria has to offer: our cultural diversity, our youth, our talents, our resilience and happiness. We still cherish our traditions and we still fear God. Isn't this something to be proud of?

Ifemelu: Yes, maybe you're right.

Beispielaufgabe 2: Owen Jones, „Brexitland"

Thematischer Bezug gemäß KLP (Soziokulturelles Orientierungswissen):
Das Vereinigte Königreich im 21. Jahrhundert – Selbstverständnis zwischen Tradition und Wandel: *Tradition and change in politics and society – The UK in the European context*

Auszug aus einem englischsprachigen Sachtext (741 W.)

Quellenangaben:
Owen Jones, „Brexitland: So much for the fractured nation – I haven't found it", *The Guardian,* London, 20.04.2017, https://www.theguardian.com/commentisfree/2017/apr/20/brexitland-fractured-nation-politicians-unite-labour (Zugriff: 01.04.2024, gekürzt); Copyright Guardian News & Media Ltd 2024

Aufgabe

1. Point out people's motivations and conflicts when voting in the referendum, according to Jones's article. *(Comprehension)*

2. Examine Owen Jones's language and argumentative strategies when dealing with "fractured" British society. Consider the way he composes his text as well as his use of language and imagery. *(Analysis)*

3. Choose one of the following tasks:

3.1 Considering the personal backgrounds and statements of the people interviewed, evaluate the usefulness of the Brexit referendum as well as referendums in general in a modern democracy. *(Evaluation: Comment)*

3.2 You are asked to take part in a debate on the role of supranational bodies in the globalised world at your partner school in Britain. Write your initial statement about the role of the EU with regard to ecological challenges as well as working and studying. *(Evaluation: Re-creation of text)*

Brexitland: So much for the fractured nation – I haven't found it (excerpt)   *Owen Jones*

[...]

We'll hear a lot about Britain being a bitterly divided nation as we head into a general election. And it would be delu-
5 sional to deny the referendum has created rifts. But having spent the last few months travelling between English communities that plumped for Brexit, I didn't find much evidence of ordinary voters brimming
10 with venom for each other. People who voted leave didn't regard remainers as effete metropolitan elitist saboteurs; remainers didn't see leavers as knuckle-dragging bigoted Neanderthals. The appetite to turn neighbour against neighbour over the ref-
15 erendum – and to transform the aftermath into a full-blown culture war – certainly exists in certain media and political circles. My suspicion is that people are growing pretty weary of it. I found that most are too
20 decent and busy to hate each other.

Take Laura and Dan: they are a couple in the South Yorkshire town of Doncaster in their early 20s who have just moved in together. Laura is a hairstylist who voted to
25 remain: she thinks "people voted to leave because of immigrants" and bemoans the loss of her freedom of movement. Her part-

ner Dan, who repairs domestic appliances, did indeed vote to leave because of "refugees". I press him, and he actually means Romanians, rather than refugees – and he notes there was an expectation of "instant change", not least over the promise of extra cash for the NHS.

But he said something that summed up how so many people I met seem to feel. "It's not that I particularly needed it or wanted it to happen. We were asked to vote so I voted, and that was the answer I came up with, with the information I had." Politicos live in a world where breathlessly scanning through Twitter for crumbs of gossip is one of the first and last rituals of the day. It is not a world most live in. Politics provokes little passion among most people, even if individual issues do. As I left them, remainer Laura and leaver Dan kissed and got on with their lives.

Or take 55-year-old Lynne, a communications manager for an IT company in Fareham, Hampshire. Her husband voted remain; she voted leave, but, like so many on both sides of the divide, was conflicted about her vote. We are not as polarised as the binary choice of "remain" or "leave", she says. As it happens, she was motivated to vote leave because she felt there was a democratic deficit, yet she believes the post-referendum rhetoric on immigration "is a disaster", and thinks "it'll be a great pity if it damages positive migration and immigration policies".

In Stockport, Greater Manchester, it's easy to find different democratic choices but little sign of bitter division. Karen, 43, is a proud, working-class Stopfordian who couldn't get a council house. She's on a weekly shop in Tesco when we speak. She was a passionate remainer, and worries about how the NHS will cope if foreign doctors and nurses leave. "Where will that leave us then?" she asks.

It's an anxiety about the future that she shares with many who voted to leave. It is difficult to divorce the pessimism that 64-year-old Tony, for instance, feels about his hometown and his democratic decision. "It's going downhill fast," he says, pointing at the empty shops in a town centre that is undoubtedly struggling to thrive. A mother and daughter I met in its Merseyway shopping centre voted for remain, but they also feel the sense of abandonment that many leavers have felt for a long time.

Do small towns such as Stockport get a bit forgotten? "Definitely!" was their immediate response. But, again, with all the people I have spoken to, there's no bitterness, no hatred, no contempt for the other side. We were asked a question, is the general gist, and we answered it.

From Doncaster and Sheffield in the north of England, down to Barking and Dagenham in London and South Thanet in Kent, I found an abundance of reasons why millions voted to leave. Low pay, a sense of decline, feeling abandoned or ignored, a housing crisis, immigration, a perceived democratic deficit, wanting to give the establishment a kicking. For some, their choice was based on a passionate inner belief; for others, their vote was made with a shrug of the shoulders.

[...]

Annotations

effete – affected and incapable of effective action; **knuckle-dragging** – i. e. dragging their knuckles over the ground; **NHS** – National Health Service; system providing free medical treatment in Britain; **politico** – person strongly involved in politics

Bearbeitungsschritte und Musterlösungen

Anforderungsbereich I (Teilaufgabe 1)

> 1. Point out people's motivations and conflicts when voting in the referendum, according to Jones's article. *(Comprehension)*

Was den Text angeht, so verlangt der Operator „point out" eine zusammenfassende Darstellung der Ausführungen und Argumente des Autors. Die entsprechenden Schlüsselbegriffe werden im Text unterstrichen oder mit Textmarker farbig markiert. Hier werden wir auflisten, was im Ausgangstext markiert sein sollte:

passage	key phrases
ll. 1–21	"bitterly divided" – "didn't find much evidence" "exists in certain media"
ll. 22–49	Laura: "remain", "bemoans the loss of her freedom of movement" Dan: "leave", "refugees"/"Romanians", "extra cash for the NHS", "asked to vote, so I voted"
ll. 50–63	Lynn: "leave", "democratic deficit", "pity if it damages positive [...] immigration policies"
ll. 64–86	Karen: "couldn't get a council house", "passionate remainer", "worries about [...] foreign doctors and nurses leav[ing]", "anxiety [...] she shares with many who voted to leave" Tony: "leave", "downhill fast", "mother and daughter [...] voted for remain", "also feel sense of abandonment"
ll. 87 – end	"no bitterness, no hatred, no contempt" "asked a question, [...] answered" "abundance of reasons why [...] leave": "a sense of decline, feeling abandoned or ignored, a housing crisis, immigration, a perceived democratic deficit, wanting to give the establishment a kicking" "passionate inner belief" vs. "shrug of the shoulders"

Nachdem diese Vorarbeiten abgeschlossen sind, geht es nun darum, Ihre Notizen und Markierungen in einen zusammenhängenden Text zu bringen. Es bietet sich an, die einleitende Aussage Jones's als *topic sentence* voranzustellen, dann seine Beispiele und Argumente anzuführen und mit seinem Fazit abzuschließen.

Beginnen Sie mit einem Einleitungssatz, der sich auf die jeweilige Textvorlage bezieht (s. S. 201), und vergegenwärtigen Sie sich die Grundsätze für das Verfassen von Zusammenfassungen.

Vermeiden Sie Wendungen wie „in the first paragraph", „from line x to line y", „then the author says". Dies sind Wendungen, die eine Strukturanalyse charakterisieren; sie gehören nicht in eine Zusammenfassung.

Hier eine mögliche Umsetzung:

The text "Brexitland: So much for the fractured nation – I haven't found it" by Owen Jones, which was published in "The Guardian" on 17 April 2017, deals with the alleged bitter divide of the British nation after the Brexit referendum. Jones claims that this image exists in certain media but that it is not true for ordinary voters.

Laura, a hairstylist from Doncaster, for instance, voted remain, whereas her partner, who is an electrician, voted to leave. While Laura's motivation was free movement, her partner's vote was directed against EU immigrants and also motivated by the promise of extra money for the NHS. But their votes did not divide them, as they do not attribute great importance to political issues.

Another example is Lynne, a communications manager from Hampshire, who voted leave and whose husband voted to remain. Yet she is conflicted about her vote. Her motivation was the EU's democratic deficit, but she seriously worries about the new aggressive rhetoric on immigration.

Karen from Greater Manchester voted remain, but she also shares her worries with many people who voted to leave, namely for the future of the NHS without staff from the EU or the declining infrastructure of their hometown. This sense of abandonment is something leavers have felt for a long time, but which remainers feel too. Reasons to vote to leave were low wages, the declining infrastructure, a feeling of being ignored, housing costs, immigration, the feeling of not having a say in Brussels or simply protest. Some believed in their decision passionately, others just voted without giving it much thought. Yet, there is no bitterness, no hatred and no contempt for the other side. People say they were asked a question and they simply answered it.

Anforderungsbereich II (Teilaufgabe 2)

> 2. Examine Owen Jones's language and argumentative strategies when dealing with "fractured" British society. Consider the way he composes his text as well as his use of language and imagery. *(Analysis)*

Die Aufgabe verlangt eine Analyse der Textstruktur und eine Analyse der Stilmittel. Diese Analysen sollten Sie getrennt voneinander angehen.

Die Struktur des Textes zeigt sich schon in den Notizen zum Inhalt. Untersuchen Sie die einzelnen Sinnabschnitte auf ihre Funktion für den Aufbau des Textes und notieren Sie sie auf der Textvorlage.

Hier stellen wir dies wieder als Tabelle dar.

argumentative structure	key phrases
introduction: claim ll. 1–21	"bitterly divided": "didn't find much evidence" "exists in certain media"
evidence/example ll. 22–49	Laura: "remain", "bemoans the loss of her freedom of movement" Dan: "leave", "refugees"/"Romanians", …
evidence/example ll. 50–63	Lynn: "leave", "democratic deficit", "pity if it damages positive [...] immigration policies"
evidence/example ll. 64–86	Karen: "couldn't get a council house", "passionate remainer", … Tony: "leave", "downhill fast", …
conclusion ll. 87 – end	"no bitterness, no hatred, no contempt", …

Innerhalb dieser Struktur bedient sich der Autor verschiedener Strategien, seine Leserschaft zu überzeugen. Ohne dass wir die Textpassagen hier einzeln aufführen müssen, werden Sie leicht erkennen, wie nicht nur beispielhaft Menschen aus der britischen Bevölkerung angeführt werden, sondern sie auch zitiert werden, was dem Text Glaubhaftigkeit verleiht. Überdies werden immer stets *leavers* und *remainers* einander gegenübergestellt – ein Kontrast, den wir auch in den Stilmitteln wiederfinden.

Es handelt sich hier um einen persuasiven Text – einen Text, der den Leser überzeugen möchte. Ein solcher Text bedient sich neben seiner Argumente auch der Stilmittel, wie sie im Kapitel zur Analyse einer Rede dargestellt sind. Wenn Ihnen diese nicht sofort ins Auge fallen, suchen Sie gezielt nach den Ihnen bekannten Stilmitteln (Checkliste im Kopf) und markieren Sie sie im Text (vgl. S. 93 f.).

Im Einzelnen finden wir in diesem Text:

lines	words/phrases	stylistic devices
title	"fractured nation"	imagery
l. 3	"bitterly divided nation"	choice of words
l. 6	"rifts"	imagery
ll. 9 f.	"brimming with venom"	imagery
l. 12	"effete metropolitan elitist saboteurs"	choice of words / imagery
ll. 13 f.	"as knuckle-dragging bigoted Neanderthals"	choice of words / imagery
ll. 14 f.	"The appetite to turn neighbour against neighbour"	choice of words
l. 16	"aftermath"	choice of words
l. 17	"full-blown culture war"	choice of words

l. 21	"decent and busy"	choice of words
l. 41	"Politicos"	choice of words
l. 42	"breathlessly scanning"	choice of words / exaggeration
l. 43	"crumbs of gossip"	imagery
l. 44	"first and last rituals of the day"	choice of words
ll. 90 f.	"no bitterness, no hatred, no contempt"	enumeration/parallelism
ll. 98 ff.	"Low pay, a sense of decline, feeling abandoned or ignored, a housing crisis, immigration, a perceived democratic deficit, wanting to give the establishment a kicking"	enumeration
ll. 102 ff.	"For some […] for others"	antithesis

Nennenswerte Stilmittel fallen zwischen Zeilen 45 und 89 nicht auf. Das ist dann eben so. Suchen Sie nicht krampfhaft etwas, was Sie dann selbst nicht glauben! Der Text wurde ja nicht für die Schule geschrieben.

Wenn Sie nun Ihren Text verfassen, ordnen Sie die Resultate wieder, anstatt textchronologisch vorzugehen. Auffällig sind die Wortwahl und die Metaphorik, aber auch emphatische Strukturen fallen ins Auge. Sinnvollerweise beginnt man mit dem vorherrschenden Stilmittel.

Bei der Umwandlung Ihrer Notizen in einen zusammenhängenden Text, müssen Sie darauf achten, nicht den Inhalt, sondern die Funktion sowohl der einzelnen Abschnitte als auch der rhetorischen Mittel wiederzugeben. Mit dem Inhalt haben sie sich hinreichend in Teilaufgabe 1 befasst. Inhaltliches wir hier auf ein Mindestmaß reduziert. Bitte paraphrasieren Sie nicht endlos den Ausgangstext!

Überdies wird verlangt, dass Ihre Klausur aus einem zusammenhängenden Gesamttext besteht. Fangen Sie also nicht mit einem neuen Einleitungssatz an, sondern schließen Sie nahtlos an Teilaufgabe 1 an. Bitte schreiben Sie nicht: *„Now I am going to examine Owen Jones's language …"* – do it, don't talk about it!

TIPP zum Punktesammeln

Im Anforderungsbereich II ist Ihr Thema nicht Brexit. Ihr Thema ist Sprache – es geht um Wörter, Ausdrücke und Sätze. Eine Formulierung wie „The author says that" führt daher in die falsche Richtung.

Denken Sie auch daran, dass eine Analyse Belege in Form von Verweisen oder Zitaten verlangt!

Hier eine mögliche Umsetzung:

Jones tries to prove his evaluation of people's attitudes by giving his text a classic structure. He introduces his article by referring to the alleged divide and hatred between leavers and remainers (ll. 2–18). In order to disclaim this allegation, he gives various examples. From lines 22 to 49, he illustrates his point with a married couple who voted for opposite sides without any damage to their relationship. His next example (ll. 50–63) shows that voting to leave does not always follow clear-cut political views but can be rather conflicted. A further example (ll. 64–86) reveals how people's worries about their daily lives are very much the same on both sides. Thus, Jones concludes (ll. 87 – end) that a lot of people did not give particular weight to the referendum.

The people referred to by Jones do not only serve as examples of one or the other side. Quoting their opinions in direct speech makes them witnesses, experts on the topic, thus giving the text credibility. Jones contrasts leavers and remainers in each example, in each case coming to the conclusion that there is no hostility. In the case of Laura and Dan (ll. 48–50), he confirms this by stating that "remainer Laura and leaver Dan kissed and got on with their lives".

As early as in the title and again in line 6, Jones uses geological metaphors to illustrate the alleged division of Britain. He speaks of "a fractured nation" and "rifts" that divide the country. The word "bitterly" (l. 3) underlines this division, suggesting hardship, sorrow, grimness, disappointment and hatred at the same time. This hatred is then illustrated with the metaphor "brimming with venom" (ll. 9 f.), which conjures the image of venomous snakes or a witch's cauldron.

People with contrasting attitudes are referred to as "effete metropolitan elitist saboteurs" (ll. 11 f.) or described with the metaphor "knuckle-dragging bigoted Neanderthals" (ll. 13 f.). Thus, people in favour of the EU are allegedly and stereotypically regarded as Londoners, who profit from comfortable professional life in the big city, do not know what hard work is and are unpatriotic or even traitors as they destroy traditional political structures. On the other hand, leavers are regarded as retarded, as having regressed to some pre-homo sapiens state and thus having lost their minds (ll. 13 f.).

Words and expressions from the semantic field of war and aggression ("turn neighbour against neighbour", "aftermath", "full-blown cultural war", ll. 14–17) underline this opposition. As the author rejects this view, he also uses the positively connotated words "decent" and "busy" (l. 21), which in turn instead allude to the typical British characteristics of reserve and politeness, of avoiding confrontation and wanting to keep harmony. In the end, what is left of the harsh contrast of leavers and remainers is simply an unspectacular, antithetical sentence saying "For some, their choice was based on a passionate inner belief; for others, their vote was made with a shrug of the shoulders" (ll. 102–105).

According to Jones, it is the politicians and politically strongly involved people that may be too agitated by the results of the referendum. He therefore ridicules them and their activity with the word "[p]oliticos" (l. 41), who "breathlessly" scan the media for "crumbs of gossip" (ll. 42 f.) with almost religious zeal ("first and last rituals", l. 44) – words and images that contrast them sharply with "decent" (l. 21) people and makes them appear almost insane and obsessed.

The last part of Jones's text is rather marked by emphatic structures than by a particular choice of words. He hammers his thesis home by using enumeration and parallelism in line 90 f.: "no bitterness, no hatred, no contempt". He also lists reasons why people voted leave (ll. 98 ff.), i. e. the factors that make people unhappy and disappointed in today's Britain in order to emphasise what is wrong with the nation and what one should be aware of shortly before a general election (l. 3 f.).

Anforderungsbereich III (Teilaufgabe 3.1)

> 3.1 Considering the personal backgrounds and statements of the people interviewed, evaluate the usefulness of the Brexit referendum as well as referendums in general in a modern democracy. *(Evaluation: Comment)*

Im Anforderungsbereich III wird von Ihnen eine Stellungnahme verlangt. Nachdem Sie sich intensiv mit der Textvorlage befasst haben, sollten Sie in der Lage sein, sich eine eigene Meinung zu bilden. Wichtig ist,
– dass Sie Ihre Stellungnahme auf den Ausgangstext bzw. die Ausgangstexte beziehen,
– dass Sie ihre eigenen Behauptungen mit Argumenten und Beispielen untermauern und
– dass Sie zu einer dezidierten persönlichen Stellungnahme gelangen, einer persönlichen Meinung, die sich aus Ihren Ausführungen ergibt.

Markieren Sie im Text diejenigen Elemente, die Sie für Ihre Stellungnahme heranziehen möchten. Sammeln und ordnen Sie Ihre Gedanken auf Ihrem Konzeptblatt. Wählen Sie dazu eine Mindmap oder auch eine Liste.

people involved	personal backgrounds and statements (should be highlighted in the text)	comment
Laura	"hairstylist", "people voted to leave because of immigrants", "bemoans the loss of her freedom of movement"	education: ability to understand consequences of vote? freedom of movement relevant?
Dan	"repairs domestic appliances", "did indeed vote to leave because of 'refugees' [...] he actually means Romanians, rather than refugees", "expectation of 'instant change', not least over the promise of extra cash for the NHS" "We were asked to vote so I voted, and that was the answer I came up with, with the information I had"	education: does not see the difference between Romanians and refugees, i. e. between the right of free movement and the refugee policy of the EU

Lynn	"communications manager for an IT company", "conflicted about her vote", "We are not as polarised as the binary choice of 'remain' or 'leave'"	complexity of political and economic issues, more multifaceted than yes or no
Karen	"a proud, working-class Stopfordian", "remainer", "anxiety about the future that she shares with many who voted to leave"	no simple solutions, causes of social and economic problems not necessarily linked to EU membership
Tony	"pessimism", "It's going downhill fast"	as above

TIPP zum Punktesammeln

Beginnen Sie Ihre Stellungnahme nicht mit „In my opinion", „I think" etc.! Beziehen sie sich auf den Ausgangstext! Beziehen Sie sich vor allem nicht mit einem „this" oder „it" auf die Aufgabenstellung der Teilaufgabe! Ihre Gesamtaufgabe ist ein zusammenhängender Zieltext, der ohne Kenntnis der Formulierung der Teilaufgaben verständlich sein muss. Beenden Sie Ihre Stellungnahme mit Ihrem persönlichen Fazit!

Hier eine mögliche Umsetzung:

The examples and statements of ordinary British citizens brightly illustrate the usefulness – or rather uselessness – of a referendum on British membership in the EU and of referendums in general. In the film "Brexit – The Uncivil War", Benedict Cumberbatch's Dominic Cummings says that referendums are "the worst way to decide anything" and calls it "a really dumb idea". Looking at what the citizens interviewed by Jones say, it becomes clear that this fictional Cummings is right in what he says, be it authentic or not. Lynn is a hairdresser, who cannot be expected to fully understand the consequences of a political decision as fundamental as the membership of the European Union. She says she'll miss her freedom of movement, which shows she is not really informed. She does not seem to have planned to move to Spain with her husband in order to work there, and her travelling as a tourist in Europe will not be restricted by Brexit. Like her, Dan, a repairman, does not seem to give much thought to academic matters and does not see the difference between those that seek asylum and EU migrants. He too was deceived by the campaign's lie about funding for the NHS. Yet, he voted "with the information [he] had" (l. 41).

A complex political decision cannot be made on the basis of two opposed views. The conflicting votes of the people interviewed in Hampshire and Greater Manchester undeniably reveal that there are no clear-cut boundaries along which people could have voted for one or the other option. This will be the case in any referendum on far-reaching issues. The example of the made-up promise of "extra cash for the NHS" shows how much a referendum is decided by populist strategies. The leave campaign were able to claim whatever they wanted without taking responsibility for it afterwards. Remain, as backed by the government, was held accountable for everything they said. Thus, the leave campaign was able to get away with fearmongering on Turkey's joining the EU, with lies on the actual costs of EU membership and the false promise of extra funding of the NHS. Considering how emotionally loaded many political questions are – just think of penal law or immigration policy –, populist manipulation is generally to be expected in any referendum.

It has also been proved that people in Britain were manipulated by being microtargeted with advertising on social media. This may seem normal in today's digital world, but, again, it is definitely easier to manipulate voters into giving a simple yes or no vote than into voting for a party programme, which also involves traditional affinity or social identity.

Turnout is another issue. The referendum turnout was a little over 70 percent. About 17 million people voted leave. The electorate was 46.5 million with a total population of 65 million people. Referring to those 17 million voters as "the people" is highly questionable to me. Polls on binary issues will always have results like this. They cannot represent the people's will. We are faced with the same pitfall as in the first-past-the-post system in parliamentary or presidential elections.

Lastly, a yes-or-no decision can also be easily influenced just by the wording of the question. A good example is the outcome of a poll in Germany in which people opted for the continuous use of daylight saving time. The German word "Sommerzeit" ('summertime') sounds so pleasant that people voted for it. Another poll avoiding this word had contrary results.

In short, I totally agree with what the Dominic Cummings character says in the film „Brexit": A referendum is the dumbest idea to decide anything. Political decisions have to be made in parliament in accordance with the required procedures.

Anforderungsbereich III (Teilaufgabe 3.2)

> 3.2 You are asked to take part in a debate on the role of supranational bodies in the globalised world at your partner school in Britain. Write your initial statement about the role of the EU with regard to ecological challenges as well as working and studying. *(Evaluation: Re-creation of text)*

Dieses Aufgabenformat ist neu seit 2021. Das Format ist Ihnen aus Ihren Klausuren nicht bekannt, weil wir in Nordrhein-Westfalen eine enge Anbindung an den Ausgangstext verlangen. Im Abitur wird eine der beiden Teilaufgaben 3 nur thematisch an den Ausgangstext angebunden sein. Zudem ist diese Aufgabe dann themenübergreifend. Deshalb werden Sie eine solch offene Aufgabe in Ihren Oberstufenklausuren, die ja Kursthemen abschließen, eher nicht finden.

Der Anspruch dieser Aufgaben, dass man sich nach stundenlanger Beschäftigung mit dem einen Thema nun auch noch einem weiteren Thema zuwendet, legt den Schluss nahe, diese Teilaufgabe zu vermeiden und in jedem Fall die andere zu wählen.

Es mag aber sicher gute Gründe geben, dieser Teilaufgabe eine Chance zu geben:
- Das jeweils andere Textformat (*comment* oder *re-creation of text*) liegt Ihnen gar nicht.
- Die Thematik liegt Ihnen oder Sie haben das Thema sehr intensiv vorbereitet.
- Sie kennen sich mit der Thematik über die Inhalte eines anderen Faches bestens aus.
- Sie mögen sich zum Ausgangstext nicht äußern.

Zur Bearbeitung dieser Aufgabe lassen Sie nun Jones's Text beiseite und sammeln Ihre Gedanken zu den beiden Kursthemen „Ecological challenges and sustainable lifestyles" und „Studying and working in a globalised world" in einer Mindmap oder Liste.

ecological issues
- climate change – no frontiers
    - international regulations
    - international research
    - cooperation on technology and green energy
    - strong power against corporations
    - international prosecution
    - distribution of climate refugees

working and studying
- Erasmus programme, benefits
    - EU money
    - personality-/character-building
    - independence
    - language learning
    - meeting people and cultures
    - widen horizons
- freedom of movement
    - working for international companies
    - opening businesses in EU countries
    - Gen Z: flexibility (working from home / availability around the clock)

conclusion: national borders are an anachronism; words like freedom and independence in this context are simply buzzwords

Hier eine mögliche Umsetzung:
I was asked to take part in this debate and I agreed with pleasure because I am an ardent internationalist and I still can't really get over what Britain did in the referendum. In my statement, I will share a few thoughts on the role of the EU, focussing on two aspects which are very close to my heart. The first aspect is ecology, the second aspect is the issue of working and studying abroad.
As far as ecology is concerned, climate change is the most important issue of our times. It can't be targeted on a national basis. Climate and weather don't stop at national bor-

ders. It's a worldwide issue, it's true, but with the EU being one of the most powerful economies in the world, effective measures can be introduced on a European footing. With the relevant institutions in place and working, it should be easy to take the appropriate steps in a minimal amount of time. And, of course, although it seems nothing has been done to improve the situation, we have to admit that steps in the right direction have been taken already. There are regulations on emissions and there are regulations on carbon dioxide reduction and, above all, there is awareness. There's no need to say that coordinated criminal prosecution of environmental offenders is likewise only possible if there's international law enforcement.

But it's not just the politicians and their regulations that have to target climate change. There is a network of international cooperation between all kinds of institutions, above all universities, so that the full impact of international expertise is ready to be used against this threat. Again, this being an international issue, international research should target climate change and indeed does so. Of course, close ties between different countries, like in the EU, immensely facilitate international cooperation and exchange.

Being an enormous economic power, the EU may also have a powerful stance when facing international corporations that don't comply with climate protection measures. One country alone can do little against global players. But even corporations that have learned the lesson themselves will be a lot more effective on a European basis when it comes to introducing new technologies like photovoltaics or green hydrogen or with respect to responsible production.

The consequences of climate change, which we are already experiencing, can also only be dealt with internationally. And again, with a supranational body already in place, it will be far easier to attend to those issues. One of the gravest consequences of climate change is and will be the number of climate refugees. The challenge of fair and equal distribution of refugees can only be addressed with international consent. Even though the EU has so far failed in this respect, the handling of refugees from Ukraine seems to show the potential of this supranational body.

The other issue I'd like to broach is studying and working. With the Erasmus programme the EU provides a scheme that facilitates studying abroad immensely. The benefits of this are obvious: With scholarships from the EU, students are able to learn about different cultures, master new languages, develop their personalities. They become independent, get fresh views, meet people and make friends with people from all over Europe, broaden their horizons. In this respect the EU is really the peace project that it was originally designed as.

The same is true for work. Without worrying about immigration and visa regulations or even restrictions, the principle of freedom of movement gives you the chance of working anywhere between Greece and Ireland or Portugal and Finland. You can work for international or national companies, you can open your own business, you can be as flexible as you want, working from home in different countries or even on your smartphone from anywhere. To Generation Z, national borders are really an anachronism. It's truly a shame that certain countries are rebuilding or seeking to rebuild borders.

Thank you for your attention.

Beispielaufgabe 3: Joseph R. Biden, Inaugural Address

Thematischer Bezug gemäß KLP (Soziokulturelles Orientierungswissen):
Amerikanischer Traum – Visionen und Lebenswirklichkeiten in den USA: *American myths and realities: freedom and equality*
Chancen und Risiken der Globalisierung: *Globalisation and global challenges: economic, ecological and political issues*

Auszug aus einem englischsprachiger Sachtext (987 W.)

Quellenangaben:
Joseph R. Biden, Inaugural address, 20 January 2021, https://www.whitehouse.gov/briefing-room/speeches-remarks/2021/01/20/inaugural-address-by-president-joseph-r-biden-jr/ (Zugriff: 01.04.2024, gekürzt)

Aufgabe

1. Sum up what challenges America faces and what has to be done to meet them according to Biden. *(Comprehension)*

2. Analyse the rhetorical means and strategies that Biden uses to convince his listeners. *(Analysis)*

3. Choose one of the following tasks:

3.1 Comment on lines 1 f. ("This is America's day. This is democracy's day. A day of history and hope, of renewal and resolve.") against the background of the speech and your work in class about the US and the American Dream. *(Evaluation: Comment)*

3.2 The debating club of your American host school deals with the challenges America and the world are facing in the 21st century. You are asked to contribute to the debate on climate change from your European perspective. Write your initial statement to the debate. Refer to work done in class on ecological issues of globalisation. *(Evaluation: Re-creation of text)*

Inaugural address, January 20th, 2021 (excerpt) *Joseph R. Biden*

[...]

This is America's day. This is democracy's day. A day of history and hope. Of renewal and resolve. Through a crucible for
5 the ages America has been tested anew and America has risen to the challenge. Today, we celebrate the triumph not of a candidate, but of a cause, the cause of democracy. The will of the people has been heard and the will of the people has been heeded.
10 We have learned again that democracy is precious. Democracy is fragile. And at this hour, my friends, democracy has prevailed.

15 So now, on this hallowed ground where just days ago violence sought to shake this Capitol's very foundation, we come together as one nation, under God, indivisible, to carry out the peaceful transfer of power as we have 20 for more than two centuries. We look ahead in our uniquely American way – restless, bold, optimistic – and set our sights on the nation we know we can be and we must be.

I thank my predecessors of both parties 25 for their presence here. I thank them from the bottom of my heart. You know the resilience of our Constitution and the strength of our nation. As does President Carter, who I spoke to last night but who cannot 30 be with us today, but whom we salute for his lifetime of service.

I have just taken the sacred oath each of these patriots took — an oath first sworn by George Washington. But the American 35 story depends not on any one of us, not on some of us, but on all of us. On "We the People" who seek a more perfect Union.

This is a great nation and we are a good people. Over the centuries through storm 40 and strife, in peace and in war, we have come so far. But we still have far to go.

We will press forward with speed and urgency, for we have much to do in this winter of peril and possibility. Much to re- 45 pair. Much to restore. Much to heal. Much to build. And much to gain.

Few periods in our nation's history have been more challenging or difficult than the one we're in now. A once-in-a-century virus 50 silently stalks the country. It's taken as many lives in one year as America lost in all of World War II. Millions of jobs have been lost. Hundreds of thousands of businesses closed. A cry for racial justice some 400 years in the 55 making moves us. The dream of justice for all will be deferred no longer. A cry for survival comes from the planet itself. A cry that can't be any more desperate or any more clear. And now, a rise in political extremism, white supremacy, domestic terrorism that we 60 must confront and we will defeat.

To overcome these challenges – to restore the soul and to secure the future of America – requires more than words. It requires that most elusive of things in a de- 65 mocracy: Unity. Unity.

In another January in Washington, on New Year's Day 1863, Abraham Lincoln signed the Emancipation Proclamation. When he put pen to paper, the President 70 said, "If my name ever goes down into history it will be for this act and my whole soul is in it."

My whole soul is in it. Today, on this January day, my whole soul is in this: Bringing 75 America together. Uniting our people. And uniting our nation. I ask every American to join me in this cause. Uniting to fight the common foes we face: Anger, resentment, hatred. Extremism, lawlessness, violence. 80 Disease, joblessness, hopelessness.

With unity we can do great things. Important things. We can right wrongs. We can put people to work in good jobs. We can teach our children in safe schools. We can over- 85 come this deadly virus. We can reward work, rebuild the middle class, and make health care secure for all. We can deliver racial justice. We can make America, once again, the leading force for good in the world. 90

I know speaking of unity can sound to some like a foolish fantasy. I know the forces that divide us are deep and they are real. But I also know they are not new. Our history has been a constant struggle be- 95 tween the American ideal that we are all created equal and the harsh, ugly reality that racism, nativism, fear, and demonization have long torn us apart. The battle is perennial. Victory is never assured. 100

Through the Civil War, the Great Depression, World War, 9/11, through struggle, sacrifice, and setbacks, our "better angels" have always prevailed. In each of 105 these moments, enough of us came together to carry all of us forward. And, we can do so now.

History, faith, and reason show the way, the way of unity. We can see each other 110 not as adversaries but as neighbors. We can treat each other with dignity and respect. We can join forces, stop the shouting, and lower the temperature. For without unity, there is no peace, only bitterness and fury. 115 No progress, only exhausting outrage. No nation, only a state of chaos.

This is our historic moment of crisis and challenge, and unity is the path for-ward. And, we must meet this moment as the United States of America. If we do that, 120 I guarantee you, we will not fail. We have never, ever, ever failed in America when we have acted together.

And so today, at this time and in this place, let us start afresh. All of us. Let us 125 listen to one another. Hear one another. See one another. Show respect to one another. Politics need not be a raging fire destroying everything in its path. Every disagreement doesn't have to be a cause for total 130 war. And, we must reject a culture in which facts themselves are manipulated and even manufactured.

[...]

Annotations

inaugural address – first speech of the President on the day of his inauguration

we the people – first words of the US constitution

Bewertungskriterien

Anforderungsbereich I (Teilaufgabe 1)

Die Schülerin / Der Schüler	max. Punkte
benennt die Herausforderungen, denen sich die USA stellen müssen: – die Coronapandemie und ihre Folgen (Arbeitslosigkeit, Insolvenz), – die Klimakrise, – Rassismus, der sich seit Jahrhunderten fortsetzt, – Extremismus, Terrorismus und Glaube an weiße Vorherrschaft, – generell: Hass, Unmut, Kriminalität, Gewalt, Hoffnungslosigkeit.	8
führt aus, wie diese Krisen nur gemeinsam bekämpft werden können.	4
	12

Anforderungsbereich II (Teilaufgabe 2)

Die Schülerin / Der Schüler	max. Punkte
führt den Patriotismus in Bidens Rede aus, der sich manifestiert in z. B. – Schlüsselwörtern (*America, democracy, nation, unity strength, great* etc.), – historischen Bezügen (Washington, Lincoln, historische Ereignisse) und	4

– religiöser Überhöhung: „hallowed ground" (Z. 14), „under God" (Z. 17), „sacred oath"(Z. 31) „better angels" (Z. 103 f.).	
erläutert den Gebrauch figurativer Sprache in ihrer jeweiligen Funktion, z. B. – die Metapher „a crucible for the ages" (Z. 4 f.), – die Metonymie/Metapher „shake this Capitol's very foundation" (Z. 15 f.), – die Metapher „storm" (Z. 38), – die Metapher „winter of peril" (Z. 43), – die Personifikation „cry for survival" (Z. 55 f.), – die Personifikation „virus silently stalks" (Z. 48 f.).	6
benennt die emphatischen Mittel in ihrer jeweiligen Funktion, z. B. – zahlreiche Wiederholungen, – Alliterationen und Aufzählungen (auch Fakten und Zahlen) zur besonderen Betonung der Missstände, – Kontraste (Antithese) zusammen mit Parallelismen bzw. Anaphern zur Betonung der Stärke und Größe Amerikas, der Größe der Herausforderungen und der Bedeutung der Einheit, – Anaphern und Aufzählungen zur Betonung der Größe der Aufgaben und der Entschlossenheit und Stärke Amerikas, die Situation zu verbessern, – Parallelismen und Wiederholungen zur Betonung einzelner Kernsätze, – kurze oder elliptische Sätze.	4
benennt die Zielgruppenorientierung durch – collective „we" (durchgehend), – „my friends" (Z. 13), – „We the people" (Z. 35 f.), – Appelle („Let us .. ", „We must …" Z. 125 ff.). – Zuhörer und Redner als zusammenstehende Amerikaner	4
	18

Anforderungsbereich III (Teilaufgabe 3.1)

Die Schülerin / Der Schüler	max. Punkte
knüpft an den Ausgangstext an, indem sie/er sich auf den Beginn der Rede bezieht.	2
erläutert die Grundsätze des Amerikanischen Traums, die sich aus der Unabhängigkeitserklärung und dem Pioniergeist und Nationalstolz ergeben (Glaube an Erfolg, Streben nach Glück, Anpacken von Schwierigkeiten, Freiheit und Gleichheit, Einigkeit)	6
beschreibt die derzeitige (von Biden beschriebene oder allgemein bekannte) Situation als dem Amerikanischen Traum widersprechend, z. B. – Ungleichheit und Privilegien Einzelner, – Rassismus, – Spaltung der Gesellschaft,	4

– Unglück und Tod.	
kommt zu einer dezidierten persönlichen Einschätzung.	2
	14

Anforderungsbereich III (Teilaufgabe 3.2)

Die Schülerin / Der Schüler	max. Punkte
formuliert eine Einleitung ihres/seines Statements, z. B. mit Hinweis auf die Flutkatastrophe in NRW und RLP 2021.	2
benennt die Ursachen der Klimakrise, insbesondere die Konzentration von Treibhausgasen, z. B. durch Verkehr, Industrie, Landwirtschaft, Rodungen.	4
benennt die Folgen der Klimakrise, z. B. Anstieg des Meeresspiegels, Extremwetter, Dürre, Kälte, Unbewohnbarkeit von ganzen Regionen, Massenmigration, Krieg um Land und Wasser.	4
benennt notwendige Maßnahmen, z. B. Verzicht auf fossile Energieträger, Einschränkung von Konsum und Produktion, Verzicht auf tierische Produkte, massive Systemveränderungen, weltweite Bildungsoffensive, Infragestellung des Bevölkerungswachstums, technologische Lösungen.	4
	14

Beispielaufgabe 4: Jordan Hall, „The Donation"

Thematischer Bezug gemäß KLP (Soziokulturelles Orientierungswissen): Chancen und Risiken der Globalisierung: *Globalisation and global challenges: economic, ecological and political issues*
Auszug aus einem englischsprachigen Drama (1000 W.)
Quellenangaben: Jordan Hall, „The Donation", C. Bilodeau und T. Petersen, *Lighting the Way. An Anthology of Short Plays About the Climate Crisis,* The Arctic Cycle, 2020, S. 169–176

Aufgabe

1. Sum up Tommy's arguments for his decision to make a "donation" and Jen's reaction towards it. *(Comprehension)*

2. Analyse the way the play develops and how it reveals the two characters' attitudes. In doing this, consider both Jen's and Tommy's behaviour and their communicative strategies. *(Analysis)*

3. Choose one of the following tasks:

3.1 Discuss the issue of climate change and assess the individual's role in it. *(Evaluation: Comment)*

3.2 Write an ending to the play taking the characters' attitudes into account. *(Evaluation: Re-creation of text)*

The Donation (excerpt) *Jordan Hall*

JEN sits at her desk. She's an overworked nonprofit kind of girl.

Jen: Alright. So if we lower the thermostat by another two degrees ...

TOMMY, a discharged soldier, a little drunk, starts hammering on JEN's office window.

Tommy: Anyone?

5 **Jen:** ... and get Alison to wear a goddamn sweater instead of using that bloody space heater ...

Tommy: Hello? Anyone?

Jen: That could save us another fifty kilos or so ...

Tommy: I can see you there ignoring me!

10 *With a sigh, JEN opens the window. Just a crack.*

Jen: We aren't open. If you're here for a canvassing job, there's another intake on Monday.

Tommy: I'm here to make a donation.

Jen: That's terrific. You can do that on the website.

15 **Tommy:** It's not that kind of donation.

Jen: Oh. No. We don't accept gifts-in-kind. We're a nonprofit so we don't have the infrastructure –

Tommy: I want to give you my life.

There's a beat. TOMMY pushes the window open the rest of the way and hops inside.

20 **Jen:** What?

Tommy: I want to donate my life.

Jen: Do – you mean you want to volunteer? God. If I had a nickel for every guilt-ridden drunk who rolls up wanting to save the world. Look. I'm just the office manager. There are pamphlets outside, you sign up and – you might not get to kayak in front of an oil rig

25 right away, but –

Tommy: No – I mean, the kayaking sounds exhilarating. But I want to donate my life.

Jen: I'm missing something, aren't I?

Tommy: I thought if I came here the donation would be properly recorded. And you could advise me about the most carbon-neutral way to do it? Because I was thinking about

30 pills – but then I might be sending the toxins into the groundwater? And there's always a gun – but that would mean supporting weapons manufacturing and I'm not really comfortable with that.

Jen: Are you – are you talking about killing yourself? Can I call somebody to help you? Like a friend? Or a therapist? Or a hotline?

35 **Tommy:** This isn't a suicide thing.

Jen: It kinda sounds like one.

Tommy: No. I know. I get it. But think of it like this. If we were in a foxhole, taking fire, and I could cover you to get to the Jeep – but laying down cover was gonna get me shot? If I did that – knowing I was gonna get shot – that's not suicide. Not really.

40 **Jen:** But you aren't talking about –

Tommy: Of course I am. I've seen the UN report. Droughts. Sea-level rise. Climate change casualties are at 400,000 per year, and it's gonna get higher. And in order to stop it, we need to hit net zero by 2050. That's how we get to the Jeep. I'm 25. Say I've got 50 years left, that's 900 tons of carbon. I can give that back to you. I can give you that much cover.

45 **Jen:** That's oddly noble – and – I can see you've thought about this – but neither I nor the organization I represent want you to do that. There are – there are better ways for you to help.

Tommy: Not really. Not that'll save us 900 tons.

Jen: Green living. Public transit. Vegetarian diet.

50 **Tommy:** 300 at best.

Jen: Well then, make a bigger difference. Protest, lobby for green candidates.

Tommy: Because that's been a roaring success for the last 50 years, hasn't it. Look. I'm not here to make you feel bad. You seem lovely. With your night school law books, here at 7 a.m. If you really don't want my life, I'll just nip over to Greenpeace –

55 **Jen:** No!

Tommy: It's really no trouble.

Jen: No. You should stay here. Stay here, and I'll make a cup of tea, and we'll talk.

Tommy: You're just going to keep trying to talk me out of it.

Jen: Well, I – Yes. Please. Have some tea. Things always seem better after a cup of tea.

60 Give me that long. And if I can't talk you out of it, I'll let you go … donate to Greenpeace.

Tommy: … Alright.

Jen: Alright. Alright. Now you just stay … Stay …

Keeping her eyes on him at all times, she nips offstage for a second, and then dashes back on.

65 **Jen:** There. Kettle's on. So. So-so-so. How did you – how did you think of your – donation?

Tommy: Oh. Well. I was down at the pub. Nowhere else to be. And the news came on with the UN report and I looked at my beer – leaving this half-moon of wet on the bar – and I wondered how much carbon went into it? Into me. All the cold beers and steak pies and my Da's car. What had I done to be worth so much? What had I done at all? Except

70 get discharged –

Jen: Discharged?

Tommy: That's not the important part. And anyway, it all comes back to this.

Jen: Comes back to this how?

75 **Tommy:** All of it. Army. Police. We say democracy. Human rights. But mostly we help old men say where the money goes. Or the oil. Or the mine. You know it because when it

really is about democracy or human rights, they tell you to protect the pipeline, and not the people.

    Jen: Is that what happened?

80   **Tommy:** I told you that doesn't matter. What matters is I can do this now. And it will save lives. 900 tons. That's five people in South America. Fifteen in India. Thirty-six in Maldives.

    Jen: Or one here.

    Tommy: Pretty much my point.

85   **Jen:** Well then, maybe I should do it too.

    Tommy: Do what?

    Jen: Donate my life.

    Tommy: But – no. I don't want you to do that.

    Jen: Oh. I see. It's fine for you, but not for me?

90   **Tommy:** Yes. I'm a grotesque waste of resources, and you're – you're –

    Jen: What? I'm worth at least 600 tons. And what am I doing, really? Looking for improvements in heating technology and paperless office procedures? Going to law school at night so that in five years I can intern for a lawyer who supports Indigenous land claims or environmental class action suits? Band-Aid on a bullet hole. Your way is much better

95 – all the good I'm ever going to do, all rolled up into one moment. And best of all, I don't have to stick around and find out the hard way if it doesn't work. Or – y'know – for the cleanup.

Annotations

discharged soldier – person that is no longer working for the military, in this case because of wrongdoing

canvassing – trying to convince people – usually strangers – to support a certain cause

nickel – 5-cent coin (US)

toxins – highly unhealthy substances

UN report – annual report by the United Nations on climate change

Indigenous – people who are native to a certain place (usually before the arrival of European colonists)

class action suit – a case brought to court by one person acting on behalf of a group of people

Band-Aid – a sticky plaster used to cover small wounds

Bewertungskriterien

Anforderungsbereich I (Teilaufgabe 1)

Die Schülerin / Der Schüler	max. Punkte
führt Tommys Vorschlag an, wegen seiner persönlichen Ressourcenverschwendung sein Leben für den Klimaschutz zu geben.	2
führt Tommys Argumente an: – die Folgen der Klimakrise (Dürre und Anstieg des Meeresspiegels verbunden mit 400.000 Toten pro Jahr),	6

– seine Rechnung, auf diese Weise 900 Tonnen CO_2 zu sparen, – seine Zurückweisung von Alternativen als zu ineffektiv, – seine Drohung bei Ablehnung zu Greenpeace zu gehen, – die Hinterfragung seines Fußabdrucks, – seine Kapitalismuskritik.	
benennt Jens Positionen dazu: – die Alternative ökologisch zu leben, – die Alternative des politischen Aktivismus, – ihre Drohung, es Tommy gleichzutun.	4
	12

Anforderungsbereich II (Teilaufgabe 2)

Die Schülerin / Der Schüler	max. Punkte
beschreibt die Entwicklung des Dialoges: – die anfänglichen Missverständnisse, – Jens plötzliches Entsetzen über das Anliegen, – die sachliche Argumentation Tommys, – seine Analogie zum bewaffneten Kampf, – seine ironisch-spöttische Widerlegung der Argumente Jens, – seine Ausführungen zu seinem persönlichen CO_2-Fußabdruck, – Jens Entschluss, es ihm gleichzutun, – Tommys Zurückweisung des Entschlusses, – Jens Argumente.	6
beschreibt Jen als engagierte Klimaschützerin, die – sich in einer Organisation engagiert, – individuelle Beiträge zum Klimaschutz forciert (Thermostat, Pullover), – sich für papierlose Büroarbeit einsetzt, – nachhaltiges Leben und Essen befürwortet, – politischen Aktivismus im realistischen Rahmen befürwortet, – Anwältin für indigene Völker und Umwelt-Sammelklagen werden will, – Tommy voller Empathie von seinem Vorhaben abbringen möchte, – schließlich den Nutzen ihres ökologischen Engagements infrage stellt.	7
beschreibt Tommy als angetrunkenen Soldaten, der die individuelle Verantwortung für die Klimakrise in letzter Konsequenz akzeptiert, dies jedoch von Jen nicht erwartet.	4
	17

Anforderungsbereich III (Teilaufgabe 3.1)

Die Schülerin / Der Schüler	max. Punkte
knüpft an den Ausgangstext an, indem sie/er sich z. B. auf Tommys radikalen Ansatz bezieht.	2
benennt – Ursachen der Klimakrise, insbesondere die Konzentration von Treibhausgasen, z. B. durch Verkehr, Industrie, Landwirtschaft, Rodungen, und – Folgen der Klimakrise, z. B. Extremwetter, Dürre, Kälte, Unbewohnbarkeit von ganzen Regionen, Massenmigration, Krieg um Land und Wasser.	5
benennt zu treffende Maßnahmen, z. B. Verzicht auf fossile Energieträger, Einschränkung von Konsum und Produktion, Verzicht auf Fleisch, massive Systemveränderungen, weltweite Bildungsoffensive, Infragestellen des Bevölkerungswachstums, technologische Lösungen.	4
führt die Bedeutung individuellen Handelns aus, mit Blick auf Bewusstmachung, Vorbildfunktion und Glaubwürdigkeit, aber betont das Primat staatlichen und supranationalen Handelns.	4
	15

Anforderungsbereich III (Teilaufgabe 3.2)

Die Schülerin / Der Schüler	max. Punkte
knüpft plausibel an den Text an unter Berücksichtigung der herausgearbeiteten Merkmale der Charaktere.	2
führt den Text fort, z. B. mit einer kontroversen Auseinandersetzung über Jens Vorschlag, mit der Akzeptanz des Vorschlags und der gemeinsamen Planung oder mit dem vollständigen Rückzug Tommys.	9
gelangt zu einem plausiblen Ende.	4
	15

Beispielaufgabe 5: Roger McGough, „The Lake"

Thematischer Bezug gemäß KLP (Soziokulturelles Orientierungswissen): Medien in ihrer Bedeutung für den Einzelnen und die Gesellschaft: *Visions of the future – utopia and dystopia*
Englischsprachiger literarischer Text (235 W., Gedicht)
Quellenangaben: Roger McGough, „The Lake", *Selected Poems*, London: Penguin 2006.

Aufgabe

1. Describe the physical and biological state of the lake in detail. *(Comprehension)*

2. Examine the way the speaker presents people and their environment and the results of pollution. In doing this, consider the speaker's choice of words and the syntax and imagery of the poem. *(Analysis)*

3. Choose one of the following tasks:

3.1 Evaluate the criticism inherent in the poem. Give arguments and examples to support or refute the author's negative view of the way people treat the environment. *(Evaluation: Comment)*

3.2 Imagine you are an environmentalist in the town where the lake is situated. Write an article for the local newspaper, stating how bad the environmental situation has become. *(Evaluation: Re-creation of text).*

The Lake   *Roger McGough*

For years there have been no fish in the lake.
People hurrying through the park avoid it
like the plague. Birds steer clear
and the sedge of course has withered.
5 Trees lean away from it,
and at night it reflects, not the moon,
but the blackness of its own depths.
There are no fish in the lake.
But there is life there. There is life.

10 Underwater pigs glide between reefs of coral debris.
They love it here. They breed and multiply
in sties hollowed out of the mud
and lined with mattresses and bedsprings.

15 They live on dead fish and rotting things,
drowned pets, plastic and assorted excreta.
Rusty cans they like the best.
Holding them in webbed trotters
their teeth tear easily through the tin,
and poking in a snout, they noisily suck out
20 the putrid matter within.

There are no fish in the lake.
But there is life there. There is life.
For on certain evenings after dark
shoals of pigs surface
25 and look out at those houses near the park.
Where, in bathrooms,
children feed stale bread to plastic ducks,
and in attics,
toy yachts have long since run aground.
30 Where, in living-rooms,
anglers dangle their lines on patterned carpets,
and bemoan the fate of the ones that got away.
Down on the lake, piggy eyes glisten.
They have acquired a taste for flesh.
35 They are licking their lips. Listen ...

Annotations

sedge – kind of grass growing in water; G.: Schilf

debris – small pieces of rubbish

sty – very dirty building or room (compare *pigsty*: pen where pigs are kept)

trotter – pig's foot

putrid – rotten; stinking

shoal – large group of fish

Bewertungskriterien

Anforderungsbereich I (Teilaufgabe 1)

Die Schülerin / Der Schüler	max. Punkte
beschreibt das dunkle Aussehen der Oberfläche des Sees, in der sich nicht einmal der Mond spiegelt.	2
führt an, dass keine Fische darin leben und das Riedgras verwelkt ist.	2
führt an, dass Tiere und Menschen gleichermaßen den See meiden.	2

beschreibt, was sich an Unrat in dem See befindet, z. B. – tote Haustiere, – Plastik, – Fäkalien, – alte Matratzen, – rostige Büchsen.	4
beschreibt die mutierten Monsterschweine, die den See bewohnen.	2
	12

Anforderungsbereich II (Teilaufgabe 2)

Die Schülerin / Der Schüler	max. Punkte
analysiert die Wortwahl des lyrischen Ich, die Ekel, Fäulnis, Tod und Bedrohung suggeriert *(plague, withered, blackness, debris, sties, dead, rotting, excreta* etc.).	4
analysiert syntaktische Merkmale des Gedichtes, insbesondere – die sich wiederholenden Zeilen 8 f. und 20 f. („There are no fish in the lake. / But there is life there. There is life."), – die Wiederholung innerhalb der Zeilen, die Bedrohung suggeriert, – die Auslassung in der letzten Zeile („Listen ..."), die ebenfalls bedrohlich wirkt.	4
erläutert die Symbolik der sich neigenden Bäume zur Illustration der Widerwärtigkeit und die Symbolik der Schweine als – Indikator für den Verschmutzungsgrad (Schweinestall), – Mutanten und damit Resultat der Veränderung der Natur durch den Menschen, – Bedrohung, die eines Tages über den See hinaus spürbar wird und dem Menschen selbst gefährlich wird.	6
erläutert die Bedeutung des Verhaltens der Menschen sowie die Symbolik ihrer Gegenstände, die immer wieder Widernatürlichkeit, Unappetitlichkeit sowie Verfall suggerieren und somit den Verfall der Umwelt widerspiegeln, z. B. – altes Brot, – Plastikenten im Badezimmer (statt Enten in der Natur), – vergessene Spielzeugjachten (nutzlos, kaputt, als Pendant zum See), – Angeln auf dem Teppich (statt in der Natur).	4
	18

Anforderungsbereich III (Teilaufgabe 3.1)

Die Schülerin / Der Schüler	max. Punkte
nimmt einleitend Bezug auf die Intention des Gedichtes.	2
erläutert anhand von Beispielen den Zustand unserer Umwelt, der dem Gedicht Recht gibt oder führt an, dass allerdings auch viele Anstrengungen zum Schutz der Umwelt unternommen werden.	8
wägt die Punkte gegeneinander ab und kommt zu einer begründeten Schlussfolgerung.	4
	14

Anforderungsbereich III (Teilaufgabe 3.2)

Die Schülerin / Der Schüler	max. Punkte
wählt den Zustand des Sees als Aufhänger für seinen Artikel.	2
führt die Konsequenzen der Verschmutzung aus und/oder benennt und beschreibt weitere Bereiche, in denen Umweltschutz geboten ist.	6
benennt Lösungsvorschläge für das Problem des Sees und andere Probleme der Umweltverschmutzung.	4
appelliert an die Lesenden, zu einer Verbesserung beizutragen.	2
	14

Klausurteil B: Sprachmittlung (Teilaufgabe 4)

Die Schülerin / Der Schüler gibt die wesentlichen Inhalte im Sinne der Aufgabenstellung sinngemäß zusammenfassend wieder:	max. Punkte
der scheinbar vorbildliche Umgang mit Plastikmüll in Deutschland,	18
die Verschiffung ins Ausland,	
das hohe Aufkommen trotz Recycling,	
die Kritik an bestimmten Produkten (*coffee to go,* Gummibärchen),	
die mangelnde Akzeptanz recycelter Materialien,	
die steigenden Kosten.	

Beispielaufgabe 6: Hannah Jewell, „Gen Z Workers Should be Proud of Being ‚Snowflakes' Rather than Martyrs"

Thematischer Bezug gemäß KLP (Soziokulturelles Orientierungswissen): Lebensentwürfe, Studium, Ausbildung, Beruf international – *Englisch als lingua franca: The international world of work; Questions of identity and gender*
Auszug aus einem Sachtext (970 W.)
Quellenangaben: Hannah Jewel, „Gen Z workers should be proud of being 'snowflakes' rather than martyrs", in: *The Guardian,* London, 27.01.2022, zitiert nach: https://www.theguardian.com/commentisfree/2022/jan/27/gen-z-workers-snowflakes-bad-treatment-bad-pay (Zugriff: 01.04.2024); Copyright Guardian News & Media Ltd 2024

Aufgabe

1. Describe the image of young people in the workplace today and the author's attitude towards this. *(Comprehension)*

2. Examine the way the author defends the young. Consider the structure of her text, her use of language and other rhetorical strategies. *(Analysis)*

3. Choose one of the following tasks:

3.1 Assess the writer's claim that young people show a tendency to the political left (e. g. trade unions, fairness, anti-discrimination) against the backgrounds of your work in class and your own experience. *(Evaluation: Comment)*

3.2 Imagine and write a dialogue between the young employee and her uncle which is hinted at in lines 27–35. *(Evaluation: Re-creation of text).*

Gen Z workers should be proud of being 'snowflakes' rather than martyrs   *Hannah Jewell*

There's nothing older generations enjoy more than complaining about the young. Their childhoods are too coddled and full of non-dangerous toys, then they get to school where they are not beaten with sticks and therefore do not build character, then they go to university where they bully statues and either have too much or not enough sex.

Now, as millennials have aged into their uncool middle-manager era, and Gen Z enter the workforce, they have inspired a number of books and articles and speeches about how kids these days don't know the value of a hard day's work.

As many columnists, business book authors and upper managers would often have it, the younger set are simply terrible workers. They ask for too much, they do too little, they do not respect hierarchies, they don't want to pay their dues, they say "like" too much, they have tattoos on their arms, they're always looking at their phones, and they quit their jobs instead of miserably sticking it out. Snowflakes!

This was what a friend of mine was once called by her own uncle, in fact, when she decided to quit a job just a few weeks in, because the boss was horrible and abusive. He was also drunk at work much of the time. Why would leaving such a job draw such an insult, suggesting she should have toughed it out in a terrible situation? She was, to his mind, entitled and too sensitive.

But it isn't actually true that young people work less hard than their elders. And even if it were – why shouldn't we aspire to a future with less work?

Last year, a New York Times headline declared that "The 37-year-olds are afraid of the 23-year-olds who work for them". It gestured to a division between anxious, conscientious millennials, many of whom had entered the workplace in the shadow of the 2008 crash; and their Gen Z counterparts, who feel comfortable "delegating to their boss".

The Harvard Business Review has similarly written about the "work martydom" of millennials, citing American studies that find young people feel more shame about taking time off for holidays and are more likely to forfeit unused vacation days. The author Malcolm Harris describes millennials not as overly rebellious but rather as "servile, anxious [and] afraid". In a precarious economy marked by historic inequality, the importance of getting and maintaining a good job is more acute than ever. And for those who entered the workforce after the double whammy of the recession and the invention of the iPhone, we are never really able to not be at work.

Nevertheless, young people are critiqued for their attempts to set boundaries at work. One young woman in the New York Times piece about Gen Z workers shocked her bosses by asking if she could leave work after finishing her tasks for the day, rather than sticking around in the name of the traditional 9 to 5. Maybe she's on to something.

For the millions who have quit their jobs in the "great resignation", the pandemic and a tight labour market have made once radical propositions – such as not sticking out a miserable job – feel more possible. Why put up with abuse, discrimination and poor pay when you could just go get another job?

While the pandemic has opened up such possibilities, it also laid bare the extreme divides between those workers who could work from home and those who had to show up and risk their lives. It showed how many businesses were willing to put their employees at risk in the name of profits, and how many privileged people were unwilling to sacrifice their creature comforts for another person's safety.

At both ends of this divided economy of work, though, we are seeing a newly invigorated labour movement – even in the generally union-unfriendly United States – and young people are playing a central role. A 2018 Pew Research survey found that American adults under 30 are the only group in which a larger share hold a favourable view of labour unions than feel the same way about corporations. The United Auto Workers union wrote in 2019 about the momentum of unionisation in unexpected places – at nonprofits, coffee shops, and digital media outfits. Meanwhile, workers at places like Amazon fulfilment centres are also seeking to form unions for the first time.

171

Wherever you find them, though, workers who demand better conditions meet with similar-sounding scrutiny. They are told that they are asking for too much, and that they should be grateful, that actually a company is like a family and they are better off without a union, which would just get in between the company and the employees.

This is what I was told in my previous digital media job when we attempted (and failed) to gain union recognition. This is also exactly what Amazon warehouse workers were told when they attempted to form a union in Alabama.

In my own experience, I saw the ways in which problems at work could be pinned on employees' lack of character, fortitude and work ethic, rather than structural faults of the company. We brought up concerns about pay gaps along gender and racial lines, lack of transparency in raises and promotions and lack of support for mental health. In response, we were given subscriptions to an app to sort out our mental health, but were expected to do it on our own time.

If management can successfully dismiss employees' demands as those of spoiled, narcissistic young people – of snowflakes – then they may save themselves the trouble and the cost of creating a fair workplace. But the problem of modern work is not that young people lack character. Their only crime is a disinclination to make themselves miserable in the name of making the rich richer. Is that so unreasonable?

Annotations

"great resignation" – current mass phenomenon in Britain of leaving one job for another one

traditional 9 to 5 – regular job

Bewertungskriterien

Anforderungsbereich I (Teilaufgabe 1)

Die Schülerin / Der Schüler	max. Punkte
beschreibt das Bild, das viele in der Arbeitswelt von der jungen Generation haben: – ohne Arbeitsmoral, – fordernd, – respektlos gegenüber Hierarchien, – zu bemängelnde Sprache, Tattoos und Handys, – kein Durchhaltevermögen im Job, – lassen lieber ihren Chef arbeiten, – setzen Obergrenzen bei der Arbeit, – finden sich nicht mit miserablen Bedingungen ab.	4
beschreibt, dass junge Millennials andererseits als servil und ängstlich gelten, sich scheuen freizunehmen, weil sie um den Job fürchten, und immer erreichbar sind.	2

	6
beschreibt, wie sie in der jungen Generation eine neu belebte Arbeiterbewegung sieht: – positivere Sicht auf Gewerkschaften, – Gründung von Gewerkschaften.	
stellt die Sicht der Autorin dar, die die Probleme eher auf Seiten der Unternehmen sieht: – strukturelle Fehler, – unfaire Gehälter (Frauen, People of Colour), – Intransparenz bei Beförderungen, – mangelnde Gesundheitsfürsorge.	
führt ihr Fazit an, dass nicht Charakterschwäche die jungen Menschen ausmacht, sondern ihre Weigerung, ihr Leben nach der Bereicherung Anderer auszurichten.	
	12

Anforderungsbereich II (Teilaufgabe 2)

Die Schülerin / Der Schüler	max. Punkte
beschreibt die Struktur des Textes: – allgemeingültige Einleitung, – spezifischer Bezug auf die heutige junge Generation, – persönliches Beispiel, – Verweis auf drei beispielhafte Zeitungsartikel, – Bewertung mit Blick auf die Corona-Pandemie, – Interpretation mit Blick auf eine neu erwachte Kultur des Arbeitskampfes, – Belege, – Umgang der Arbeitgeber/-innen damit, – Belege, persönliche Erfahrungen, – Fazit.	6
benennt die zahlreichen Beispiele und Zitate, mit denen die Autorin ihre Ausführungen unterstützt.	2
benennt die Adressatenorientierung, z. B. – durch wiederkehrende rhetorische Fragen, – durch die klare Positionierung in der Überschrift.	2
erläutert den in Teilen spöttischen, ironischen Ton, der die Haltung der Autorin von Anfang an verdeutlicht.	4
benennt emphatische Mittel, z. B. Aufzählungen und Anaphern.	4
	18

Anforderungsbereich III (Teilaufgabe 3.1)

Die Schülerin / Der Schüler	max. Punkte
knüpft an den Ausgangstext an, indem sie/er z. B. auf Aussagen aus Zeilen 91–107 verweist.	2
betrachtet die junge Generation hinsichtlich ihrer politischen Ausrichtung mit Blick auf z. B. – Inhalte im Englischunterricht, – die letzte Bundestagswahl, – Protestbewegungen (Fridays for Future / Ukraine / Brexit / Black Lives Matter / Demos gegen rechts), – Einstellung zum politisch korrekten Sprachgebrauch, – Einstellung zu Minderheiten (Migranten, LSBTIQ*), – persönliche Einstellungen, – persönliche Erfahrungen.	6
bewertet ihre/seine Betrachtungen im Sinne der Aufgabenstellung.	4
kommt zu einem dezidierten Fazit.	2
	14

Anforderungsbereich III (Teilaufgabe 3.2)

Die Schülerin / Der Schüler	max. Punkte
schreibt einen situationsangemessenen Dialog, indem sie/er die Nichte die Umstände ausführlich schildern lässt, die zu ihrer Kündigung führten (s. 30 ff.).	6
den Onkel als unverständig darstellt, indem er z. B. – ihre Schwäche kritisiert, – Missstände und Fehlverhalten herunterspielt, – die Einstellung der Jugend allgemein herabwürdigt.	6
kommt zu einem plausiblen Ende mit verhärteten Positionen.	2
	14

Beispielaufgabe 7: William J. Harris, „Modern Romance"

Thematischer Bezug gemäß KLP (Soziokulturelles Orientierungswissen):
Fortschritt und Ethik in der modernen Gesellschaft: *Visions of the future – ethical issues of scientific and technological progress*
Lebensentwürfe, Studium, Ausbildung, Beruf international – *Englisch als lingua franca: Questions of identity and gender*

| literarischer Text (Gedicht) (222 W.) |
| Bildimpuls für Teilaufgabe 3.1 |

Quellenangaben:
William J. Harris, „Modern Romance", in: Baldus, J. et al. (Hrsg.), *Invitation to Literature,*
Cornelsen, Berlin, 1990, S. 82 f.
iStockphoto.com, Calgary: guoya

Aufgabe

1. Sum up what story is implied by this poem. *(Comprehension)*

2. Analyse the different attitudes towards the affair with particular regard to the language the speakers employ. *(Analysis)*

3. Choose one of the following tasks:

3.1 The poem dates back to 1977. Comment on the advancement of AI as well as on its dangers with reference to the poem, the picture and to your work in class. *(Evaluation: Comment)*

3.2 Write the story of the romantic affair between the husband and the robot as it develops after the dismissal of the robot. *(Evaluation: Re-creation of text).*

Modern Romance   *William J. Harris*

One: The Wife

The reason
we got rid
of the robot
5   was
she was an
absolute slut.
You must
understand,
10   my Mortimor
is a strong
man
but how long
can even a good
15   man resist
temptation?

The way
she used to
look at him
20   and rub
against
him
every chance
she got. She
25   was a tramp,
that fancy
vacuum cleaner
with tits.

175

Two: The Husband

30 My wife never understood Doris.
I mean, the domestic robot.
She was a delight.
Intelligent yet submissive.
Sexy but didn't mind housework.
35 And she knew her place.
The perfect woman.
Must have been designed by a man.
Of course, a flesh and blood woman
is preferable to a machine
40 no

matter how perfect
and beautiful
and understanding
and responsive.
45 Poor Annie was so upset
by this whole mess.
I think a vacation would do her
a world of good.
The Grand Canyon? That's the place …

50 Three: The Robot

Imagine me, marrying
a man like Mortimor
Why this is the
happiest day of
55 my life & a true
advancement for
my people. I am
the first robot
in history
60 to marry a man
of Mortimor's stature.
Oh, he's so

brave to withstand
public opinion
65 and so strong
to
overcome that
tragedy
of last weekend
70 when his wife accidentally
fell to her death
from a great height
in Arizona.

Bewertungskriterien

Anforderungsbereich I (Teilaufgabe 1)

Die Schülerin / Der Schüler	max. Punkte
beschreibt, dass die Geschichte in der Zukunft spielt, in der die Technologie so weit fortgeschritten ist, dass man in der Lage ist, menschenähnliche Roboter zu produzieren.	3
benennt die Affaire des Hausherrn mit dem Roboter, die mit Abschaffung des Roboters zunächst beendet wird.	3
führt den mysteriösen Tod der Ehefrau am Grand Canyon an, dessen Ursache im Unklaren bleibt.	3
führt an, dass Ehemann und Roboter schließlich heiraten.	3
	12

Anforderungsbereich II (Teilaufgabe 2)

Die Schülerin / Der Schüler	max. Punkte
beschreibt, wie die Ehefrau – als verständnisvolle Gattin erscheint, die ihrem Mann einen Seitensprung nicht nur verzeiht, sondern die Schuld seiner Geliebten zuweist (Z. 13 ff.), – durchweg abfällig, von dem Roboter spricht: (Z. 2, 7, 25). „that fancy / vacuum cleaner / with tits", Z. 26 ff.), – den Roboter damit auf die zwei Funktionen Hausarbeit und Sexualobjekt reduziert, was ihre Verachtung unterstreicht.	6
führt die Haltung des Ehemanns aus, der – deutlich positiver von dem Roboter spricht („Doris" (Z. 30), „domestic robot" (Z. 31), „delight" (Z. 32), „perfect" (Z. 36), „beautiful" (Z. 42), „understanding" (Z. 43), „responsive" (Z. 44)), – den Roboter dennoch auf ein Sexualobjekt reduziert: „Intelligent yet submissive. / Sexy but didn't mind housework. / And she knew her place", (Z. 33 ff.), „Must have been designed by a man" (Z. 37), – die traditionellen sozialen Unterschiede zwischen Herrschaft und Dienstmädchen („a flesh and blood woman / is preferable", Z. 38 f.) zum Ausdruck bringt, – die Affaire nicht so ernst zu nehmen scheint („whole mess" (Z. 46), „poor Annie" (Z. 45)), – sich aber uneindeutig zum Aufenthalt am Grand Canyon äußert („That's the place" (Z. 49).	6

führt aus, wie die Roboterfrau – in Hochstimmung erscheint („imagine me" (Z. 51), „why" (Z. 53), „happiest day" (Z. 54), „oh" (Z. 61)), – die Heirat nicht nur als persönliches Glück, sondern als politischen Erfolg sieht („true advancement for my people", Z. 55 ff.), wobei „my people" auch insbesondere auf den Status der Schwarzen Bevölkerung in der Geschichte der USA anspielt, – je nach Interpretation der Haltung des Mannes und der Geschehnisse am Grand Canyon hier entweder als naiv oder besonders in den Zeilen 62 ff. höchst zynisch erscheint.	6
	18

Anforderungsbereich III (Teilaufgabe 3.1)

Die Schülerin / Der Schüler	max. Punkte
beschreibt den Stand der technologischen Entwicklung künstlicher Intelligenz im Gedicht als *strong AI,* als fiktiv und in verschiedenen Belangen unserer heutigen Technologie als weit voraus.	2
führt aus, wie heutige KI, insbesondere ChatGPT, weitgehend vom Menschen nicht mehr unterscheidbar ist und in letzter Konsequenz auch Gefühle wecken kann, wobei sie/er auch auf den Bildimpuls eingeht.	8
bewertet schlussfolgernd allgemein die von KI ausgehende Gefahr hinsichtlich Transparenz, Falschinformation und/oder Menschenwürde.	4
	14

Anforderungsbereich III (Teilaufgabe 3.2)

Die Schülerin / Der Schüler	max. Punkte
schließt ihre/seine Geschichte plausibel an die Entscheidung zur Beendigung der Affaire an.	2
erzählt die Ereignisse, die zum Unfall oder Mord am Grand Canyon führen.	6
entwickelt die Beziehung des Mannes zum Roboter, die schließlich zum Eheversprechen führt.	6
	14

NRW Abitur Englisch
Original-Prüfungsaufgaben 2023

Quelle der Aufgabenstellung

Qualitäts- und UnterstützungsAgentur – Landesinstitut für Schule[1]

Hinweis: Bitte beachten Sie, dass das Hörverstehen erstmalig in die Abiturprüfungen 2025 einfließt. Die hier angebotenen Originalprüfungen enthalten diesen Aufgabenteil daher nicht.

GK Literarischer Text mit Beispiellösungen

Klausurteil A: Leseverstehen und Schreiben integriert

AUFGABENSTELLUNG

1. Outline the concept and aim as well as the proceedings of the global Climate Audit.
   (Comprehension) (12 Punkte)

2. Analyze how Bill's state of mind is presented. Focus on point of view and use of language.
   (Analysis) (16 Punkte)

3. Choose **one** of the following tasks:

3.1 With regard to the severe consequences of the climate crisis, comment on the question whether a state should be allowed to regulate individual lifestyles on the way towards more sustainability.
   (Evaluation: comment) (14 Punkte)

3.2 After completing the questionnaire, Bill leaves the house and takes a walk to think about his situation. He reflects on the audit and the consequences it might have for himself and his family. Write his interior monologue.
   (Evaluation: re-creation of text) (14 Punkte)

---

[1] Die Lösungen sind keine amtlichen Lösungen.

Klausurteil B: Sprachmittlung isoliert

AUFGABENSTELLUNG

4. Your school is taking part in an international project promoting scientific research activities for students. Participants are asked to introduce an example of a science talent competition.
   Write an internet article for the project website, outlining the development and the goals of "Jugend forscht". *(Mediation) (18 Punkte)*

Materialgrundlage:

Klausurteil A:
Rachel May, „The Audit", in: Mary Woodbury, *Winds Of Change: Short Stories About Our Climate,* Coquitlam, British Columbia: Moon Willow Press 2015, S. 42–44 (gekürzt)
Wortzahl: 792

Klausurteil B:
Stiftung Jugend forscht e.V. (Hrsg.) (o. D.), „Historie: Einzigartiges Netzwerk zur Talent-förderung mit herausragender Erfolgsbilanz", in: *jugend-forscht.de,* Hamburg: zitiert nach: https://www.jugend-forscht.de/stiftung-jugend-forscht-e-v/historie.html (Zugriff: 01.04.2024, gekürzt)
Wortzahl: 567

Zugelassene Hilfsmittel:

- Ein- und zweisprachiges Wörterbuch
- Herkunftssprachliches Wörterbuch für Schülerinnen und Schüler, deren Herkunfts-sprache nicht Deutsch ist
- Wörterbuch zur deutschen Rechtschreibung

Klausurteil A

The Audit   *Rachel May*

The short story is set in North America in the near future.

[...]

"Dad! You've got to come. We got the Audit." The boy's normally high voice took on a husky rasp as he pronounced the last words.

5

"An audit? You make it sound like a fatal illness," Bill responded to his anxiety-prone son with a practiced calmness, as David grabbed his hand and started pulling him towards the house. "Relax, Davey. It's not that

10

big a deal. Our taxes are all in order." [...]

As soon as they entered the house, Bill felt David's hand tighten and his shoulders stiffen. Bill's wife Laurie was standing at the computer in the family room, biting

15

her lip, while their daughter Jess looked on with an inscrutable expression.

"C'mon, everybody. It's just an audit, right?" Bill tried the soothing tone again. "What's the big deal? We're as likely to get

20

taxes back as to owe them."

"It's not a tax audit, honey. It's the new one." Laurie's voice had a touch of the same husky terror he had heard from David.

"Yeah, Dad. You know, the GCA?" Jess

25

added, with the practiced superiority of a 14-year-old.

"GCA?"

David's voice rose to a squeak. "I heard they take your house and car and every-

30

thing!"

Laurie came over to give David a hug while Bill sat down, bewildered, at the computer.

"Now I'm sure it's not that bad. Let me

35

take a look." He was embarrassed to admit he hadn't heard of the GCA, when even his fifth-grader seemed to know all about it.

Big yellow letters on a dark blue screen spelled out GLOBAL CLIMATE AUDIT.

40

Every effort to surf away from the page resulted in the same message: "You have been selected for the GCA. Internet service will be restored after you complete your climate footprint calculation."

45

"You have to do it, Dad. It's international law." Jess said. [...]

It didn't give Bill much confidence as he stared at the Climate Footprint Calculator on the screen. It was essentially a detailed

50

inventory of their daily habits. The GCA already had a surprising wealth of information about them: the amount of gas they bought each week for the SUV, how many BTUs it took to heat and cool their six-

55

bedroom house, how much hot water they used, even what percentage of strawberries they bought came from Chile. At one point he called his credit card company to complain that this outfit had hacked into

60

his records.

"No worries, sir. That's the GCA. They have treaty rights to that information. It will not be used for any purpose other than calculating your carbon overdraft."

65

Overdraft. That sounded ominous. Bill finished the online questionnaire. Shortly after he hit SEND, a graphic appeared showing three round pictures of Earth and an additional wedge with most of the

70

Americas. The caption read:

"Your carbon footprint is 3.4 times the acceptable global mean. If everyone generated your level of greenhouse gases, 3.4 planet Earths would be required to ac-

75

commodate the emissions. The terms of the

Global Climate Accord require that you reduce your footprint as follows …"

They were giving the family a year to get the number down below three, and two more years to get it to one, on penalty of severe fines. Bill had two weeks to present the GCA with a plan. [...]

Bill didn't think he could blithely hit "ACCEPT" the way he did whenever iTunes updated its terms of service. This GCA was deep in his credit card data and might have the power to hold him to it. He called Laurie's sister, who was a lawyer.

"Sorry, Bill. The GCA is the real deal. The US and every other nation on Earth signed an agreement this year to enforce its terms. I can't believe you hadn't heard about it. World leaders have been trying to pass a global climate policy framework for decades, but the best the cowards could do was shift the burden from governments onto individuals. People all around the world are getting audited, and credit card companies and utilities are obligated to furnish quantitative information about their consumption patterns."

"Tell me about it. It's as if they had informers everywhere – our gas tank, our fridge, probably my underwear drawer. So you're saying I should accept the terms?"

"I don't think you have a choice. There's some fine print you can read at the website that may give you a way around their requirements, but they tried to make this treaty have teeth."

So Bill went ahead and nervously clicked the fateful button. It was a relief to see his browser pop up as if nothing had happened. Except that in one corner there hovered a blue box with yellow letters, which periodically flashed a message, saying "You have 14 days remaining to complete your climate action plan."

Anmerkung:

55	**BTU** – British Thermal Unit, used as a unit of energy in the US and Canada
73	**mean** – *here:* average
84	**blithely** – without any worries
85	**iTunes** – free software program developed by Apple which acts as a media player
111	**to have teeth** (*informal*) – to be powerful and effective

Beispiellösung

(Aufgabe 1) In the extract from Rachel May's short story "The Audit", first published in Mary Woodbury's *Winds of Change: Short Stories About Our Climate*, households are randomly chosen to take part in an audit which evaluates their carbon footprint. If their footprint is deemed too large by the Global Climate Audit (GCA), which organises the audit, participants must submit a detailed plan on how to match the goals set by the GCA. The audit is carried out worldwide, and citizens – not governments – are held accountable for their emissions. To evaluate a household's carbon footprint, the GCA collects relevant data, e. g. credit card transactions, a household's heating emissions and the amount of energy used for their vehicles. Further data must be supplied by the participants themselves, filling in an online questionnaire.

Once a household is chosen to take part in the audit, there is no way to refrain from completing the online questionnaire as internet access is blocked until the survey has been completed. The carbon overdraft is then calculated, and online services are restored.

Depending on the respective carbon overdraft, each household must meet certain requirements as to how to reduce carbon emissions. This plan has to be submitted to the GCA within two weeks. Should someone fail to present the plan or should they fail to reduce their emissions, they are fined.

(Aufgabe 2) The protagonist of the short story is Bill, a married father of two. The short story is narrated by a third person narrator from his point of view. This allows the reader to get an insight into his thoughts and feelings and allows them to relive Bill's changing state of mind.

The narrative starts with Bill's son David informing his dad with increasing apprehension that their family has been selected for the audit. Bill "respond[s …] with a practiced calmness" (ll. 7 f.). His son's agitation thus stands in stark contrast to his own controlled response (cf. ll. 8–11).

Inside the house Bill meets his wife and daughter, who are also both worried about the audit (cf. ll. 14–17). Bill continues to treat their concerns with slight condescension ("Relax, Davey", l. 10; "C'mon everybody", l. 18), mistakenly believing it to be a tax audit (cf. ll. 20 f.).

It becomes clear that he is ignorant of the GCA and the consequences it might have for their family, and he is "embarrassed to admit he hadn't heard of the GCA, when even his fifth grader seemed to know all about it" (ll. 36–38). This ignorance seems to indicate that financial rather than environmental concerns are his topmost priority.

As he sits down in front of the computer, the narrative focus shifts away from the scene and Bill's interactions with his family to his own reflections (cf. ll. 48 f.). In addition, narrated time is conflated considerably (cf. ll. 58–61), giving his thoughts a rushed feel. Accordingly, his ignorance and relaxed mood vanish, and it dawns on him that his family's enormous carbon footprint might have consequences for them (cf. ll. 51–58).

The following paragraphs (cf. ll. 66–111) offer a bulk of background information on the GCA, informing the reader as well as Bill. His own incredulity therefore matches the reader's potential difficulties in envisioning this treaty. Bill therefore finds himself unable to "blithely hit 'ACCEPT' the way he did whenever iTunes updated its terms of service" (ll. 84–86), realising that there is no way to cheat on the GCA, a view seconded by a lawyer (cf. ll. 107–111). Embracing the inevitable, Bill finally hits the "fateful button" (l. 113) and feels briefly relieved when internet services is restored, but the feeling is only temporary: like the sword of Damocles, a countdown in one corner of his screen constantly reminds him of the number of days left until their climate action plan has to be submitted (cf. ll. 115–119).

Interestingly, his wife and his children, who were far more knowledgeable about the situation than Bill and who were the ones to inform him about the details of the audit, are not mentioned any further towards the end of the excerpt. The focus of the narrative has shifted on Bill alone, isolating him in his responsibility to come up with a plan to reduce their emissions.

Bill's changing state of mind is underlined by a matching choice of words: Whereas he uses a "soothing tone" (l. 19) to calm down his son at the beginning of the short story, he is "bewildered" (l. 33) and "embarrassed" (l. 36) when he learns about the impact the audit will have on his family. Consequently, he is rather nervous when he submits the completed questionnaire by pressing what he feels to be a "fateful button" (l. 113). It is also worth noting that words and phrases referring to the GCA, such as "GLOBAL CLIMATE AUDIT", l. 40; "SEND", l. 68; "ACCEPT" l. 85), are printed in capital letters and immediately catch the reader's attention. The typesetting thus expresses the significance and inevitability these words have to Bill.

In contrast to Bill's growing state of panic, the language used to describe the audit itself and the procedure of filling in the questionnaire is matter-of-fact (cf. ll. 50–58). The result of the family's audit (cf. ll. 72–78), too, is described in an unemotional, neutral style even though it requires them to drastically change their lifestyles.

(**Aufgabe 3.1**) At a time of a growing awareness of the dangers of climate change, environmental pollution and exploitation of natural resources, one might ask oneself whether a state should be allowed to regulate individual lifestyles on the way towards more sustainability.

Under the status quo climate change and global warming are pressing challenges that already take their toll on our every-day lives, e. g., with floods, heatwaves, droughts and rising sea levels. These challenges are not temporary but will certainly affect generations to come. The degree to which future generations will be impacted by our lavish and often careless lifestyles is yet to be determined and depends on whether we manage to actively adapt our lifestyles to current challenges.

A growing number of people agree that sustainability is the word, and, in some ways, governments are already regulating individual lifestyles by increasing taxes on oil and petrol but also through governmental support programmes for citizens that buy electric vehicles or invest in modernising their houses, subsidising public transportation to encourage people to refrain from driving their cars.

There are various arguments that speak for governmental regulation of individual lifestyles. Many people still close their eyes when it comes to challenges like climate change and/or do not consider it their responsibility to tackle these issues. In this case, laws and regulations are necessary to make people reconsider their non-sustainable lifestyle choices.

One should not forget that governmental regulations do not necessarily need to have negative consequences for citizens but might also lead to innovations, e. g., the ban of single-use plastics in many countries across the world led to innovations regarding sustainable alternatives.

A government should also take seriously its duty of care for its citizens which means that an individual's lifestyle that has a negative impact on the lives of others should not be promoted.

Nevertheless, the dose makes the poison: the right to make one's own life choices without being overruled by the state is also a fundamental one.

When looking at the world at large, it is important to notice that these global challenges do not affect all countries in the same way, but that developing countries are hit extremely hard by the consequences of climate change. The same is true on a national scale, where poorer people will usually be more adversely affected than the wealthier. For instance, those without residence or those working outside, e. g. in construction, are more likely to suffer the hardships of increasingly severe climate phenomena.

A growing gap between the rich and the poor also emphasises that western countries need to stop abusing developing countries as their landfills for electronic waste and plastics and close their eyes to the detrimental effects their way of life has on the poor. However, it is crucial that not one state alone regulates its citizens' individual lifestyles on the way towards more sustainability, but that countries around the world collaborate to do their best to pave the way for leaving a healthy planet for generations to come.

(**Aufgabe 3.2**) Oh, I'm such a fool! How could I be so ignorant regarding the GCA and the consequences it will have for my family? I must admit that I never thought about our lifestyle and whether it's sustainable. Now I see that it's anything but! How can our footprint be so big compared to others'? OK, we do have a pretty big house. Six bedrooms for four people – not everyone has that much space. And the SUV. Well, it's a practical car, especially for holidays, which means we don't take the plane every time. But I suppose we don't really need it to get the kids to school. And what can be so wrong with strawberries? Everybody loves strawberries!

Maybe I'm wrong. I guess not everyone can afford a big house and strawberries twice a week. And, yes, I think it's fair to say that these things add up. Maybe getting exotic or unseasonal fruit now and then is OK. Maybe driving an SUV on holiday is OK. Maybe buying new clothes is OK. But in combination ... it gets too much.

It feels so weird that the GCA should have such an in-depth insight into all our family's habits, the way we spend our money and any other preferences we have. It feels so intrusive. Who gets to see all this data? And getting no say in all of this. We HAVE to take part in the GCA, no matter what. That feels really unfair, inappropriate.

Maybe I'm underestimating this whole thing. If the government is ready to do away with all these rights to privacy – they wouldn't do it without good reason because they're really risking their necks.

Well, I guess we'll all have to change and evaluate beloved habits and fulfil the GCA's requirements. I'll have to relinquish strawberries, Laurie will have to leave the car in the garage more often and the kids will have to make do with a warm sweater rather than crank up the heating in autumn. Maybe I'll start with bringing the bikes in for a check-up next week.

I guess all these changes won't be easy; there'll definitely be a lot of arguments in the family. Nobody will find it easy letting go of their privileges; I certainly won't. But I don't see any alternative – the heavy fines they'll punish us with if we fail to meet the GCA's requirements hang over our heads like the sword of Damocles ...

We should – no! we have to – set up a plan that helps us fulfilling the GCA's orders but also allows us to gradually change our lifestyles to make the transition easier.

I worry whether we'll really be able to do it, reach these goals, and what happens if we don't. One thing is certain: things will have to change.

Klausurteil B

Jugend forscht: Einzigartiges Netzwerk zur Talentförderung mit herausragender Erfolgsbilanz *ohne Verfasserangabe*

„Sputnik-Schock" und „Bildungsnotstand": Schon in den 60er Jahren des vergangenen Jahrhunderts stand das deutsche Bildungssystem in der Kritik. Der damalige
5 stern-Chefredakteur Henri Nannen jedoch ließ es nicht bei journalistischen Schlagworten bewenden. Er startete eine gesellschaftlich breit angelegte Initiative, um den qualifizierten Nachwuchs an jungen
10 Wissenschaftlerinnen und Wissenschaftlern in der Bundesrepublik Deutschland zu fördern. Unter dem Motto „Wir suchen die Forscher von morgen!" rief Nannen im Dezember 1965 erstmals zur Teilnahme an
15 „Jugend forscht" auf.

Das Vorbild für „Jugend forscht" kam aus den USA. Dort hatten „Science Fairs" bereits eine lange Tradition: Bei den im Stil von Messen organisierten Wettbewerben
20 stellten junge Menschen ihre Forschungsprojekte und Erfindungen neben einer fachkundigen Jury auch der breiten Öffentlichkeit vor. [...]

Für die Idee, „Science Fairs" auch in der
25 Bundesrepublik durchzuführen, fand Nannen auf Anhieb tatkräftige Unterstützung. Mehrere große Unternehmen übernahmen Patenschaften für die Wettbewerbe in den einzelnen Bundesländern. Heute wie da-
30 mals richten die Partner die Wettbewerbe aus, stiften Preise und fördern weitere Aktivitäten wie etwa Ehemaligentreffen. Seit über fünf Jahrzehnten ist dieses Konzept ein zentrales Erfolgsrezept des Wettbe-
35 werbs. Mittlerweile unterstützen rund 250 Partner „Jugend forscht" mit einer jährlichen Summe von rund 10 Millionen Euro. [...]

1990 stellte die deutsche Wiedervereinigung auch „Jugend forscht" vor eine gro-
40 ße Herausforderung. Binnen kurzer Zeit musste die Infrastruktur des Wettbewerbs auch in den neuen Ländern aufgebaut werden. Trotz anfänglicher Schwierigkeiten, Patenunternehmen zu finden, stand die
45 Organisation in wenigen Monaten. Bereits im März 1991 wurden in den fünf neuen Ländern Landeswettbewerbe ausgetragen; zwei Monate später fand der erste gesamtdeutsche Bundeswettbewerb statt. [...]
50

Die zunächst eingeführte Bewertung der Teilnehmerinnen und Teilnehmer nach Geschlecht bzw. Zugehörigkeit zu einer Gruppe wurde bereits 1967 zugunsten ver-
55 schiedener Fachgebiete aufgegeben. Zunächst standen die klassischen Schul- und Studienfächer Biologie, Chemie, Mathematik und Physik zur Wahl. 1968 kam das Fachgebiet Technik hinzu, ein Jahr später
60 Geo- und Raumwissenschaften sowie 1975 Arbeitswelt. Dieses Fachgebiet sollte vor allem junge Auszubildende in stärkerem Maße für den Wettbewerb gewinnen.

Sehr bald stellte sich auch heraus, dass
65 man für die zahlreichen Mädchen und Jungen der unteren Jahrgangsstufen eine eigenständige Sparte innerhalb des Wettbewerbs benötigte. Seit 1969 gibt es daher neben „Jugend forscht" auch die Junioren-
70 sparte „Schüler experimentieren" für alle Teilnehmer bis 14 Jahre.

In den zurückliegenden 50 Jahren waren „Jugend forscht"-Projekte immer auch ein Spiegelbild der sich wandelnden Fragestel-
75 lungen in der naturwissenschaftlich-technischen Forschung: So überzeugte der erste

Bundessieger 1966 die Jury mit seiner Entwicklung eines elektronischen Rechenapparats. Knapp 50 Jahre später waren zwei Bundessieger mit einem selbst konstruierten 3-D-Rotationsdrucker erfolgreich. [...]

Der Bundespräsident begleitet den Wettbewerb seit 1977 als Schirmherr und Preisstifter. Eine Preisstifterin mit Tradition ist auch die Bundeskanzlerin, einer ihrer Vorgänger lobte 1971 zum ersten Mal den Preis für die originellste Arbeit aus. Seit 1981 reisen neben dem Gewinner dieses Sonderpreises auch alle Platzierten des Bundeswettbewerbs zum Kanzlerempfang in die deutsche Hauptstadt. [...]

„Jugend forscht" ist ein äußerst wirksames Instrument zur Talentförderung. Neun von zehn erfolgreichen Wettbewerbsteilnehmenden studieren später ein naturwissenschaftlich-technisches, mathematisches oder medizinisches Fach. Im Anschluss an das Studium ist etwa die Hälfte der ehemaligen Bundessiegerinnen und Bundessieger im Bereich Forschung und Entwicklung an Hochschulen, außeruniversitären Forschungseinrichtungen oder in Unternehmen tätig. Für eine ganze Reihe wissenschaftlicher Karrieren war „Jugend forscht" der Ausgangspunkt. Dies gilt etwa für die Physik-Professorin und Leibniz-Preisträgerin Gisela Anton, den SUN-Microsystems-Gründer Andreas von Bechtolsheim oder den Vater der Pisa-Studie Andreas Schleicher. [...]

Die seit Jahren steigenden Anmeldezahlen bei „Jugend forscht" beweisen, dass es trotz der weiterhin bestehenden Kritik am deutschen Bildungssystem möglich ist, junge Menschen für Naturwissenschaften zu begeistern.

Anmerkung:

1 **Sputnik-Schock** – die politischen und gesellschaftlichen Reaktionen in der westlichen Welt auf den Start des ersten künstlichen Erdsatelliten Sputnik im Oktober 1957 durch die Sowjetunion

85 **Bundeskanzlerin** – zum Zeitpunkt der Veröffentlichung führte noch Angela Merkel die Bundesregierung an

Beispiellösung

Aufgabe 4

"Jugend forscht" – The Development and Goals of the German Science Competition
When thinking of a German example for science talent competitions, many Germans immediately think of "Jugend forscht", which can be roughly translated to "Teenage research".
"Jugend forscht" was established in the 1960s by Henri Nannen, former chief editor of the German magazine *stern*, with the first competition taking place in December 1965. It was Nannen's intention to actively support German scientists-in-the-making, instead of merely complaining about the flaws in Germany's educational system at the time. American "Science Fairs" functioned as role models for Nannen's vision of a German science competition in which children and teenagers got the chance to present their research in a field of interest of their choice to expert judges as well as the public. Nannen's idea immediately took off, and major German companies and institutions teamed up with him, sponsoring competitions in all German federal states.

Today, about 250 companies donate prizes, organise the competitions as well alumni meetings and follow-up programmes for successful candidates. With an annual support of 9 million euros, these partners are crucial for the competition's constant success and public recognition.

The initial distinction between genders and groups was superseded by a delineation along the different disciplines. Whereas the initial categories focussed on projects affiliated with classic science subjects taught at school, e. g., biology and chemistry, additional categories like technology and earth sciences were later added to the portfolio. Competitions for younger participants were also established and shortly after the reunification of Germany, both local competitions in each of the 16 German federal states as well as a nationwide competition were carried out. Dignitaries and politicians take on the patronage for local competitions and sponsor participants.

The aims of "Jugend forscht" are to spark an interest in science in children and teenagers from a young age onward and to acknowledge scientific projects and research among youngsters. Furthermore, their scientific research garners public acclaim, thereby encouraging a growing number of students to study sciences after graduating from school.

LK Literarischer Text mit Beispiellösungen

Klausurteil A: Leseverstehen und Schreiben integriert

AUFGABENSTELLUNG

1. Summarize what we learn about life in Kosawa and Pexton's role in it.
   (Comprehension) (12 Punkte)

2. Analyze the atmosphere created in the text and its effect on the reader. Focus on narrative techniques and use of language. *(Analysis) (16 Punkte)*

3. Choose **one** of the following tasks:

3.1 Steve Killelea, founder of the Institute for Economics and Peace, warns that "ecological threats pose serious challenges to global peace. [...] In the absence of action, civil unrest, riots and conflict will most likely increase."[1] Comment on this prediction, referring to economic, ecological and political issues of globalization.
   (Evaluation: comment) (14 Punkte)

3.2 Having committed her life to fight against oil drilling in Nigeria, Thula, the narrator, has been awarded an international prize for her outstanding achievements for sustainable development in Nigeria. In consequence, she has been invited to write an article for *The Guardian* about how her childhood in Kosawa has motivated her to become an environmental activist and about her demands for the future. Write the article. *(Evaluation: re-creation of text) (14 Punkte)*

---

[1] https://www.theguardian.com/environment/2020/sep/09/climate-crisis-could-displace-12bn-people-by-2050-report-warns (Zugriff: 08.08.2023)

Klausurteil B: Sprachmittlung isoliert

AUFGABENSTELLUNG

4. Your British friend is doing research on projects promoting multicultural partnerships in the arts and has asked you about corresponding initiatives in Germany.
   Write an email to your friend in which you outline the information about the project "Writing On". *(Mediation) (18 Punkte)*

Materialgrundlage:

Klausurteil A:

Imbolo Mbue, *How Beautiful We Were,* Edinburgh: Canongate 2021, S. 3–7 (gekürzt).
Wortzahl: 935

Zitat:
Jon Henley, „Climate crisis could displace 1.2 bn people by 2050, report warns", in: *The Guardian*, London, 9. September 2020, zitiert nach: https://www.theguardian.com/environment/2020/sep/09/climate-crisis-could-displace-12bn-people-by-2050-report-warns (Zugriff: 01.04.2024)

Klausurteil B:

Lara Sielmann, „Berliner Literaturprojekt ‚Weiter Schreiben': Briefe aus dem Krisenge-biet", in: *Der Tagesspiegel,* 25. Mai 2020, zitiert nach: https://www.tagesspiegel.de/berlin/briefe-aus-dem-krisengebiet-6601948.html (Zugriff: 01.04.2024, gekürzt)
Wortzahl: 648

Zugelassene Hilfsmittel:

- Ein- und zweisprachiges Wörterbuch
- Herkunftssprachliches Wörterbuch für Schülerinnen und Schüler, deren Herkunftssprache nicht Deutsch ist
- Wörterbuch zur deutschen Rechtschreibung

Klausurteil A

How Beautiful We Were   *Imbolo Mbue*

This is the beginning of the novel. The story told from Thula's perspective and is set in the fictional African village Kosawa in the 1980ies.

We should have known the end was near. How could we not have known? When the sky began to pour acid and rivers began to turn green, we should have known our
5 land would soon be dead. Then again, how could we have known when they didn't want us to know? When we began to wobble and stagger, tumbling and snapping like feeble little branches, they told us it would
10 soon be over, that we would all be well in no time. They asked us to come to village meetings, to talk about it. They told us we had to trust them.

We should have spat in their faces, heaped
15 upon them names most befitting – liars, savages, unscrupulous, evil. We should have cursed their mothers and their grandmothers, flung pejoratives upon their fathers, prayed for unspeakable calamities to befall
20 their children. We hated them and we hated their meetings, but we attended all of them. Every eight weeks we went to the village square to listen to them. We were dying. We were helpless. We were afraid. Those meet-
25 ings were our only chance at salvation.

[…]

In the square we sat in near silence as the sun left us for the day, oblivious to how the beauty of its descent heightened our
30 anguish. We watched as the Pexton men placed their briefcases on the table our village head, Woja Beki, had set for them. There were always three of them – we called them the Round One (his face was
35 as round as a ball we would have had fun kicking), the Sick One (his suits were oversized, giving him the look of a man dying of a flesh-stealing disease), and the Leader (he did the talking, the other two did the
40 nodding). We mumbled among ourselves as they opened their briefcases and passed sheets of paper among themselves, covering their mouths as they whispered into each other's ears to ensure they had their
45 lies straight. We had nowhere more important to be so we waited, desperate for good news. We whispered at intervals, wondering what they were thinking whenever they paused to look at us […].

50 We inhaled, waited, exhaled. We remembered those who had died from diseases with neither names nor cures – our siblings and cousins and friends who had perished from the poison in the water and the poi-
55 son in the air and the poisoned food growing from the land that lost its purity the day Pexton came drilling. We hoped the men would look into our eyes and feel something for us. We were children, like their
60 children, and we wanted them to recognize that. If they did, it wasn't apparent in their countenance. They'd come for Pexton, to keep its conscience clean; they hadn't come for us.

65 Woja Beki walked up to the front and thanked everyone for coming.

"My dear people," he said, exposing the teeth no one wanted to see, "if we don't ask for what we want, we'll never get it. If we
70 don't expunge what's in our bellies, are we not going to suffer from constipation and die?"

We did not respond; we cared nothing for what he had to say. We knew he was

75 one of them. We'd known for years that though he was our leader, descended from the same ancestors as us, we no longer meant anything to him. Pexton had bought his cooperation and he had, in turn, sold 80 our future to them. [...]

In the glow of the fading sun our village looked almost beautiful, our faces almost free of anguish. Our grandfathers and grandmothers appeared serene, but we 85 knew they weren't – they'd seen much, and yet they'd never seen anything like this.

"We'll now hear from Mr. Honorable Representative of Pexton, all the way from Bézam to speak to us again," Woja Beki 90 said, before returning to his seat.

The Leader rose up, walked toward us, and stood in the center of the square.

For several seconds, he stared at us, his head angled, his smile so strenuously earnest 95 we wondered if he was admiring a radiance we'd never been told we had. We waited for him to say something that would make us burst into song and dance. We wanted him to tell us that Pexton had decided to leave and 100 take the diseases with them.

His smile broadened, narrowed, landed on our faces, scanning our stillness. Seem-

ingly satisfied, he began speaking. He was happy to be back in Kosawa on this fine day, he said. What a lovely evening it was, 105 with the half-moon in the distance, such a perfect breeze, was that the sound of sparrows singing in one accord? What a gorgeous village. He wanted to thank us for coming. It was great to see everyone again. 110 Incredible how many precious children Kosawa has. We had to believe him that the people at headquarters were sad about what was happening to us. They were all working hard to resolve this issue so every- 115 one could be healthy and happy again. He spoke slowly, his smile constant, as if he was about to deliver the good news we so yearned for.

We barely blinked as we watched him, 120 listening to lies we'd heard before. Lies about how the people who controlled Pexton cared about us. Lies about how the big men in the government of His Excellency cared about us. Lies about how hundreds of 125 people in the capital had asked him to relay their condolences to us. "They mourn with you at the news of every death," he said. "It'll be over soon. It's time your suffering ended, isn't it?" 130

Annotations:

18 **to fling pejoratives** – *here:* to speak in a very negative way about someone

89 **Bézam** – fictional African town

Beispiellösung

(**Aufgabe 1**) The excerpt from Imbolo Mbue's novel *How Beautiful We Were*, which was published in 2021, tells the fictitious story of the conflict between an oil drilling company and the inhabitants of an African village in the 1980s.
Apparently, the oil drilling has wrought immense environmental destruction. Air pollution is causing acid rain, water pollution is so bad that it has turned the rivers green, agricultural products are poisoned. People's health is severely affected: many suffer from diseases which have been unknown so far and others have even died.
Pexton holds regular meetings with the people of the village just to pretend that the company cares. In fact, they only tell lies, pretending that they are working hard to

improve the situation. From the beginning the village leader has been bribed by them, so they can recklessly pursue their own interests. The people from the village therefore have no trust in their leader, let alone in the Pexton company.

(Aufgabe 2) It is especially the narrative point of view that conveys the village people's fear, despair, contempt and disillusionment. The point of view of a child as a first-person narrator conveys the thoughts and feelings of the people of the village. As the narrator continuously uses the first-person plural, it becomes clear that she is a representative of the village children, if not all the people in the village, who all feel the same. She begins by reflecting on the situation with the help of questions (cf. ll. 1, 3), which insinuates right from the beginning that things have gone seriously wrong. She uses the conditional in lines 7 ff., which again is a critical subjective reflection of the past and which immediately suggests to the reader that the Pexton people are hypocritical and untrustworthy. Her choice of words colours the presentation of the Pexton company, and also the villager's rage and helplessness, as she uses numerous derogatory words and words with negative connotations ("spat", "heaped upon them names", "liars, savages, unscrupulous, evil", "cursed", "flung pejoratives", "hated", "dying", "afraid", ll. 5–10).

Moreover, images are employed to illustrate the diseases that they all suffer from ("wobble and stagger, tumbling and snapping like feeble little branches", l. 4). The image and personification of the sunset (cf. l. 13 f.) serves various purposes. Symbolic as it is, it suggests abandonment, descent, darkness as it is going down, paradoxically leaving the village in beauty. This may be a nostalgic note referring to a better past, but it also alludes to hypocrisy, which is a central theme of the text, and contributes to the irony of the situation (see below).

The narrator's description of the Pexton representatives together with their nicknames is again highly subjective. Neither their outward appearance (cf. ll. 16–19) nor their behaviour is in any way pleasant, as the narrator observes them "covering their mouths as they whisper into each other's ears to ensure they get their lies straight" (ll. 20 f.).

Also, the villagers' contempt for their corrupt leader becomes clear by means of the narrative point of view. Woja Beki's smiling is described as "exposing teeth no one wanted to see" (l. 32). It suggests falseness and insinuates ugliness and disgust as well.

Together with the direct-speech announcement by Beki (cf. l. 43) and the description of the smile that "broadened, narrowed, landed on our faces, scanning our stillness" (l. 49), the reported speech by "the Leader" (l. 44) is full of irony. Against the background of the narrator's, the villagers' and the reader's knowledge of the environmental destruction and the deadly diseases, his happiness and his description of the evening atmosphere ("lovely evening", "half-moon in the distance", "perfect breeze", "sparrows singing in one accord", "gorgeous village", "precious children", ll. 51 ff.) contrasts starkly with the reality of life in the village, thus creating very strong irony.

Apart from her lexical choices, the narrator makes use of emphatic means of language, too, employing enumeration (cf. l. 25), parallelism and alliteration (cf. l. 26) and repetition (cf. l. 28, ll. 58 ff.) in order to enhance the atmosphere of despair, rage and anxiety.

(Aufgabe 3.1) This example of injustice, of indifference on the side of those in power on the one hand, namely corporations and governments, and of helplessness, despair and rage on the side of the ordinary people perfectly illustrates Steve Killelea's warning of the danger of civil unrest. Killelea is the founder of the Institute for Economics and Peace, and in an article in the *Guardian*, he warns that "ecological threats pose serious challenges to global peace". He fears that if no action is taken, "civil unrest, riots and conflict will most likely increase". Considering the situation in the fictitious village of Kosawa, it seems to be only a matter of time before desperation and rage will result in an eruption of violence. What else could be expected when people are made to suffer to an extent that is beyond human endurance?

What is true on a local level will also be true on a global scale. It is the Global North that exploits the African continent. Mining, drilling, clearing the rainforests – all this is the work of large corporations that exploit the resources directly, or it is done by locals that cater for the North's needs, ignorant of or indifferent to the ecological implications of their actions. Even more destructive to the environment and global peace is the climate crisis. Caused by the industrial countries and the oil-producing emirates of the Middle East, the climate crisis hits the African continent hardest. It leads to droughts and famines. Huge areas of land will soon be uninhabitable. War about water and soil in the Northern hemisphere is a scenario which is far too realistic. Desperate people are already flocking to other areas in the world, and it does not take much imagination to understand how this will lead to brutal fighting for sheer survival. People in Africa have all the access to the media to know about the unfairness of the global distribution of resources and wealth. In the face of death, they will no longer tolerate the rich countries to always take the lion's share.

Thus, it is high time for politicians and corporations alike to acknowledge the signs of the times. Justice has to be secured for people and countries. This means strengthening young democracies and fighting dictatorships. It also means putting up programmes that help the people and not the international world of finance. Fair trade programmes have to be encouraged, NGOs that work globally or locally have to be supported. Conflicts have to be overcome, not fuelled.

A central issue is education. People have to have access to better jobs, but in particular they have to be able to become aware of global issues, the importance of human rights, the importance of women's rights, the importance of environmental protection and the importance of sustainability in general.

And most important, the climate crisis has to be tackled. The industrial North still relies too much on fossil fuels. Conservative politicians and corporations still reiterate the mantra of gradualism and postponement. They ignore the urgency of the moment. Killelea's warning is to be taken seriously. He himself says violence and conflict "will most likely increase". I should say, violence and conflict will definitely increase. So, what are we waiting for?

(**Aufgabe 3.2**) Growing up in the village of Kosawa, I would never have dreamt of being awarded an international prize and being invited to write an article for the *Guardian*. It was my childhood experience in my little village, though, that shaped my life and made me an environmental activist and journalist.

Kosawa is a village like any other in Africa. We lived on what we produced with our hands on our fields. We lived on what the land yielded to us. We had the fish in the rivers, the mangoes from the trees and the grains from the soil. The village community was intact. There was a close network of family and friends, and we had leaders who we respected. All this came to an end when the Pexton company started drilling for oil close to the village. At the time, there were hardly any environmental regulations. There would have been a chance to prevent the drilling altogether if the villagers or the village council had not agreed in the first place. But those people who had a say in Kosawa were easily bribed. Grand corruption is a daily occurrence in Nigeria, and with oil companies having so much money, it is no wonder that they could buy our leaders.

The infrastructure developed to exploit the oil fields around Kosawa destroyed acres of forests and their wildlife. The drilling as such produced toxic emissions which caused immense air pollution and in turn acid rain. Oil spills together with other toxic liquids used in the drilling process polluted the soil and also the water. Water pollution was so bad that it was clearly visible. Rivers had literally turned green. In fact, the drilling destroyed our livelihood. Soon we did not have any clean water, the air we had to breathe was toxic and the food from the water and the soil poisoned our bodies. People developed illnesses that could not be cured, especially not in Kosawa, and many people died. Pexton never took any responsibility. They just pretended. Their hypocrisy was unbearable when they told us lies and made promises they never wanted to keep.

Luckily, I had the chance to leave the village and get an education and work in Lagos, which enabled me to dedicate myself to environmental work. My commitment to fighting against oil drilling in Nigeria has led to various achievements for sustainable development, which has won me this international prize that I am very proud of. Yet, there is no time to stop fighting. There is a lot to be done in the way of sustainable development. It is still the global corporations that profit from Africa's resources. Local workers are excluded from profits. And the environment is suffering from this economic and social injustice. To people who are struggling to stay alive, caring for the environment is a luxury. A central issue is education. People have to have access to better jobs, but in particular they have to be able to become aware of global issues, the importance of human rights, the importance of women's rights, the importance of environmental protection and the importance of sustainability in general. People without education are not aware of the impact of pollution, and people without education will not be able to work for technological innovation that will make us independent of fossil fuels.

With Africa's ecological footprint being a lot smaller than that of the Northern countries, i.e. with Africans producing a lot less CO_2, they still have to bear the brunt of climate change. They are forced to pay for the North's luxury and consumption with climate catastrophes like droughts, heatwaves, storms and flooding. With Africa's dependence on agriculture, it is particularly hard to adjust to the climate crisis.

Thus, one important demand has be to that drilling stops altogether. Fossil fuels must be abandoned; alternative renewable sources of energy have to be developed. In Africa, the sun should be able to produce more energy than is needed. Thus, drilling for oil could be considerably reduced. In turn, I will further commit myself to the restoration of the environment that has been destroyed. Ecosystems have to be regenerated.

I have proudly accepted this prize, but I will not rest. Sustainability in Nigeria, in Africa, in the world is crucial for the survival of humanity.

Klausurteil B

Berliner Literaturprojekt „Weiter Schreiben": Briefe aus dem Krisengebiet   *Lara Sielmann*

Das Projekt bringt Autoren aus Krisengebieten und Deutschland zusammen. Ausländische Schriftsteller erhalten so leichter Zugang zum deutschen Literaturpreis.

„Früher konnte ich das ganze Haus beobachten, während ich den Innenhof schrubbte. Ich erinnere mich an das Wasser, das ich aus dem Eimer goss, ich erinnere mich an das Geräusch des Schrubbers, ich erinnere mich daran, wie ich das Wasser verteilte und wie das Wasser allen Staub und Schmutz verschluckte, wie es alle meine Sünden in den Gully mit der gelben Abdeckung schwemmte", schreibt die syrische Schriftstellerin Lina Atfah, die mittlerweile in Nordrhein-Westfalen lebt, ihrer Brieffreundin Nino Haratischwili über das Haus ihrer Kindheit in Salamiyya. [...]

Der digitale Brief ist bereits der dritte der beiden Schriftstellerinnen, der in „(W)Ortwechseln" erschienen ist. Insgesamt sechs Autorenpaare sind Teil des Projektes, das seit Ende April im Zwei-Wochen-Rhythmus das gesamte Jahr über auf der dazugehörigen Homepage veröffentlich wird.

Mit dabei sind Autoren aus Syrien, dem Irak, dem Iran, Kroatien, Russland, Georgien, Österreich und Deutschland, unter anderem Pegah Ahmadi und Monika Rinck, Abdalrahman Alqalaq und Katerina Poladjan, Mariam Al-Attar und Sabine Scholl. Der Leser erhält persönliche und künstlerische Einblicke und erfährt etwas über die Bedingungen des Schreibens der jeweiligen Briefverfasser.

[...]

Hervorgegangen ist „(W)Ortwechseln" aus dem Berliner Literaturprojekt „Weiter Schreiben", das seit 2017 deutsche Autoren mit Autoren aus Krisengebieten in Tandems zusammenbringt, mit dem Ziel, die ausländischen Schriftsteller und Schriftstellerinnen im deutschsprachigen Literaturbetrieb zu etablieren.

„Alle Autorinnen und Autoren aus diesen Gebieten, die nach Deutschland gekommen sind, hatten einen Wunsch, nämlich weiter zu schreiben", erzählt die Schriftstellerin und Gründerin des Projektes, Annika Reich. Bereits vor acht Jahren hat die Wahlberlinerin zusammen mit der Malerin Katharina Grosse einen Kreis von 100 Frauen aus dem Bereich Wissenschaft, Kunst und Kultur gegründet.

Sie sollen sich gegenseitig unterstützen und gemeinsam Projekte umsetzen. [...]

2015 wurde aus diesem Verband die NGO „Wir Machen Das" gegründet, die Menschen aus Krisengebieten aus dem Bereich Kultur und Journalismus den Einstieg in den deutschen Kulturbetrieb erleichtern soll. Das Projekt „Weiter Schreiben" richtet sich vor allem an Autoren, die auf Arabisch schreiben.

[...]

„Die deutschsprachigen Autorinnen und Autoren des Tandems sind hier bekannt und etabliert. Dadurch wurde von den großen Literaturinstitutionen von Anfang an auch die literarische Qualität der Partnerinnen und Partner nicht infrage gestellt, auch wenn sie hier noch nicht bekannt sind", erzählt Reich.

Die 47-Jährige unterbrach für die Arbeit bei der NGO das eigene Schreiben für fünf

Jahre. Vor der Corona-Pandemie war das Projekt in Berlin gut erlebbar: Es gab ver-
75 schiedene Lesungen in Buchhandlungen und bekannten Literaturinstitutionen wie dem Literarischen Colloquium am Wannsee oder dem Literaturhaus in der Fasanenstraße.

80 Daneben erscheint seit 2019 auch das „Weiter Schreiben"-Magazin, in dem die Autoren und Autorinnen des Projektes publiziert werden. Interviews und Essays zu einem Themenschwerpunkt stehen auch
85 darin. Die aktuelle Ausgabe beinhaltet erste Auszüge der Briefkorrespondenz der deutschen Lyrikerin Monika Rinck mit ihrer iranischen Tandempartnerin Pegah Ahmadi.

Besonders groß ist der Markt an über-
90 setzter arabischsprachiger Literatur in Deutschland noch nicht, vor allem, was die Gegenwartsliteratur betrifft.

„Es ist erschreckend, wie wenig generell aus dem Arabischen übersetzt wird", sagt
95 Reich. „So transportieren sich ja auch kein neues Wissen oder Einblicke in die arabischsprachige Literaturwelt oder in das, worüber aktuell geschrieben und nachgedacht wird."

Allerdings laufe es für die Autorinnen 100 und Autoren von „Weiter Schreiben" ganz gut, fünf haben schon Bücher veröffentlicht. Drei weitere Verträge sind geschlossen. Insgesamt 17 aktive Tandems gibt es zurzeit, viel mehr Kapazitäten hat das 105 Team um Reich herum nicht.

Das alles sei auch eine Geldfrage: „Für die nächsten drei Jahre sind wir zum Glück gefördert, viel Luft nach oben, also für alle Autorinnen und Autoren, die wir ger- 110 ne aufnehmen würden, lässt uns das aber trotzdem nicht."

Für dieses Jahr hatten sie sich viel vorgenommen, das Netzwerk sollte über Deutschland hinaus wachsen. Das geht we- 115 gen der aktuellen Krise gerade nicht, soll aber nachgeholt werden, sobald es wieder möglich ist. „Unsere Briefkorrespondenzen kommen somit zur richtigen Zeit", sagt Reich. 120

Im Herbst soll der dazugehörige Podcast in Kooperation mit dem rbbKultur folgen. In insgesamt drei Folgen wollen die Autoren das bis dahin Geschriebene und Veröffentlichte näher beleuchten. 125

Anmerkungen:

Die Sprachrichtigkeit betreffende Fehler wurden korrigiert.

13 Nino Haratischwili – aus Georgien stammende deutsche Theaterregisseurin, Dramatikerin und Romanautorin

14 Salamiyya – Kleinstadt in Syrien

122 rbbKultur – Programm des Senders Rundfunk Berlin-Brandenburg

Beispiellösung

Aufgabe 4

Hello Sophie,

Cool, I really like the project you're doing research for. As a matter of fact, I've just come across a German project that would fit in with your project. It's the Berlin literature project "Writing on", which teams up authors from areas of conflict with authors from Germany and Austria. Part of the project is a website which consists of digital correspondences between six pairs of authors from Syria, Iraq, Iran, Croatia, Russia, Georgia, Austria and

Germany. The reader gets a personal and literary insight and gets to know about the circumstances of writing the respective writers find themselves in. The ultimate goal is to establish foreign writers in the German literary community.

All authors from these areas wish to keep writing. Starting in 2014 as an association of 100 women from science and culture, the NGO "We will do it" was founded in 2015 in order to facilitate access to the German cultural scene for journalists and artists. The project "Writing on" targets authors writing in Arabic in particular. As the German-speaking authors are well-known and well-established, the literary quality of their international partners has never been questioned, even though they are not known here yet.

Before the pandemic there were lots of readings in bookshops and literary institutions in Berlin. There is also the "Writing-on" magazine, which combines the authors' texts with interviews and essays. Unfortunately, not a lot of Arabic literature is translated into German.

As of 2022, there were 17 active partnerships, some authors have already published books and although there is always a shortage of money, a network beyond Germany has been envisaged, and also a radio podcast was planned for last autumn.

I hope I could help you with your project.

Take care

Tom

Die sprachliche Leistung im Abitur

Der Stellenwert der sprachlichen Leistung

Bei der Bewertung der Abiturprüfung können 150 Punkte vergeben werden. Davon fallen 90 Punkte für die sprachliche und 60 Punkte für die inhaltliche Leistung an. Über das Fachwissen zu den lehrplanrelevanten Inhalten hinaus ist also die sprachliche Leistung im Englischen für ein gutes Ergebnis in der Abiturprüfung von grundlegender Bedeutung. Natürlich bedingen sich die beiden Teilbereiche gegenseitig: Ohne stichhaltigen Inhalt kann nicht die volle Punktzahl im Bereich Sprache erreicht werden und umgekehrt.

Die Entwicklung der englischen Sprachkompetenz ist ein komplexer Prozess, der sich über viele Jahre hinweg bis zum Abitur hin entfaltet. Es ist an dieser Stelle nicht möglich, eine umfassende Revision der sprachlichen Grundlagen anzubieten, aber Sie finden hier Hinweise auf die wichtigsten Aspekte, die Sie zum Zeitpunkt des Abiturs beherrschen sollten. Bei Bedarf können Sie dann das eine oder andere Kapitel mit Hilfe eines grammatikorientieren Buches wiederholen.

TIPP zur individuellen Wiederholung der Grammatik

Wenn Sie das Gefühl haben, in wichtigen Bereichen der Grammatik noch Defizite zu haben, analysieren Sie gezielt Ihre persönlichen Schwachpunkte aus den Klausuren und wiederholen Sie selbstständig die entsprechenden Kapitel anhand einer Grammatik oder eines Übungsbuches auf Sprachniveau B2 des Gemeinsamen Europäischen Referenzrahmens.

Klassische Fehlerquellen sind zum Beispiel *if*-Sätze, Passivkonstruktionen, die Wahl der richtigen Zeitform oder Präpositionen nach bestimmten Verben.

Die Leistungskriterien

Eigene Fehlerschwerpunkte erkennen

Um eigene Fehlerschwerpunkte zu erkennen, ist es empfehlenswert, die Darstellungsleistung in eigenen Klausuren genau zu analysieren.

- Lesen Sie Ihre eigenen Klausuren inklusive der Randbemerkungen und Kommentare Ihrer Englischlehrkraft erneut durch und halten Sie auf einem separaten Blatt fest, welche Teilbereiche besonders „fehleranfällig" sind.
- Wenn Ihre Klausuren mittels eines Korrekturrasters bewertet worden sind, studieren Sie dieses im Hinblick auf die Darstellungsleistung genau: In welchen Teilbereichen haben Sie besonders wenige Punkte erhalten? Lesen Sie nun Ihre Klausuren im Hinblick auf diese Teilbereiche erneut durch. Halten Sie schriftlich fest, wo Ihre individuellen Fehlerschwerpunkte liegen.

Wenn Sie die eigenen Fehlerschwerpunkte identifiziert haben, sollten Sie diese beim Anfertigen – und anschließenden Korrekturlesen – schriftlicher Hausaufgaben und Klausuren besonders im Blick haben.

Defizite im Bereich der Grundgrammatik können Sie mit entsprechenden Übungsbüchern aufarbeiten. Auch hier gilt: Üben Sie konsequent über einen längeren Zeitraum hinweg und trainieren Sie immer wieder das Verfassen schriftlicher Texte, indem Sie z. B. im Unterricht angefertigte Stichpunkte ausformulieren.

In den meisten Wörterbüchern finden Sie Zusammenstellungen der unregelmäßigen Verben und der wichtigsten *phrasal verbs.* Es empfiehlt sich, diese vor Klausuren zu wiederholen.

Die Vorgehensweise in Klausuren und in der schriftlichen Abiturprüfung

Um in Klausuren und in der schriftlichen Abiturprüfung ein möglichst gutes Ergebnis zu erzielen, ist es unerlässlich, eine sinnvolle und gut strukturierte Vorarbeit zu leisten. Lassen Sie sich nicht von Mitschülerinnen und Mitschülern aus der Ruhe bringen, die nach kürzester Bearbeitungszeit und ohne Notizen sofort anfangen zu schreiben!

Je intensiver Sie sich mit der Aufgabenstellung und dem Ausgangstext auseinandersetzen und entsprechende Notizen anfertigen, desto einfacher wird es Ihnen fallen, die Aufgabenstellungen in zusammenhängenden Texten zu bearbeiten.

Die Bearbeitung in folgenden Schritten hat sich bewährt:

1. Lesen Sie zunächst die Aufgabenstellung und den Ausgangstext ein erstes Mal durch. Achten Sie hierbei auch auf eventuelle Erläuterungen, die dem Ausgangstext vorangestellt sind. Diese sind meist kursiv gedruckt und enthalten wichtige Zusatzinformationen, die Ihnen die Bearbeitung der Aufgaben erleichtern. Beim ersten Lesen sollten Sie auch Wörter unterstreichen, deren Bedeutung Sie nicht kennen und auch nicht aus dem Kontext erschließen können.

2. Schlagen Sie nun die Wörter nach, die Sie beim ersten Lesen nicht verstehen bzw. erschließen konnten, und die für das Textverständnis von Bedeutung sind. Oft lassen sich unbekannte Wörter aus dem Zusammenhang bzw. mit Rückgriff auf andere Sprachen erschließen.

3. Bevor Sie den Text nun erneut lesen, sollten Sie die Aufgabenstellungen einer genauen Betrachtung unterziehen. Achten Sie auf die verwendeten Operatoren – diese „verraten" Ihnen, was genau Ihre Aufgabe ist bzw. welche Aspekte sie untersuchen sollen. Auch im Abitur werden Sie die Dreiteilung in „Comprehension", „Analysis" und „Evaluation: Comment / Re-creation of text" vorfinden. Beachten Sie: Bei der Bearbeitung der „Comprehension"-Aufgabe sollen – im Gegensatz zur „Analysis"-Aufgabe – keine Zitate und Textverweise verwendet werden!

4. Lesen Sie nun den Ausgangstext erneut und nehmen Sie zunächst (farbige) Markierungen und Randbemerkungen für die Bearbeitung der ersten Aufgabe vor. Auf einem separaten Blatt sollten Sie darüber hinaus Stichpunkte anfertigen, die Ihnen die anschließende Bearbeitung der jeweiligen Aufgabenstellung erleichtern. Bevor Sie die Stichpunkte ausformulieren, empfiehlt es sich, diese in eine sinnvolle Reihenfolge zu bringen, etwa durch Nummerierung. Denken Sie daran, Ihre Ausführungen zur ersten Aufgabe mit einem entsprechenden Einleitungssatz (Nennung von Autor/-in, Titel, Textsorte, Erscheinungsdatum, Quelle und Thema) zu beginnen. Anschließend wenden Sie diese Verfahrensweise auf die Aufgaben 2 und 3 an. Hier ist es nicht notwendig, den Einleitungssatz der ersten Aufgabe zu wiederholen – Ihre Leserinnen und Leser wissen ja nun, welcher Ausgangstext Ihren Ausführungen zugrunde liegt! Es ist allerdings notwendig, kurz darzulegen, welche Aspekte nachfolgend untersucht bzw. bearbeitet werden.

5. Nachdem Sie alle Aufgaben bearbeitet haben, sollten Sie ausreichend Zeit (ca. 20 Minuten) einplanen, um Ihre Klausur Korrektur zu lesen. Achten Sie dabei auf Ihre individuellen Fehlerschwerpunkte!

In der schriftlichen Abiturprüfung haben Sie im Fach Englisch im Grund- und im Leistungskurs die Auswahl zwischen jeweils zwei Klausurvorschlägen.
Hierbei handelt es sich stets um einen literarischen Text und einen Sach- oder Gebrauchstext – möglicherweise in Kombination mit einem Cartoon, einer Grafik oder einer Statistik.

Sie haben 30 Minuten Zeit, sich mit beiden Themenvorschlägen zu befassen und einen der beiden zur Bearbeitung auswählen. Der nicht gewählte Vorschlag verbleibt bei Ihnen. Theoretisch könnten Sie sich nach zwei Stunden noch umentscheiden. TUN SIE DIES JA NICHT! Wenn Sie sich entschieden haben, legen Sie den Vorschlag weit weg, am besten auf den Boden, um Verwechslungen zu vermeiden!
Anschließend dürfen Sie sofort mit der Bearbeitung des von Ihnen gewählten Vorschlags beginnen, d.h. Sie müssen nicht das Ende der dreißigminütigen Auswahlzeit abwarten.

Als Hilfsmittel sind in der Klausur ein- und zweisprachige Wörterbücher sowie ein Wörterbuch zur deutschen Rechtschreibung zugelassen; Schülerinnen und Schüler, deren Herkunftssprache nicht Deutsch ist, dürfen zudem ein herkunftssprachliches Wörterbuch nutzen.
Bislang bezieht sich dies jedoch ausschließlich auf Wörterbücher in Printform. Elektronische Wörterbücher sind also im Abitur nicht erlaubt.

Kommunikative Textgestaltung

Aufgabenbezug, Textformate, Textaufbau, Ökonomie, Belegtechnik

Aufgabenbezug

Hier wird bewertet, ob der von Ihnen verfasste Text konsequent an der jeweiligen Aufgabenstellung ausgerichtet ist.

Dies hört sich recht banal an, doch aufgrund des im Unterricht erworbenen Vorwissens zu einem bestimmten Themenbereich ist in Klausuren die Versuchung oft groß, eben dieses Wissen in seiner Gesamtheit abzubilden und sich damit in Details zu verlieren. Achten Sie also genau darauf, was von Ihnen verlangt wird. Auch hier hilft Ihnen das Anfertigen von Stichpunkten zu den verschiedenen Aufgaben dabei, Ihre Gedanken zu bündeln und nicht den Überblick zu verlieren.

Die im Abitur gestellten Aufgaben enthalten stets die vom Schulministerium aufgelisteten Operatoren, die Sie auch auf S. 14–16 in diesem Buch finden.

Den verschiedenen Anforderungsbereichen („Comprehension", „Analysis" und „Evaluation") sind dabei unterschiedliche Operatoren zugeordnet, deren Bedeutung klar definiert ist.

Vor Bearbeitung der konkreten Aufgaben empfiehlt es sich, die Aufgabenstellung genau in den Blick zu nehmen. Es ist hilfreich, wenn Sie die verwendeten Operatoren farbig markieren und dann für sich die folgenden Fragen beantworten:

- Welche Operatoren werden verwendet?
- Was wird konkret von mir erwartet?
- In Hinblick auf welche inhaltlichen Schwerpunkte soll ich bei der Aufgabe „Comprehension" den Text wiedergeben? Welche Gestaltungsmerkmale / stilistischen Mittel innerhalb des Textes soll ich bei Bearbeitung der Aufgabe zur „Analysis" näher untersuchen?
- Welches Zieltextformat wird bei der Aufgabe „Evaluation: Re-creation of text" verlangt?

Textformate

TIPP zum Punktesammeln

Beim Verfassen der Zieltexte sollten Sie stets darauf achten, welche Textsorte Sie produzieren sollen. Eine Übersicht über die verschiedenen Zieltextformate, die in Klausuren von Ihnen verlangt werden können, finden Sie ab Seite 103 in diesem Buch.

Denken Sie daran, bei den oben genannten Teilaufgaben keine **short forms** wie *don't*, *isn't* oder Ähnliches zu verwenden. Davon ausgenommen sind nur informelle Texte wie persönliche Briefe/E-Mails in Aufgabe 3.

Nachfolgend finden Sie eine allgemeine **Übersicht** über die Konventionen der verschiedenen Zieltextformate innerhalb der Schreibaufgabe:

Comprehension:

Beginnen Sie Ihre Ausführungen mit einem **Einleitungssatz** (Autor/-in, Titel, Textsorte, Publikation, Ort und Jahr der Erscheinung). Sollte es sich bei dem Ihnen vorliegenden Text um einen Textauszug handeln oder sollte der Text an eine ganz bestimmte Zielgruppe gerichtet sein, dann merken Sie dies ebenfalls im Einleitungssatz an.
Zitate und Textverweise sind bei Teilaufgabe 1 **nicht angebracht.**

Analysis:

Während bei Aufgabe 1 eine erste inhaltliche Annäherung an den Text erfolgen soll, wird bei der zweiten Aufgabe **eine detaillierte Analyse des Ausgangstextes** unter Beachtung der in der Aufgabenstellung genannten Gesichtspunkte und **mit Rückgriff auf Zitate** beziehungsweise **Textverweise** verlangt.
Die Bearbeitung der zweiten Teilaufgabe sollte in einem **sachlich-neutralen Stil** erfolgen. Eine Darstellung der eigenen Meinung oder eine Wertung erfolgen also nicht.
Zu den verschiedenen Herangehensweisen an die Analyse von literarischen Texten sowie von Sach- und Gebrauchstexten sei auf das entsprechende Kapitel in diesem Buch verwiesen (S. 78–102).

Evaluation:

Bei der dritten Aufgabe („evaluation") haben Sie die Wahl zwischen zwei unterschiedlichen Aufgabentypen: der Kommentierung eines entsprechenden Sachverhalts („comment") oder einer kreativen Schreibaufgabe („re-creation of text").

Comment:

Hier sind Sie aufgefordert, Ihre **eigene Meinung** zu einem beziehungsweise **Ihre subjektive Sicht auf einen bestimmten Sachverhalt** zu erörtern und begründen.
Achten Sie darauf, Ihre Argumentation **logisch** zu entwickeln und die einzelnen Argumente sinnvoll aneinander anzuschließen.
Ihre Ausführungen sollten mit einem **abschließenden Fazit** enden.

Re-creation of text:

Sollte es bei der kreativen Aufgabe durch die Vorgabe der anzufertigenden Textsorte (z. B. Dialog, Blogeintrag, E-Mail, innerer Monolog) nicht zwangsläufig gefordert sein, sollten Sie beim Verfassen Ihres Zieltextes auch bei Aufgabe 3.2 (bzw. 4.2) auf die Verwendung umgangssprachlicher Formulierungen, Slang und Kurzformen *(can't, wouldn't, doesn't* usw.) unbedingt verzichten.
Achten Sie auch stets darauf, an wen Ihr Zieltext gerichtet sein soll. Bei Verfassen eines *speech script* ist es zum Beispiel mit Blick auf das Vorwissen und den Erfahrungsschatz der Zielgruppe ein großer Unterschied, ob Sie sich an High-School-Absolventinnen und -Absolventen oder eine Versammlung von Führungskräften richten. Dies sollten Sie durch die Verwendung passender sprachlicher Mittel kennzeichnen.

Textaufbau

Der von Ihnen verfasste Text soll leicht lesbar sein – und das nicht nur mit Hinblick auf das Schriftbild und die formale Gestaltung.

Mit „Textaufbau" ist vielmehr gemeint, dass ein für die Leserinnen und Leser leicht erkennbarer „roter Faden" durch Ihren Text führt und der von Ihnen verfasste Text klar und sachgerecht strukturiert ist.

Damit ist gemeint, dass Sie Ihren Text in klar erkennbare Abschnitte gliedern, die auch inhaltliche Sinneinheiten ergeben. Leiten Sie neue Gedanken durch die Verwendung von **signal words** (etwa *First …, Second …, Third, …*) ein. Diese ermöglichen Ihnen die sinnvolle Gliederung Ihres Textes und strukturieren diesen auch für die Lesenden in klare Einheiten.

Denken Sie daran, Ihre Argumentation logisch aufzubauen und vermeiden Sie Gedankensprünge, die den Leserinnen und Lesern das Textverständnis erschweren.

Durch Verwendung geeigneter Konnektoren gelingt es Ihnen, Ihre Argumente und Beobachtungen sinnvoll zu verknüpfen, sodass Ihre Leserinnen und Leser Ihren Ausführungen leicht folgen können.

Nachfolgend eine Übersicht über die wichtigsten **Konnektoren**:

Reihung von Argumenten

and	und
first(ly) … second(ly) … third(ly) …	erstens … zweitens … drittens …
furthermore	außerdem / darüber hinaus
in addition to	zusätzlich zu
moreover	ferner/überdies
not only … but also	nicht nur … sondern auch
as well as	sowie
finally	schließlich

Gegensatz

but	aber/sondern
although	obwohl
however	jedoch
despite the fact that	trotz der Tatsache, dass
in spite of	trotz
nevertheless/nonetheless	nichtsdestoweniger
even so	selbst dann
on the contrary	im Gegensatz dazu
on the one hand … on the other hand	einerseits … andererseits

unlike	anders als
whereas	während/wogegen/indessen
while/whilst	während (dagegen)
yet	dennoch

Bedingung

if	falls/wenn
unless	wenn nicht
otherwise	ansonsten

Folge

because	weil
since	da
so	daher
consequently	folglich
as a result	demzufolge
therefore	daher/deshalb
due to	infolge
accordingly	daher
that is why	deshalb

Vergleich

like	wie
in comparison with	im Vergleich zu
similarly	ähnlich
equally	gleichermaßen

Intention der Autorin bzw. des Autors

An mehreren Stellen in Ihrer Abiturklausur werden Sie Ihre eigenen Aussagen in Relation zur Meinung der/des Verfassenden setzen müssen. Dafür empfiehlt es sich, eine Reihe von sprachlichen Ausdrücken parat zu haben, z. B.:

He/She points out / argues that ...	Er/Sie weist darauf hin / argumentiert, dass ...
He/She implies/claims/states that ...	Er/Sie behauptet, dass ...
He/She believes/suggests ...	Er/Sie glaubt / schlägt vor ...

He/She emphasises …	Er/Sie legt sein/ihr Hauptaugenmerk auf …
His/Her idea was to …	Er/Sie wollte …
He/She writes with the intention of (+ gerund) …	Er/Sie schreibt mit der Absicht …
His/Her aim is to …	Sein/Ihr Ziel ist es …
His/Her attitude towards …	Seine/Ihre Einstellung gegenüber …
When he/she says/writes … he/she means that …	Wenn er/sie sagt/schreibt …, meint er/sie …
According to the author …	Dem Autor / Der Autorin zufolge …

Ökonomie

TIPP zum Punktesammeln

Vorweg: Der Umfang des von Ihnen verfassten Zieltextes ist nicht zwangsläufig ausschlaggebend für die Qualität Ihrer Klausur. Bearbeiten Sie die Ihnen gestellten Aufgaben zielgerichtet und hinreichend ausführlich, aber vermeiden Sie inhaltliche Doppelungen. Anstatt einen Sachverhalt zu wiederholen, sollten Sie auf bereits erfolgte Erläuterungen zurückverweisen.

Verwenden Sie konkrete Beispiele, um komplexe Sachverhalte zu illustrieren.

Belegtechnik

Um Ihre Aussagen zu belegen, fügen Sie geeignete Zitate aus dem Originaltext in Ihre Antworten ein. Setzen Sie diese in englische Anführungszeichen – diese beginnen oben und enden oben. Da es sich in der Abiturklausur um einen relativ kurzen Ausgangstext handelt, genügt als Quellenangabe die Angabe der Zeilennummer in Klammern direkt hinter dem Zitat.

Beispiel zu Shakespeare, *Romeo and Juliet:*
In his speech Prince Escalus speaks about the Montagues and the Capulets as "enemies to peace" (l. 1) and finishes by even threatening them with "pain of death" (l. 23).
Verwenden Sie nicht das ganze Zitat, können Sie die ausgelassenen Passagen mit Punkten in eckigen Klammern kennzeichnen. Genauso können Sie ein Bezugswort in eckigen Klammern einfügen, wenn dies aufgrund der Satzkonstruktion notwendig ist.
Die wörtliche Übernahme von Formulierungen aus dem Ausgangstext beziehungsweise einem anderen Text ohne entsprechende Kennzeichnung ist nicht zulässig und wird negativ bewertet.
Da mit Zitaten Aussagen belegt oder gefestigt werden, stehen sie normalerweise nach der entsprechenden Behauptung. Diese sollten Sie zunächst mit eigenen Worten paraphrasieren. Synonyme hierfür finden Sie in Ihrem einsprachigen Wörterbuch.

Ausdrucksvermögen / Verfügbarkeit sprachlicher Mittel

Eigenständigkeit, allgemeiner und thematischer Wortschatz, Textbesprechungs- und Textproduktionswortschatz, Satzbau

Eigenständigkeit

Es wird in Klausuren von Ihnen erwartet, dass Sie einen eigenständigen Text formulieren und sich vom Ausgangstext lösen. Sie sollen also nicht Formulierungen aus dem Ausgangstext in Ihren Text übernehmen, ohne diese kenntlich zu machen.

Selbstverständlich können und sollen Sie aus dem Ausgangstext zitieren, um eigene Gedanken zu stützen. Allerdings müssen Sie Zitate auch immer als solche kennzeichnen, damit die Eigenständigkeit Ihrer Leistung zu erkennen ist.

Dennoch ist natürlich stellenweise ein kreativ verarbeitendes Vorgehen mit dem Sprachmaterial des Ausgangstextes durchaus notwendig und erwünscht. Dies ist insbesondere beim Aufgabentyp 3.2 (bzw. 4.2) der Fall.

Allgemeiner und thematischer Wortschatz

Es wird erwartet, dass Sie sich sachlich und stilistisch angemessen ausdrücken. (Beachten Sie das jeweilige Zieltextformat!) In diesem Buch finden Sie eine Vielzahl von Wortlisten, die Ihnen dabei helfen können, Ihren thematischen Wortschatz zu den einzelnen Unterrichtsinhalten zu festigen und zu erweitern.

Auch Wortwiederholungen sollten Sie vermeiden. Nachfolgend finden Sie eine Übersicht über Synonyme für häufig verwendete Wörter und Begriffe. Diese ermöglichen Ihnen, sich variantenreich auszudrücken und einen abwechslungsreich formulierten Text zu verfassen.

to say (im Sinne von „sagen"/„ausdrücken")

state, remark, announce, affirm, assert, maintain, declare, express, put into words, tell, phrase, communicate, make known, convey, reveal, disclose, indicate, suggest

to see (im Sinne von „erkennen"/„verstehen")

grasp, get, comprehend, follow, take in, know, realise, discover, learn

to think (im Sinne von „denken"/„meinen")

believe, suppose, expect, imagine, surmise, conjecture, guess, consider

to understand

comprehend, apprehend, grasp, see, take in, recognise, think, believe, conclude

because / because of

> because:
> since, as, in view of the fact that, owing to the fact that, seeing that
> because of:
> on account of, as a result of, owing to, by reason of, as a consequence of, thanks to, by virtue of

many

> numerous, a large/great number of, great quantities, multiple, various, several, frequent

a few

> not many, a small number, one or two, a handful

in addition to

> additionally, besides, as well (as)

furthermore

> moreover, further, additionally, on top of that, also, as well

Vermeiden Sie auch sogenannte *false friends.* Als *false friends* werden Wörter und Begriffe bezeichnet, von denen man annimmt, dass sie in Mutter- und Fremdsprache die gleiche Bedeutung haben, weil sie sich im Schriftbild oder in der Aussprache ähneln beziehungsweise identisch sind. Ein bekanntes Beispiel ist das im Deutschen für Mobiltelefone verwendete Wort „handy", welches im Englischen zwar existiert, aber dort unter anderem „geschickt" und „praktisch" bedeutet.

Hier finden Sie eine Übersicht über häufig miteinander verwechselte *false friends:*

deutsch	englisch	*false friend*
bekommen	to get	nicht: „become"
die Kritik	criticism	nicht: „critic" – der Kritiker
die Politik	politics	nicht: „policy" – persönliche Strategie, außer in Begriffen wie „foreign policy" – Außenpolitik
sensibel	sensitive	nicht: „sensible" – vernünftig
meinen/ glauben	to think	nicht: „mean" – bedeuten (oder Adj. = gemein)

aktuell	current	nicht: „actually" – in der Tat
also	so	nicht: „also" – auch
brav	honest, good	nicht: „brave" – mutig, tapfer
Chef	boss	nicht: „chef" – der Küchenchef
engagiert	committed	nicht: „engaged" – verlobt; besetzt
eventuell	possibly	nicht: „eventually" – schließlich
Handy	mobile phone (AE: cell phone)	nicht: „handy" – handlich, praktisch
Konfession	denomination	nicht: „confession" – die Beichte
Konkurrenz	competition	nicht: „concurrence" – Zusammentreffen
konsequent	consistent	nicht: „consequently" – folglich
Lager	warehouse	nicht: „department store" – Warenhaus
mobben	to bully	nicht: „mob" – das gemeine Volk
Mörder	murderer	nicht: „murder" – der Mord
prägnant	concise	nicht: „pregnant" – schwanger
prinzipiell	fundamentally, basically, in/on principle	nicht: „principally" – hauptsächlich
Prospekt	brochure, leaflet	nicht: „prospects" – die Zukunftsaussichten
Protokoll	minutes	nicht: „protocol" – die Etikette (außer bei EDV)
Publikum	audience	nicht: „public" – die Öffentlichkeit
rentabel	profitable	nicht: „rentable" – zu mieten
Rückseite	back	nicht: „backside" – Hinterteil
spenden	to donate	nicht: „to spend" – ausgeben

Textbesprechungs- und Textproduktionswortschatz

Selbstverständlich ist es von großer Bedeutung, dass Sie nicht nur die geforderten Zieltextformate erstellen, sondern dass Sie dabei auch die entsprechenden sprachlichen Mittel verwenden.

Nachfolgend erhalten Sie einen ersten Überblick darüber, welche Art von Vokabular bei den Teilaufgaben 1, 2 und 3 des Klausurenteils A von Ihnen erwartet wird.

Teilaufgabe 1: Um diese Aufgabe erfolgreich bearbeiten zu können, sollten Sie über Vokabular zur Wiedergabe und Zusammenfassung von Inhalten verfügen.

Teilaufgabe 2: Grundsätzlich ist die Analyse eines Ausgangstextes – dies können auch Filmausschnitte, Karikaturen, Grafiken usw. sein – Gegenstand der zweiten Teilaufgabe. Vokabellisten, die Ihnen die Analyse von Texten erleichtern können, finden Sie im Kapitel „Methoden der Textarbeit" (S. 79–103) in diesem Buch.

Teilaufgabe 3.1: Zur Bearbeitung dieser Teilaufgabe ist vor allen Dingen Vokabelmaterial zur eigenen Meinungsäußerung und Bewertung von Sachverhalten erforderlich. Wichtige Redewendungen sind in der nachfolgenden Übersicht enthalten.

Teilaufgabe 3.2: Bei dieser Teilaufgabe müssen Sie darauf achten, welches Zieltextformat von Ihnen verlangt wird, und das von Ihnen verwendete Vokabular entsprechend anpassen. Die verschiedenen Zieltextformate werden Ihnen auf den Seiten 103–112 genauer vorgestellt.

Eine sichere Behauptung oder Fakten ausdrücken

The fact is that ...	Es ist eine Tatsache, dass ...
It cannot be denied that ...	Man kann nicht leugnen, dass ...
It goes without saying that ...	Selbstredend ...
Undoubtedly, ...	Zweifellos ...
I am convinced that ...	Ich bin überzeugt davon, dass ...
It is indisputable/obvious that ... / There is no doubt that ...	Es ist unbestreitbar / offensichtlich / ohne Zweifel, dass ...
It is inevitable that ...	Es ist unvermeidbar, dass ...

Eine Vermutung ausdrücken

Apparently, ...	Anscheinend (am Satzanfang) ...
They will probably ...	Sie werden wahrscheinlich ...
It seems highly likely that ...	Es scheint äußerst wahrscheinlich, dass ...
It may be the case that ...	Es kann sein, dass ...

Einen Zweifel ausdrücken

It is doubtful whether ...	Es ist zweifelhaft, ob ...
I wonder if ...	Ich frage mich, ob ...
There is no proof/evidence that ...	Es gibt keine Beweise, dass ...

Einen Sachverhalt betonen

In order to stress that …	Um hervorzuheben, dass …
to emphasise	betonen
I would like to make it clear that …	Ich möchte klarstellen, dass …

Eine Meinung ausdrücken

In my opinion … / To my mind … / From my point of view …	Meiner Meinung nach …
My thoughts on the subject are …	Meine Meinung zu diesem Thema ist …
Personally, I think … / My personal view is that …	Ich persönlich denke, dass …
As far as I am concerned …	Was mich angeht …
From my point of view	Aus meiner Sicht
I assume …	Ich vermute, dass …
I am (not) convinced that …	Ich bin (nicht) überzeugt davon, dass …
I cannot help thinking that …	Ich kann nicht umhin zu denken, dass …
I get the impression that …	Ich habe den Eindruck, dass …
I am afraid that …	Ich fürchte, dass … (abschwächend)
Honestly … / To be honest …	Ehrlich gesagt …
I cannot judge …	Ich kann … nicht beurteilen.
I am in no position to say …	Es steht mir nicht zu, mich zu … zu äußern.

Einen Widerspruch einräumen

in contrast to	im Gegensatz zu
on the contrary	ganz im Gegenteil
whereas …	während … hingegen …
I strongly object to …	Ich spreche mich deutlich gegen … aus.
One could argue that … but …	Man könnte argumentieren, dass … , aber …
Although it is true that …, it would be wrong to claim that …	Obwohl es wahr ist, dass …, wäre es falsch zu behaupten, dass …

Zustimmung ausdrücken

Fortunately, …	Glücklicherweise …

I entirely agree with … / I share the opinion that …	Ich stimme vollkommen mit … überein.
I support his view.	Ich unterstütze seine Meinung.
I share her views.	Ich teile ihre Meinung.
I am of the same opinion (as) …	Ich bin der gleichen Meinung (wie) …
I approve of his/her opinion.	Ich bin mit seiner/ihrer Meinung einverstanden.
I take your point about …	Ich akzeptiere Ihre Meinung über …
I am in favour of …	Ich bin für …
He rightly mentions that …	Zu Recht betont er, dass …
I will not object to …	Ich widerspreche … nicht.
It cannot be justified that …	Es gibt keine Rechtfertigung für …
Nobody would disagree with that statement.	Niemand würde dieser Behauptung widersprechen.
This statement is very convincing.	Diese Aussage ist sehr überzeugend.
I have to admit that the author …	Ich muss zugeben, dass der Autor / die Autorin …

Ablehnung ausdrücken

It is only partly true that …	Es entspricht nur teilweise der Wahrheit, dass …
I disagree completely with …	Ich muss … vehement widersprechen.
I see things differently.	Ich sehe den Sachverhalt anders.
I have to disagree on this matter.	Ich bin in dieser Angelegenheit anderer Meinung.
One cannot possibly accept that …	Man kann unmöglich akzeptieren, dass …
I must object to …	Ich muss … widersprechen.
I have to criticise strongly that …	Ich muss scharf kritisieren, dass …
I doubt whether …	Ich bezweifle, dass …
however	jedoch
It is not as simple as it seems.	Es ist nicht so einfach wie es scheint.
Unlike the author, I think …	Abweichend vom Autor / von der Autorin glaube ich …
I cannot share the author's view on …	Ich kann die Meinung des Autors / der Autorin über … nicht teilen.
This statement entirely contradicts …	Diese Behauptung widerspricht ganz und gar …

Einen Grund angeben

As/Since …	Da/Weil …
In view of the fact that …	Angesichts der Tatsache, dass …
The reason for this development lies in …	Der Grund für diese Entwicklung liegt bei …
This causes confusion.	Das sorgt für Verwirrung.
That is why …	Aus diesem Grund …
Given that …	In Anbetracht der Tatsache, dass …
therefore	deshalb
This was caused by …	Das wurde verursacht durch …
for this reason/purpose	aus diesem Grund

Eine Folge darstellen

Consequently, … / As a consequence, …	Folglich …
In view of this statement …	In Anbetracht dieser Behauptung …
in order to	um zu
as a result of	als Folge von

Vergleiche anstellen

to be comparable	vergleichbar sein
compared to / in comparison with	im Vergleich zu
to be different from	sich unterscheiden von
differentiate between (A and B)	(A von B) unterscheiden
to be considerably better than	wesentlich besser sein als
get more and more difficult	immer schwieriger werden
Nowadays, it is less and less common that …	Heutzutage ist es immer weniger üblich, dass …
superior/inferior to	überlegen/unterlegen
the former … the latter …	der erstere … der letztere …
They have little in common.	Sie haben wenig gemeinsam.
They are equal in price.	Sie haben den gleichen Preis.

Beispiele anführen

for example/instance	zum Beispiel
Let me give you an example.	Lassen Sie mich ein Beispiel anführen.
such as	wie (zum Beispiel)
Look at …	Sehen wir uns einmal … an.

Conclusion

To sum up, …	Zusammenfassend kann man sagen, dass …
I come to the conclusion that …	Ich komme zu der Schlussfolgerung, dass …
In short, …	Kurz gesagt: …
(to put it) in a nutshell	um es auf den Punkt zu bringen
I can support the author's view on …	Ich kann die Ansicht des Autors / der Autorin über … unterstützen.
To summarise, …	Um das zusammenzufassen …
All in all, I believe that …	Insgesamt glaube ich, dass …

Satzbau

Ein abwechslungsreicher und klarer Satzbau erhöht die Lesbarkeit Ihres Textes.

TIPP zum Punktesammeln

Versuchen Sie nicht krampfhaft, mehrere Gedanken in einen Satz zu packen.
Bedenken Sie: Überlange Sätze sind fehleranfälliger als mehrere kurze, prägnante und sinnvoll miteinander verbundene Sätze.

Machen Sie sich gegebenenfalls noch einmal mit den grammatischen Eigenschaften von z. B. Aktiv- und Passivkonstruktionen sowie Gerundial-, Partizipial- und Infinitivkonstruktionen vertraut.

Korrekturlesen

Beim Verfassen eines Klausurtextes passiert es schnell, dass sich Rechtschreibfehler einschleichen.
Daher ist es wichtig, dass Sie zum Korrekturlesen Ihres Textes genug Zeit einplanen.
Achten Sie insbesondere auf Wörter, deren Aussprache oder Schreibweise zwar ähnlich oder sogar identisch ist, deren Bedeutung aber eine vollkommen andere ist, beispielsweise „sale" (Verkauf) und „sail" (das Segel, segeln).

Stichwortverzeichnis